Arts & Economics

Analysis & Cultural Policy

Springer
*Berlin
Heidelberg
New York
Barcelona
Hong Kong
London
Milan
Paris
Singapore
Tokyo*

Bruno S. Frey

Arts & Economics
Analysis & Cultural Policy

With 2 Figures
and 9 Tables

 Springer

Prof. Bruno S. Frey
University of Zürich
Institut für Empirische Wirtschaftsforschung (IEW)
Blümlisalpstrasse 10
CH-8006 Zürich
Switzerland

ISBN 3-540-67342-3 Springer-Verlag Berlin Heidelberg New York

Library of Congress Cataloging-in-Publication Data
Die Deutsche Bibliothek – CIP-Einheitsaufnahme
Arts & Economics: Analysis & Cultural Policy / Bruno S. Frey. – Berlin; Heidelberg; New York; Barcelona; Hong Kong; London; Milan; Paris; Singapore; Tokyo: Springer, 2000
    ISBN 3-540-67342-3

Springer-Verlag is a company in the BertelsmannSpringer publishing group.
© Springer-Verlag Berlin · Heidelberg 2000
Printed in Germany

Hardcover-Design: Erich Kirchner, Heidelberg

SPIN 10734342   43/2202-5 4 3 2 1 0 – Printed on acid-free paper

Preface

To put the ARTS and ECONOMICS next to each other, as in the title to this book, may be shocking to some readers. Must not creative art be free of economic constraints, must it not lead a life of its own? And is economics not the realm of mean commercial dealings? This book argues that it is not so: the ARTS and ECONOMICS go well together, indeed need each other. Without a sound economic base, art cannot exist, and without creativity the economy cannot flourish.

There is a second way in which the Arts and Economics go together, namely in the sense of applying economic thinking to the arts. Over the last decades, this scholarly endeavor has been established under the name of "The Economics of Art" or "Cultural Economics". But this may also sound revolting to some readers as it suggests an imperialistic extension of a lowly benefit-cost calculus to the world of art. This fear is unwarranted. On the contrary, cultural economists stress the social value of art and defend it against a crude business view of art. Rather than dismissing art without direct commercial profit, art economists seek ways and means of supporting it. This book is not a textbook summarizing the achievements attained by the economics of art. Such books already exist, among them the author's own, *Muses and Markets, Explorations in the Economics of Art*, written jointly with Werner Pommerehne.

ARTS & ECONOMICS charters little known territories. I focus on so far disregarded aspects of the relationship between the arts and the economy. Novel aspects are introduced into economic analysis in order to better understand the world of art. At the same time, I seek to maintain the strength of the economic approach. The book is written so that it can be understood by social scientists in general and all persons interested in the arts. At the same time, it is hoped that my economist colleagues find challenging and unorthodox views and results worth noting.

The content of the book is based on ideas, which were presented at many different conferences, and have subsequently been published in various scholarly journals and book collections. Chapter 5 is based on an article jointly written with Isabelle Vautravers-Busenhart, chapters 6 and 7 on joint work with Werner Pommerehne, and chapter 9 with Reiner Eichenberger. The papers have been rewritten, and brought up to date, to form a coherent whole. Several chapters contain new material not previously published. Part I presents a personal survey of art economics and introduces the particular characteristics of the economic approach to culture. Part II deals with various aspects of museums, such as the management of the collections and superstar museums, as well as special exhibitions and festivals which have become prominent over the last decades. Part III, which follows, discusses how the arts can be supported by the public, whether the arts may be left to direct democratic decisions, and how artistic creativity is affected by government support. The final part IV inquires whether art is a financially lucrative investment, how the value of cultural property can be evaluated, and what can and should be done about fakes.

The ideas and the research results presented here have been influenced by intensive discussions with the members of the invisible – and sometimes visible – college of economists and social scientists interested in the arts. I wish to record my debt of gratitude to those I feel not only scientifically close to, but also with whom I have regularly met over the last years. In addition to the forerunners, in particular William Baumol, Sir Alan Peacock, Dick Netzer and Mark Blaug, I want to explicitly mention Françoise Benhamou, Trine Bille, Giorgio Brosio, Reiner Eichenberger, René Frey, Victor

Ginsburgh, John O'Hagan, Michael Hutter, Arjo Klamer, Gianfranco Mossetto, Dominique Sagot-Duvauroux, Walter Santagata, Mark Schuster, Bruce Seaman, David Throsby, Ruth Towse and Michele Trimarchi, and last but not least, the late Werner Pommerehne, former co-worker and dear friend whom I sorely miss.

Special thanks go to Reto Jegen and Rosemary Brown, who greatly helped me with the preparation of this book.

Zurich, in March 2000.

Table of Contents

Chapter 1 -
Economics of Art: A Personal Survey

1. Art Economics Today

The economics of art has established itself as a major discipline within the *economic approach to the social sciences*. This approach is based on a systematic study of the interaction between the behavior of individuals and institutions existing in society[1].

The economic approach to the social sciences champions a totally new kind of *inter-disciplinarity*. Up till now, inter-disciplinarity has been understood to be a combination of various disciplinary approaches. This has often led to a meeting of minds at a rather low quality level, often not more than just well-formulated trivialities. In contrast, the new kind of inter-disciplinarity proposed here is based on a unique analytical method (the economic way of thinking), which has been used to study a large variety of problems and issues. The model of human behavior applied here carefully distinguishes preferences, i. e. what people desire, and constraints imposed by social institutions, income, prices and the amount of time available. It has been successful in accounting for phenomena in and beyond economics.

---

[1]   See more fully Chapter 2.

Efforts to use this so-called rational choice framework have sometimes been welcomed, but have more often remained controversial, and have in many cases been rejected. But its innovative feature has been fully recognized in the form of Nobel Prizes, most specifically to Gary Becker in 1992. Other Nobel Prize winners in economics, employing the rational choice approach, are Kenneth Arrow (1972), Herbert Simon (1978), Theodore Schultz (1979), James Buchanan (1986), Ronald Coase (1991), Douglass North and Robert Fogel (1993), and Amartya Sen (1998).

One of the most fascinating applications of the rational choice approach has been to the *arts*. This new area is also known as *Cultural Economics*. It actually has quite an old history (but was not known under this name in the past). Economists in German-speaking countries have for a long time been interested in economic aspects of the arts[2]. Public finance issues have received special attention, in particular the role of the state in financing culture[3]. On the whole, it was taken for granted that the public should subsidize the arts, as they produce (what would today be called) positive external effects on the society at large. These externalities are called "non-user benefits" because they also accrue to persons not consuming a particular cultural activity, but to the population at large. They consist of "existence value" (the population benefits from the fact that culture exists even if a person does not attend any artistic activities), "option value" (persons benefit by being able to attend cultural events even if they do not presently attend them) and of "bequest value" (persons benefit from culture by being able to leave it to future generations, even if they themselves do not participate in any artistic events). The same normative question of why the state should support the arts was also taken up by famous British economists such as Lord Lionel Robbins (1963, 1971) or Sir Alan Peacock (1969), both of whom, incidentally, were actively involved

---

[2]   E.g. Kindermann 1903, Drey 1910, Seelig 1914, Haalck 1921, Reusch 1922, or Bröker 1928. A special issue of the "Volkswirtschaftliche Blätter" has been devoted to "Kunst und Volkswirtschaft" (art and economics) already in 1910.

[3]   Examples are Epstein 1914, Marggraff 1922, Herterich 1937.

in the arts, as was the towering economist of the 20th century, Lord John Maynard Keynes[4].

The birth of art economics as a discipline of its own within modern economic science can be dated exactly: it occurred with Baumol and Bowen's book on the *Performing Arts – The Economic Dilemma*, published in 1966. The dilemma referred to is created by an ever increasing level of economic welfare (per capita income) and the concomitant increase in the cost of staging the lively arts. As a result, procedures in the performing arts are under continually rising financial pressure. It seems that precisely because societies are rich, and become ever richer, they have more and more problems in entertaining the lively arts.

Subsequent to Baumol and Bowen's pathbreaking book, cultural economics has started to flourish. In Anglo-Saxon countries, the books by Moore (1968) on the *American Theatre*, Peacock and Weir (1975) on *The Composer in the Market Place,* and Netzer (1978) on the *Subsidized Muse* are good examples. Soon, Blaug (1976) collected the first book of readings, and Throsby and Withers (1979) wrote the first textbook on *The Economics of the Performing Arts*. Cultural economics was early on taken up in other countries and in other languages, in particular in France[5], Italy[6] and Switzerland[7].

In the last decade, the literature on the economics of art has expanded greatly. A small, and subjective, selection of only a few important works can be mentioned here (a survey of the earlier work is given in Frey and Pommerehne 1989a). Three recent texts in

---

[4] Keynes was a great art lover and an important figure in British art administration. He financed and partially ran the theatre in Cambridge, as well as being married to a prima-ballerina. However, Keynes did not make any noteworthy contributions to art economics.

[5] Examples are Moulin 1967, Gallais-Hamonno 1972, Leroy 1980, Dupuis 1980, Menger 1983, Sagot-Duvauroux 1985, Greffe 1985, Dupuis and Greffe 1985.

[6] E.g. Mazzocchi 1971, Gerelli 1974, Villani 1978, Trimarchi 1985 a, b.

[7] E.g. R. L. Frey and Neugebauer 1976, Pommerehne and Frey 1980 a,b, Pommerehne 1982, Pommerehne and Schneider 1983, Schneider and Pommerehne 1983.

English are Heilbrun and Gray's (1993), O'Hagan's (1998), based on a welfare economic point of view, and Throsby's (2000) focusing on value creation. There are excellent text-books available in French: Farchy and Sagot-Duvauroux (1994), Greffe, Pflieger and Rouget (1990), and Benhamou (1996).

Among monographs devoted to specific aspects of, and issues in the arts, there is Feldstein's (1991) *Economics of Museums*, Peacock's (1993) *Paying the Piper* with a selection of his articles, Towse's (1993) *Singers in the Market Place*, or Mossetto's (1993) *Aesthetics and Economics*. French contributions include e.g. Greffe's (1990, 1999), or Rouget, Sagot-Duvauroux and Pflieger's (1991) books. An interesting economic analysis of the arts in Italy is Brosio and Santagata (1992). Tietzel (1995) is an excellent German contribution on the economics of literature, dealing amongst others with Goethe who, despite appearances, turns out to be a very astute homo oeconomicus.

There are several useful readers in the area. Without a doubt, the most extensive was edited by Towse (1997a), but those compiled by Peacock and Rizzo (1994), Blaug (1976), Ginsburgh and Menger (1996) and Towse (1997b) are also worthy of note. Two collections of essays are devoted to the economics of heritage, and were edited by Hutter and Rizzo (1997), and Peacock *(1998). The Journal of Cultural Economics* carried useful special issues on the Economics of Intellectual Property Rights (Vol. 19, 1995), on the Art Market (Vol. 21, 1997), and on the Economics of Museums (Vol. 22, 1998).

The study of the economics of arts has been institutionalized by the *Association for Cultural Economics International*, which regularly organizes conferences and edits a review entitled *Journal of Cultural Economics*. The bulk of articles relating to the subject are published there, but some contributions also appear in other (often leading) journals such as the *American Economic Review,* the *Journal of Political Economy,* or *Kyklos,* as well as in other reviews devoted to the social science aspects of art (e.g. *Cultural Policy, Empirical Studies in the Arts, International Journal of Cultural Property,*

International Journal of Arts Management). There are also centers devoted to the subject, the most prominent being ICARE (*International Center for Art Research in Economics*), founded by Gianfranco Mossetto and associated with the University of Venice.

The emergence of an economic (or rational choice) approach to the arts has not hindered close relationships with other disciplines devoted to the arts. In particular, the sociology of art is in many respects quite similar (see e.g. Moulin 1986, DiMaggio 1986 or Foster and Blau 1989, as well as the specific view by Bourdieu 1979, and Bourdieu and Dardel 1966). In contrast, there are so far only few contacts with art history. This may be due to a misunderstanding of the economic approach. Art historians seem to think that economists only value what is profitable in monetary terms, and that they therefore propose to commercialize art. Art historians are surprised to hear that most economists favor state support of the arts, and go to great pains to empirically demonstrate "non-economic" values such as existence, prestige, education or bequest values. Another reason why art historians are reluctant to deal with art economics is the conscious or unconscious effort to keep newcomers out. There are first signs that both fears are losing force; there are promising efforts under way to bridge the gap between art history and economics, particularly with respect to cultural property.

2.   Why a Personal View?

There is no need to give a general survey of the economics of art; this task has been well fulfilled by Throsby's (1994) and Mossetto's (1992) articles. I prefer to present my own thoughts and views. They are, of course, also reflected in the subsequent chapters, but I wish to discuss them in a more coherent form here.

2.1   Broadening Art Economics

The dominant neoclassical methodology has proved very useful in the study of culture: it is based on a clear behavioral model, which helps to capture the demand and supply of art. On the basis of the resulting equilibria, it is possible to derive empirically testable implications. Most of the predictions conform to "common sense", but others are unexpected and surprising. An example is Baumol and Bowen's (1966) analysis of the performing arts: the richer societies become, the more difficult it is for them to maintain live performing arts.

Because of its demonstrable usefulness, most art economists stick closely to the traditional neoclassical method of analysis. Examples are Throsby in his major survey article for the *Journal of Economic Literature* (1994), or O'Hagan in his *The State and the Arts* (1998).

In my opinion, it may be fruitful to transcend the rather rigid limits of orthodox neo-classics. This view is shared by most economists, as far as explicitly taking *institutions* into account. Thus, the difference between the public and private supply of art has been the center of attention for many art economists. Similarly, incentive problems, due to principal-agent relationships within theatres, opera houses, and other art suppliers, have been variously studied.

However, I wish to argue that it may often be useful to go even further, beyond the existing limits of the neoclassical approach. In particular, *psychological* aspects are important to consider in certain instances. *Behavioral anomalies* are one such aspect, suggesting that human beings deviate systematically from what is predicted by rational choice analysis (or more precisely, by subjective expected utility maximization) under identifiable conditions (for a survey, see chapter 11 in Frey 1999a). To provide an example: many owners of paintings become subject to the "endowment effect": they are not prepared to sell a painting for a given sum (say 10 000 Euros), though they would not buy it for that price (even disregarding transaction costs). As discussed in chapter 9 on "Art Investment Returns", this behavioral anomaly is likely to influence prices paid on the art market.

Another important contribution of psychology to art economics refers to *human motivation*. There is no doubt that artists systematically respond to monetary (i.e. extrinsic) incentives, like all other people. Salvador Dalí is reported to have said "All that interests me is money"; statements to the same effect have been made by several other artists. Nevertheless, strong evidence exists that (successful) artists have had a strongly developed intrinsic motivation, i.e. they pursue art for art's sake. This applies particularly for the first years in an artist's career. Commonly, this is the most innovative and productive period in an artist's life. The extent and the specific ways in which an artist is motivated intrinsically or extrinsically are crucial when it comes to the public support of culture. Do public subsidies, in particular direct income transfers to individual artists, raise or damage creativity? This issue is discussed more fully in chapter 8 on "State Support and Creativity". To focus on both extrinsic and intrinsic motivation, and to look at the dynamic interaction between the two (the so-called Crowding Effect), goes beyond traditional neo-classically based art economics. But the present author is convinced that it is crucial both for understanding, and supporting, the arts.

One of the characteristics of this book on art economics is an effort to go beyond generally accepted ideas and to explore new avenues. The conventional analysis of culture essentially using basic neoclassical methods has greatly enriched our knowledge of the social aspects of the arts, and in particular the relationship between the monetary and artistic realms. The application of economic cross-section and time series analyses has often been most useful. It has added an empirical slant. But there is always the danger of running into diminishing, or even negative returns (see Hirshleifer 1985). Not all applications of economic thinking to culture yield interesting insights. Sometimes it boils down to renaming observations in the economic terminology. This has, in my opinion, not occurred yet to any notable extent, one reason being that many art economists, who

– from the point of view of traditional economics – venture into such an "outlandish" subject[8], are an unorthodox lot.

Novel and challenging insights can be gained by transgressing established boundaries, and venturing into new (methodological) territory. Indeed, art economics is one of those areas in economics most open to new approaches. An example is Klamer's (1996) *The Value of Culture,* which is based on the idea that an actively sought discourse between all the participants in the artistic process produces insights, and shows ways to solve problems. Perhaps more than in other areas, such an exchange of views is fruitful in the arts. Another unconventional approach is championed by Hutter (1996a), who does not look at how economics can be used to study culture, but how cultural economics impacts on economic theory.

2.2   Aspects of Interest

This survey, as well as this book as a whole, strongly reflects the author's view of what he considers to be important and interesting. This evaluation is subjective and cannot be objectively established. It must be left to the reader whether he or she shares the author's predilections.

Two issues run through all the chapters of this book:

1. *Economic and political influence.* There is no sense in restricting the analysis to purely economic aspects of culture. Obviously, the state plays a most important role in directly (via subsidies) and indirectly (via regulations such as tax laws) supporting the arts. At the same time, the government may cripple the arts, not only in dictatorships but also in democracies. In both cases, the decisions made by the state are based on political (and bureaucratic) considerations. Political aspects are relevant in the arts beyond the state. Many more actors are involved in influencing the arts, and are in turn influenced by them (see e.g.

---

8   There are a surprisingly large number of professional economists who have never heard that there is such a thing as the economics of art.

Hutter 1986, 1987). Hence, there is for me no doubt that a *political economy* of the arts is needed.

2. *Institutions shape culture*. It matters greatly how the fundamental decisions about art are taken, i.e. the role accorded to politics, the market, and bureaucracy. The arts, generated by an unfettered market, differ strongly, both in quality and quantity, from the arts emerging through democratic decisions, and from the arts produced by bureaucratic rules. Hence, all the chapters in this book engage in a "comparative analysis of institutions". An example is chapter 3, dealing with the policy of museums with respect to their holdings ("For Art's Sake – Open Up the Vaults"). It has been demonstrated that the readiness of museum directorates to put holdings in their vaults to good use by selling at least some of the objects, and acquiring new ones which serve them more, strongly depends on the extent of legal independence of the museum in question from the government, i.e. an institutional factor.

2.3   Value Judgements

Each scholar has his or her basic values, even when undertaking scientific research. This is also visible in the present book. My position does not lend well to definition in the traditional left-right spectrum. Consonant to the view of most modern economists, I see the advantages of using markets. They tend to be efficient and allow the different artistic preferences of the population to be met. Art is not only what (often self-defined) art experts call "art". Art experts have often been unable to grasp new art movements; the market has often been much quicker to respond. An example is impressionism, which was rejected by established art critics and the art establishment in Paris. Those who are praised today as the great masters of impressionist art, had to at the time resort to private initiative ("Salon des Refusés"), as well as to the market (Monet's paintings were first bought in sizeable numbers by private American collectors). Impressionist paintings were traded at high prices on markets before that particular art movement was acknowledged by the art establishment.

But I also see the limits of markets. In my view, relevant external effects and other market failures exist. These cannot simply be overcome by bargaining between the actors involved, not least because the consumers are unorganized. I therefore deviate from the view championed by Grampp (1989a) that the market works wonderfully where the arts are concerned, and that it should be left to itself. But I do not agree that market failures in the arts necessarily mean that the government must intervene. As a political economist, I clearly see the limits of state activity, also with respect to the culture.

The following chapters propose the view that the arts flourish, provided the appropriate *constitutional rules* are set. A constitutional contract can be reached behind the "veil of ignorance" (Buchanan 1987 and Frey 1983). Most important of all, freedom of expression must be guaranteed. I also believe – and this belief is based on empirical evidence, see chapter 7 on "Public Support for the Arts in a Democracy" – that, to a large extent, the direct participation of citizens is beneficial to the arts. Culture is lively when the ground rules of society support as great a variety of forms and types of art as possible. Thus, it is important to prevent monopolistic positions where art is concerned. The government and its bureaucracy should be restricted so as not to become monopolistic supporters, and therefore final judges of art. But the same holds for the efforts of private actors to monopolize the supply of, and trade in, art.

3. Fascinating Art Economics

In this section, two issues are discussed. They serve to illustrate why I find art economics so fascinating. This specific approach to the arts presents a viewpoint of its own, offering new insights. The results reached, and the policy conclusions suggested, often stand in complete contrast to commonly held opinions. They should therefore command special attention.

The two issues dealt with are the role of the market, and the role of democracy, for the arts. It is not intended to provide a full treatment of all aspects (many of them are discussed in the subsequent chapters of this book as well as in earlier sections of this chapter). Rather, this section endeavors to bring to light what – in my view – are particularly challenging aspects.

3.1   Does the Market Produce Bad Art?

Most people believe that the market produces low quality art. Complaints about "mass culture" and "commercialization" abound. This view dominates not only amongst the general public, but (perhaps even more strongly) in intellectual discussions. A considerable part of the philosophical discourse is devoted to rejecting the market as a decision-making mechanism for culture. Behind this deep-seated conviction is a general suspicion of the market on the part of intellectuals (pointed out so well by Schumpeter 1942), and also the more specific belief that a public support of culture is needed to maintain high quality. Not only must the state subsidize the arts, but it must also produce cultural activities itself by running museums, theatres and opera houses, ballet companies and orchestras.

This extremely wide-spread view that the market only produces low quality mass culture is based on a misunderstanding of the way the market works. Moreover, it is empirically simply incorrect. In fact, the market *can* produce high quality culture, and even art of the highest quality. To understand this statement, it is necessary to look behind "the" market. The market is an institution which responds to demand: if low quality art is asked for, it produces low quality art – but if high quality art is asked for, it produces high quality art. There is no reason to assume that such a demand for high quality culture does not exist. In reality, we observe that there are indeed persons spending money to enjoy good art (see e.g. the many examples in Cowen 1998). A case in point is the many art festivals (including film festivals) where art of the highest quality is performed. Such festivals are normally the result of private initiative, with the intention of avoiding the crippling political, administrative and artistic constraints typical of government-run theatres, opera and concert halls (see chapter 5 on "Special Exhibitions and Festivals"). Some of these festivals cater for a small minority of lovers of a particular art form such as modern music, which does not find a sufficiently large audience in the established artistic venues. The market thus does *not* require a mass audience. The general and wildly popular statement that "the market produces bad art" is untenable[9].

But another statement is true: much commercially produced art is of low, if not very low, quality. But this is not surprising. The vast majority of people have such tastes, and the market simply reflects them. This tendency may be reinforced in some cases by economies of scale. They allow the production of large quantities at a lower price than small quantities. An example is the production of CDs. It costs very little to produce another 100,000 or another million pieces. Nevertheless, we observe that the same market also produces serious music of superb quality, in particular recordings of classical music. It is therefore important not to focus on the mass aspects of the market only, but to see that the price system is normally very well able to cater for high quality demand.

As has been pointed out in a previous section, economists of art are not equipped to judge what is "good" or "bad" art. The criteria must, of course, be decided by the respective sciences. But it has been known for centuries that there is no consensus: "de gustibus non est

---

9   A comparison with the market for newspapers and journals might be helpful. A quick glance at any kiosk immediately reveals that the market provides for the reading demands of very specialized tastes. There are certainly not less than a dozen journals solely devoted to the opera or to art museums, but also to collectors of toy soldiers or old furniture. If publications in different languages are considered, the supply even in such very specialized subjects becomes virtually uncountable.

Such an opinion is most probably fuelled by tendencies such as the often lamented drop in program quality after the liberalization of European TV markets. The author doubts, however, that the market is to be held responsible; it is rather the case that (1) subsidies for programs about art that use the medium as an art form of its own go to specialized channels (e.g. ARTE), or (2) producers use wrong or doubtful measures of success (i. e. net viewer ratings instead of aggregated willingness to pay for advertised goods).

disputandum". But even if one is prepared to accept rough distinctions in quality (e.g., Verdi's operas are better than the soap operas shown on TV), which the present author is, one should keep in mind that evaluations may change over time: what was once considered outrageous junk may become accepted art, and what was once considered great art may be discarded.

One of the market's great advantages is that it permits and fosters *variety*. No commission and no group of experts need to approve the tastes reflected in the market. This raises the chances that innovative ideas spring forth, keeping art lively. An open market is an antidote to a monopoly of artistic taste.

The markets for art as they exist in reality are far from ideal: there are external effects, increasing returns and monopolistic tendencies among suppliers. The conclusion offered by marketeers that the market should only be tolerated in the arts is therefore not based on analysis but rather on an ideological conviction. The market should be seen in perspective. For the arts (as well as elsewhere), several decision-making mechanisms are available. Instead of jumping to the conclusion that the market is the only thing in culture, or the reverse, that the government is the only thing, one *must* engage in *comparing* the advantages and disadvantages of the various decision-making mechanisms.

Let us now turn to another fascinating system, namely democracy.

3.2   Can Arts Policy Be Left to Democracy?

There is a common charge against "democratizing" the arts, in particular against leaving decisions about art to the people (via popular referenda): "people do not understand what good art is". It is often claimed that the people's taste in art is terrible. Therefore, cultural decisions should certainly not be left to the members of the public.

These arguments are similar to those raised against using the market in culture. But the charge is more stringent, if democratic decisions are indeed identified with majority decisions. As we have seen, the market is well able to care for minority preferences, including those with high artistic tastes. In contrast, in a direct democracy with majority rule, it is indeed the "mass", in the sense of the majority, which decides [10]. Majority decisions on cultural issues are feared to inevitably lead to very bad, even hideous, art. It is concluded that the élite must decide. This immediately raises the question: what élite? There are many possibilities:

1. *Elected politicians*. The taste of politicians does not correspond to that of the population at large (they are, on average, better educated), but it is doubtful whether they really have better judgement concerning art. Moreover, in order to secure re-election, politicians respond to a large number of outside influences. In a democracy with stiff competition between the parties, the politicians seek to fulfil the preferences of the electorate. In that case, the decisions on art are shifted back from the élite (here the politicians) to the population at large. In most democracies, however, politicians have discretionary room with regard to making decisions on art. But exactly this capacity makes it worthwhile for interest groups to influence them. The better these groups are organized, the stronger their influence. This also applies to art decisions, where established and, therefore, essentially culturally conservative group interests have a larger say than those promoting innovative forms of culture. The latter are, almost by definition, unorganized and therefore politically weak, as they represent future, still unknown forms and types of art.

2. *Art administrators in government*. Those people employed in government, and various art organizations, are generally well-

---

[10]   This does not, however, correspond to the "mass" of the population, because average vote participation in popular referenda tends to be low. In most cases, between 30-50 percent of the eligible citizens actually participate in a vote.

Moreover, no democracy is direct in the sense that all decisions are taken by popular referenda. Rather, there are parliaments and governments (the executive) who decide on most issues, and a small part only is referred to the electorate (see e.g. Butler and Ranney 1994, Frey 1994a, Cronin 1989).

educated in art, but they also have a stake in the art that they have been supporting in the past. If they suddenly decided to support new art forms and manifestations, this would cast doubt on the activities they have undertaken so far. Thus, a museum's existing holdings would be regarded less highly if the director decided to steer a different course. Art administrators therefore have an interest in defending established art. Most importantly, they have an incentive to fight off outsiders – but this is exactly where creative and innovative art comes from. Leaving cultural decisions to art administrators introduces a marked conservative bias.

3. *The art establishment*. Art critics in the media, art historians and gallery owners, as well as private and corporate collectors, make up this type of establishment. Many of them also have a conservative slant because art, as presently en vogue, is their area of competence, which they would partly or totally lose if an innovative art form were to appear. They are at best prepared to follow a new direction that they can participate in and associate with. Real outsiders, whose raison d'être is to reject existing art, would, however, not be supported – unless their originators were prepared to succumb to the wishes and ideas of the existing art establishment. If this happens, innovative elements tend to be lost.

It might be argued that the situation has changed since the time when the art establishment in Paris rejected the new art forms of Impressionism and Expressionism. This is partly true. Today there are groups of people (and firms) who actively try to pick up the newest waves in art and fashion in order to be able to exploit this (insider) knowledge. This benefits new art forms that appear to be exploitable over a reasonably short time period, but works against new art forms where this is not the case. It should, moreover, be kept in mind that especially the firms engaged in discovering future art trends want to predict their acceptance within the population, i.e. look at the demand in order to adjust the supply. Innovative art, in contrast, takes place mainly on the supply side, and the demand thereafter does or does not adjust to it.

4. *Artists*. Decisions about culture may be left to the artists producing it. This sounds quite convincing, but only at first sight. First of all, it is far from clear whether artists are good judges with respect to art produced by *other* artists. They rightly highly value what they do themselves (otherwise they presumably would not do it), but they are often quite negative about what others do. This may partly be due to envy, but even more importantly to an incapacity to go beyond their own realm of thinking: many artists are quite self-centered, if not actual maniacs, a fact intimately related to their own creative efforts.

There is another problem with letting "artists" decide on art. Who are the artists? To be an artist is not well defined (see Frey and Pommerehne 1989a, chapter 9). Is it those who have the "right" education, i.e. who have graduated from an art academy? Or is it those who are members of an artists' association? And if so, which associations are admissible? Or is it those who are able to make a living from their artistic activity? Or is it all those people who believe themselves to be artists even if they devote only a little time to artistic activity, and earn nothing from it? In all these cases, a quite different set of people qualify as "artists". If the first two sets of people are chosen, a conservative slant is introduced, and established art will be favored. If artists are defined by income, it will include some people solely catering for low taste (but, of course, also others, as argued above). If only subjective feelings matter, very incompetent people will be able to decide on art.

There is yet another problem with leaving decisions on art to artists, which also applies to decisions by the art establishment: how are the decisions to be made? If representatives are to be elected, they are likely to lose touch with the group whose tastes they are supposed to reflect. This holds, in particular, when this group is ill-defined (as in the definitions based on income or subjective belief). As a result, the representatives may deviate more and more from what they are supposed to reflect (this is a classical principal-agent problem).

This discussion reveals that there is certainly no easy consensus to be reached as to who, in a democracy, should decide on art, if it is not to be the population at large. Decisions on art, reached by each of the groups under consideration, have grave disadvantages. This comparative evaluation is important, because it shows that while leaving decisions on art to a popular referendum may be criticized, all other decision-making groups discussed may also be criticized.

The role of democracy for the arts may moreover be seen in a very different perspective. So far, decisions on art have been discussed as they are taken by the voters, or "the élite", in the current politico-economic process. The perspective is fundamentally shifted if one moves to the level of the *constitution* – or, more generally, the level of the *basic rules of society* – which determine *how* the current decisions on art are to be taken (see Brennan and Buchanan 1985, Frey 1983). One of the most important constitutional rules for a flourishing cultural life is to guarantee *artistic freedom*. Anybody who feels that he or she wants to perform a cultural act, should be free to do so (provided it does not impose major costs on other people). It would be too simple to assume that artistic creativity can only exist under such defined democratic conditions: some great art has been produced under authoritarian rulers. An example is the Renaissance, which was accompanied by an explosion of artistic talent. The then reigning princes were far from democratic. But it may still be argued that the artist gained a considerable measure of artistic freedom in that period. Many of the great masters, among them Michelangelo Buonarroti and Leonardo da Vinci, were free enough to bargain between various masters. They thus were able to enter service with, or to produce particular pieces of art for, that master who provided them most artistic freedom relative to financial compensation. Nevertheless, in our modern world, where the population as a whole, and in particular artists, have experienced a rise in self-determination brought about by democracy, a decision-making system involving the whole population is by far the best-equipped to establish, and to safeguard, constitutional rights for artistic freedom.

4.   Conclusions

This chapter has endeavored to show why art economics is a fascinating and worthwhile subject. Its analysis is based on the rational choice approach, which has been widely used to also study other areas beyond economics, such as the economics of the environment, of politics, of history or of law. It has been argued that the economics of art would profit from going beyond the well-trodden paths, and integrating knowledge from the other social sciences, in particular psychology. This gives us the opportunity of understanding even better how human beings behave with respect to the arts.

The economics of art has dealt with a large number of different issues and subjects. Many of them will be treated in the following chapters of this book. But one of the most important aspects has been the relationship between culture and the market. Most art experts and lovers, as well as the general population, seem to believe that using the market produces bad art. People tend to focus entirely on the mass market, where indeed art is produced and created which suits the (bad) preferences of the population at large.

Such a view is mistaken, not solely because what is "good" and what is "bad" art is not fixed, but changes over time. There are many cases in which what was considered to be bad art was later highly regarded. But the view of commercialization producing bad art is also mistaken because the market is well able to produce good art, even first rate art – it all depends on who exerts the demand. The chapter argues that the art élite is badly equipped to make wise decisions on art, not least because it is unclear who this élite really is. Rather, a society's constitution must guarantee artistic freedom, in particular that new artists, and new art forms, have a chance to flourish. In an age of self-determination, this is best achieved in a democratic society.

Chapter 2 -
Art: The Economic Point of View[*]

1.   Pitfalls and Possibilities

Whenever economists study areas outside their traditional field of economy, they run the danger of misperceiving what contribution they are able to make. Only if the choice of what aspects to study is carried out carefully can a useful and novel contribution from the part of economics be expected.

The danger indicated is particularly great in the case of the arts. One reason is that no consensus as to the definition of the arts exists among experts or the public. Another reason is that the scholars engaged in art economics are invariably art lovers, and sometimes art practitioners (William Baumol, Alan Peacock and Hans Abbing are examples), so that they risk being carried away by their emotions instead of taking the same sober and rationalistic attitude as when they deal with their traditional area.

The area of the "Economics of Art" can be determined from two different points of view, which are discussed in section 2. It is

[*]   This chapter is based on Bruno S. Frey (1994), "Art: The Economic Point of View.", previously published in Peacock and Rizzo (eds.), *Cultural Economics and Cultural Policies*, pp. 3-16, used by permission of Kluwer Academic Publishers.

argued that the second point of view is preferable, and that the economics of art are not restricted to the (narrow) economic, material or monetary aspects of the arts. The following section 3 looks at the economic concept of art from the demand side (from the consumers of art) and from the supply side (from the producers of art). Section 4 suggests that the disequilibrium between the demand for, and supply of, art helps us to understand better what "art" is from the economic point of view. Section 5 offers concluding remarks.

2. Two Views on the Economics of Art

"Economics" and "art" can be combined in two quite different ways:

1. as the analysis of economic or material *aspects* of artistic activities and, in the extreme case, as commercial dealings in art;

2. the application of the "economic" or, rather, the "rational choice" *methodology* to art.

These two points will subsequently be discussed.

2.1 Economic Aspects of Art

The arts need an economic base on which to flourish. Think, for example, of:

– the dominant role of public and private subsidies to the performing arts and to museums in Europe. In America, these subsidies are substituted by tax exemptions for private and corporate donations;

– the increasing role of private sponsoring by enterprises for all kinds of art;

– the prices in, and profitability of, the market for paintings, antiques and other art objects;

– international trade in art;

- the income of individual artists;

- cultural activities which influence the economy as, for example, festivals such as Salzburg or Verona, attracting a huge crowd of additional visitors to the city.

Such connections between economics and art are rather obvious and clearly visible, and need not be further commented on here.

2.2   The Economic Approach to Art

Over the last few years, the typical way of economic thinking has been applied to many different areas. Economic methodology in the form of the rational choice approach has become a general social science paradigm, extending to all areas of *human behavior*[1].

The economic approach is characterized by four features with respect to human behavior:

1. individuals, but not groups, states or society as a whole, are the acting units (methodological individualism), but this does not mean that individuals act in isolation, rather that they constantly interact with each other;

2. behavior depends on individual preferences as well as on the constraints in terms of resources (income), time or norms an individual is subject to;

3. individuals are, on average, mostly pursuing their own interests; their behavior is determined by incentives;

4. changes in behavior are, as far as possible, attributed to changes in constraints rather than changes in preferences[2], because the

---

[1]   The main exponent is Becker (1976); see also McKenzie and Tullock (1975) and the survey article by Hirshleifer (1985). A methodologically oriented treatment is given in Kirchgässner (1991), and several applications are provided by Frey (1999a).

[2]   Changes in tastes (which occur with fixed "basic" preferences) have been analyzed most importantly by Becker and Murphy 1988, and Becker 1992, 1996.

latter are better observable. This strategy allows us to derive empirically testable propositions.

Another cornerstone in the economic approach is the importance attached to *institutions,* which shape the environment within which human beings act. Institutions may take the form of decision-making systems; norms, traditions and rules, as well as organizations. They act as constraints on human behavior and thus determine an individual's possibility set. Modern economists look at institutions from a comparative perspective, i.e. they study the effects of different institutional settings on the demand and supply of art. Thus, it is not analyzed whether a theater produces a Pareto-optimal amount and quality of performances, but how the number of plays, and their quality, is affected if the theater acts in a competitive market or as a monopolistic supplier; whether it receives subsidies from the government or gains its revenues by its own productive efforts; whether the subsidies received are unconditional or conditional on the number of tickets sold, etc. As a result, the comparative institutional approach is directly related to relevant policy questions.

2.3   Comparison between the Two Views on Art

To look at the economics of art in terms of content or in terms of approach both have their merits. Nevertheless, it is argued here that the guiding principle should be to look at the economics of art as a *methodological approach.* The reason is that the material or monetary aspects of art can also be dealt with by other social sciences. This has, for instance, been shown in an exemplary way for sociology by Hauser (1953) in his monumental *Sozialgeschichte der Kunst und Literatur* or, more recently, by Foster and Blau (1989). The distinguishing characteristics of an *economics* of the arts would be lost if it were restricted to the interrelationship of economy and art. What makes the economics of art different from other approaches is its outlook, shaped by the assumption of individuals' rational behavior and the comparative view of institutions. It may, of course, be argued that economists have a relative advantage in looking at material or monetary aspects of art. This may be true, but it should not be overlooked that many practitioners have an excellent knowledge of such aspects (e.g. auctioneers on prices of paintings, or theater managers on salaries of actors), so that the economist's relative advantage again consists of the particular way such facts and figures are analyzed.

3.   The Economic Concept of Art

3.1   The Consequences of Individualism

The concept of art, as understood by economists, starts with the preferences or values of the *individual*. This distinguishes the economic concept of art fundamentally from other definitions of art which derive from quite different principles, e.g. from a notion of aesthetic beauty based on deeper philosophical grounds. It also strongly differs from the concept of art defined by art experts (art historians, museum curators, conservationists, art critics and journalists, gallery owners and artists themselves), who have a superior professional knowledge of the various aspects of artistic activities and therefrom derive the authority to pass judgement on what art is. According to the economic approach, the individual preferences for art are recorded, but no normative judgement about it is given: art in this sense is what people think art is[3]. Economists cannot, and do not want to, say what constitutes "good" or "bad" art; this is not within the realm of their professional competence, but should be left to those sciences (such as philosophy) which have a theory appropriate to dealing with the question of art quality.

A case in point is the "authentic" reproduction of paintings which it has been suggested be put into museums to overcome the scarcity of

---

[3]   While this sounds terribly naive, such a definition of art is indeed supported by some of the most sophisticated artists and art theorists, an example being Joseph Beuys.

originals (see Banfield 1984, based on the much earlier idea by André Malraux in his "Musée Imaginaire" 1947). Economists are neutral as to whether such copies represent art. They rely on the judgement of the consumers. In contrast, other sciences concerned with art do deal with the question of whether reproductions constitute art. Thus, philosophers of aesthetics tend to argue that copies do not have the special "aura" of the original. Art lawyers, for instance, would also claim differences because the rights of the creator of the original work of art may be affected. While economists in their professional capacity do not engage in the debate of whether copies are art, they have much to say about the consequences for demand and supply of producing perfect reproductions. Presumably, if the originals are no longer distinguishable from the copies, their price tends to fall. Museum managers would find themselves in a drastically different situation because they could now afford to exhibit any painting they cared to, and protection and preservation costs would fall heavily. But would art lovers still visit such museums? Or would new groups of people be attracted? It would indeed be fascinating to analyze the many different consequences by using the economics of art tools[4].

Two different kinds of individuals' preferences for art need to be distinguished. The *basic* preferences referring to the fundamental wishes of people are taken as exogenously determined; they are not the subject of economic analysis, but are left to other sciences better equipped to deal with them. Economists have limited knowledge about the factors affecting human preferences (see e.g. Becker, 1992), in particular how experts' opinions influence what ordinary people think about art – if they are influenced at all. It is often useful, especially when deriving testable propositions, to assume that these basic preferences do not change over time and do not in general differ widely between individuals. Preferences, as revealed in behavior, on the other hand, are not only shaped by the (constant) basic preferences but also by the constraints with which individuals are confronted. The difference between basic and revealed preferences can be demonstrated by considering the preferences for

---

[4]   An attempt is made in chapter 11 on "Art Fakes – What Fakes?".

visiting the opera. A person may have a deep love of the opera. Despite this marked basic preference for this form of art, he or she may reveal low preference for the opera when one looks at his or her behavior. Perhaps the opera lover is poor and cannot afford to buy a ticket (income constraint), or he/she is very much taken up by his/her profession (time constraint), or cannot find a baby-sitter (social constraint), or the next opera house is located too far away (physical constraint). In the same way, an economist would, as a working hypothesis, not assume that the Japanese have an intrinsic or even genetically given preference for buying European Impressionists and Expressionists (Renoirs, van Goghs)[5]. Rather, an economist would study to what extent the differences in the constraints between Japanese on the one hand, and American and European collectors on the other hand, influence the preferences revealed by their behavior. Relevant factors to look at would be the differential growth in income, relative price changes (in particular of the exchange rate between the dollar and the yen), the availability of different sorts of paintings at auctions, the difference in the "use" to which the paintings are put, differences in tax treatments, but also the differences in familiarity and in cultural education (impressionist paintings seem to be more similar to classical Japanese art), which can be studied by human capital theory (see Stigler and Becker 1977).

These two examples, serving to illustrate methodological individualism in general, and basic and revealed preferences in particular, refer to the demand side, but equally apply to the supply side. The production of art in all its forms is (in principle) traced back to individual behavior: there are frequent studies made on how, and to what extent, incentives and constraints induce people to create art.

The economic approach to art focuses on the fact that *scarcity* exists with respect to resources (capital and labor, natural resources and the

---

5   Remember that a couple of the highest prices ever payed for a painting are van Gogh's *Portrait du Dr. Gachet* (auctioned for $ 82,5 million in 1989), and *Sunflowers* (auctioned for $ 39.3 million in 1987), which both went to Japan.

environment), time and the physical as well as psychic[6] potential of persons. This again distinguishes the economics of art fundamentally from other studies of art (such as aesthetics, and of most art history), which are not concerned with scarcity and therefore do not deal with the problems and aspects alluded to above.

The economic approach outlined has the following consequences for the concept, and definition, of art:

- what is "art" is defined by individual actors and not by exogenous considerations or art experts;
- there is no such thing as "good" or "bad" art;
- what is considered "art" changes over time and differs between persons as a result of changing constraints, i.e. it is a dynamic concept;
- different institutional conditions affect individuals' constraints and therewith the concept of art.

The following two subsections discuss particular aspects of the economic approach – the demand for, and supply of, art.

3.2   The Demand for Art

An individual experiences utility from enjoying (consuming) what he or she considers to be art. The economist is able to measure this demand in the form of the "marginal willingness to pay". For the various art objects and artistic activities, variations in the willingness to pay can be observed, but it would be ridiculous to attach any intrinsic "artistic" value to such measurement. If individuals are prepared to pay twice as much to see a film than to see a theatrical play (or vice versa), this does not, of course, mean that the film is

---

6   The cognitive limitations of human beings have only slowly been acknowledged within economics. Pathbreaking is Simon's (1978, 1982) "bounded rationality", and the discussion of anomalies in human behavior (Kahneman, Slovic and Tversky 1982 or Dawes 1988). For a discussion of these limitations and the respective extensions of economics see Frey (1999a).

twice as "good" as the play – economists refrain from normative statements and simply register that the individuals in question are ready to pay twice as much, depending on *their own evaluation.*

The willingness of individuals to pay is often directly visible in the price paid for art objects (e.g. at auctions for paintings), or the entrance fee paid for attending a cultural event. In other cases, it must be measured empirically, for which there are many different methods (for an extensive discussion see Pommerehne 1987). They range from direct methods, via simple surveys and budget games (where the persons are subject to an income constraint), to indirect methods such as travel costs (measuring how much people are willing to spend in the way of time and money in order to see an artistic event), or market evaluations (where the willingness to pay for art is reflected in higher house and land values, all other things being constant). While these methods are sometimes not easy to apply, they nevertheless provide a useful quantitative picture of what the individuals composing society consider to be art.

It should be noted that such estimates are not democratic in the sense that the majority of citizens decide what art is. Rather, every person decides for him- or herself; a willingness to pay is recorded even if it only refers to a very small minority in the population. Indeed, it is quite possible that a few persons make up the bulk of a society's aggregate willingness to pay for a specific art form, i.e. even rare preferences for art can be expressed.

There are many areas and instances in which individuals do not exert their demand for art directly, but prefer to leave the decisions to some representative body. This can be parliament (which determines the size of the budget allocated to the arts), public administration (which distributes the funds to the various art institutions and artists), or a group of experts (which may either exert control at "arms' length" only, or hand out the money in the form of prizes or stipends). In these cases, the individuals' willingness to pay for art is expressed indirectly in the sense that these representative bodies are ultimately given the power to decide about art. Thus, in a democracy, the voters also decide on the general arts policy when they elect their parliament and government. In Switzerland, the citizens can express their preferences about art more directly by means of initiatives and referenda (see chapter 7 on "Public Support of the Arts in a Direct Democracy").

3.3   The Supply of Art

It is useful to distinguish between individuals acting (1) as artists producing independently, and (2) in the framework of an art organization such as a theater.

1. *Self-employed artists.* In most societies, everyone is free to call him- or herself an "artist". This may have been quite different in earlier times, when an artist was a well-defined member of a profession, i.e. had to undergo a specific education (mostly as an apprentice) and, moreover, had to belong to a guild (see e.g. Montias 1982). It may also be different in more primitive societies, where custom and tradition determine who is an artist. Economic thinking can be applied irrespective of an artist's underlying motivations.

   Who is, and who is not, an artist is, however, of crucial relevance to empirical studies on the share of artists in the population, and, more importantly, on artists' incomes (see e.g. Filer 1986). If a purely subjective evaluation is used, per capita income tends to be systematically lower than if one takes a more restricted definition, such as the membership in a professional association, or the successful completion of a recognized school of art.

2. *Artists in Organizations.* Most individuals in the performing arts work in a unit such as a theater company, in a corps de ballet or in a circus. But there are, of course, independent performers also in this area of art. Art organizations are also very important in the case of all kinds of museums. In economics, art organizations are not treated as collective entities with a life and behavior of their own. Rather they are the result of individual action.

Institutional conditions strongly determine to what extent an organization is free to call itself "artistic" or "cultural". In Western industrial societies, the use of these expressions is in principle free (e.g. it may even be used for purely pornographic performances). However, the government regulates and codifies its use whenever it supports the "arts" by handing out subsidies or allowing tax exemptions and tax credits. What constitutes "art" and "culture" is, in this case, the outcome of the interactions of a large number of people active in the political sphere. The result heavily depends on the strength of organizations interested in the government support of the arts, in particular the community made up of art experts and devoted art lovers. Established art forms such as theater, opera and ballet, or museums, have long enjoyed governmental promotion, while newcomers engaged in "illegitimate" art forms find it much harder to belong to the publicly recognized sector of art and culture.

3.4 Equilibrium Between Demand and Supply

The demand and supply side of art has so far been considered separately. It should be appreciated, however, that the equilibrium between demand and supply determines to a large extent what an artist is from the point of view of economics.

While every supplier is free to call him- or herself an "artist" in today's society, the term becomes more definite when the interaction with demand is taken into account. While a young lady working as a waitress may want to consider herself an opera singer (even without adequate education), it makes little sense to count her among the artists if the demand for her artistic services is so low that she works zero hours as a singer. The same applies if demand is so low that she receives only a small share of her total income from artistic activities.

In some countries, namely those influenced by German Romanticism, such a view is rejected: there is a strong tradition suggesting that a "true artist" is poor[7]. In contrast to what has just been argued, this tradition proposes a negative relationship between the quality of art and its marketability. However, this view is purely idealistic and has little to do with reality. Empirical evidence (see Frey and Pommerehne 1989a, chapter 9) shows that:

- by no means are all artists poor (van Gogh and Gauguin are exceptions and certainly not the rule);

- artists of high income are not necessarily of "poor" quality (defined according to art historians' evaluations);

- many "top-quality" artists have received very high incomes.

Examples of the last two statements are, among painters, Rubens, Tiziano and Rembrandt[8], Lenbach and Stuck, Picasso and Beuys; among composers, Mozart[9] and Beethoven, Verdi and Wagner; among singers Domingo, Pavarotti and Carreras; among writers, Shakespeare and Goethe, Dickens, Hauptmann, Brecht and Thomas Mann.

For the purpose of practical analysis, economists often follow the common distinctions between "creative art", "performing art" and "cultural heritage". Thus, for instance, Baumol and Bowen's (1966) or Throsby and Wither's (1979) books are devoted to the performing arts only, while Wagenführ's (1965), or Feldstein's (1991) books deal with creative art in the sense of paintings and museums only. Such differentiation makes sense in so far as the demand and supply processes, and therewith the equilibrium attained, deviate systematically from each other.

---

[7]   Spitzweg's picture "Der arme Poet" (1839) in Munich's Neue Pinakothek is a good illustration of people's perception of an artist in German-speaking countries.

[8]   Rembrandt earned a lot of money, but he (almost) went broke because of risky speculations with shipping stocks.

[9]   In contrast to what Milos Forman's film and Peter Shaffer's underlying play "Amadeus" portray, Mozart was well paid for his time, but he lost much of his money gambling (Baumol and Baumol 1994).

4.   Dynamic Aspects

The reactions to disequilibrium situations when either supply exceeds demand (excess supply) or demand exceeds supply (excess demand) allow important conclusions to be drawn about the concept of art in society, and should therefore be carefully studied.

4.1   Excess Supply of Art

Consider a theater company, which plays to an almost empty house. What does this situation reveal about the economic concept of art? The economist need not jump to the conclusion that lack of demand for the performance reveals that no art is involved. Rather, the analysis of this disequilibrium situation leads him or her to concentrate on the *process* of art in society.

A lack of demand to the extent stated in our example leads to a commercial *loss* for the theater company. This disequilibrium situation cannot be maintained over an extended period. Three solutions are possible:

1. The company does not survive. In this case, "art" indeed disappears, it is no longer produced.

2. The theater company is reorganized so that costs are reduced and/or demand is increased. If this means avoiding a loss and enables the company to survive, we have an example of market produced art.

3. The company covers the losses of producing the play by outside funding. Private sources, usually benefiting from tax exemptions, may directly sponsor the activity. In this case, a change in tax laws has a strong impact on whether such privately subsidized art is able to survive[10]. The loss may also be covered by the government. What type of art survives, and what culture

---

[10]   For example, restrictions on tax exemptions in the United States have resulted in a reduction of private donations to museums of 24 percent, according to some estimates. See Fullerton (1991).

therefore is, is in that case politically determined by what parties are in   government and parliament, how well the cultural interests are organized compared to other pressure groups, what art experts' influence is, and how good the budget situation is.

As has become clear, different factors are responsible, and are studied by art economists, depending on which of the three adjustment processes equilibrate the excess supply of art.

4.2   Excess Demand for Art

Consider again an extreme example, namely that a demand for a particular artistic activity exists, but that the supply is not forthcoming. The analysis of this disequilibrium again draws attention to factors relevant to understanding art in society.

In the example given, artistic activity has not taken place and cannot be measured as part of society's output (e.g. as part of national product). However, the pertinent question is *why* the "profit" opportunities given by existing demand are not exploited by offering the corresponding supply of artistic activities. Three major reasons for a disequilibrium can be analyzed:

1. The production of the artistic output is not feasible because costs exceed the stated willingness to pay. The question then arises whether individuals' demand captures all the benefits produced by the artistic activity or, in other words, whether any (relevant, i. e. marginal) externalities exist. The literature based on economic welfare theory has identified important public good effects produced by art (see i.e. Throsby and Withers 1983 for Australia), the most important being the option value, the existence value, the prestige value, the education value and the bequest value (see chapters 1 and 10). Depending on the size of these external effects, it may normatively be argued that the corresponding artistic activities should exist, and economists can suggest policy measures designed to reflect individuals' true marginal willingness to pay.

2. The artistic activity is not forthcoming because its supply is forbidden or at least hindered. Political restrictions on the supply of art do not only exist in authoritarian regimes and dictatorships but also in democracies, especially when aspects of sexuality are involved[11].

3. Supply is not adjusted to demand in order to maintain, or willingly produce, a queue. The goal is to make consumers interpret the length of the queue as an indication of quality (see also rational for the suppliers when they are able to appropriate (part Becker 1991 for the case of queues in restaurants). Such behavior is of) the rents arising from the artificially created scarcity. In many public theaters, opera houses and festivals, the managers raise their level of power, prestige and, directly or indirectly, their income by allowing a black market for tickets (for an extensive discussion on the case of the Salzburg Festival see Frey and Pommerehne 1989a, ch. 4).

In order to understand what kind and quality of art is produced under these conditions, it is again necessary to undertake an analysis along the lines of Political Economy. It should be emphasized that the outcome of the political process does not necessarily reflect the normative considerations just discussed. In particular, it may well be that the government does not intervene though, for example, an option or existence value exists that is not reflected in the market. On the other hand, political forces often induce the government to support art even when no such external effects exist. In contrast to the welfare theoretic approach of conventional economics, the politico-economic analysis allows for the identification of the factors which determine the production of culture in these areas, and which indirectly define what "art" is from the economic point of view.

---

[11]   A recent example in the United States is Mapplethorpe's photographs.

5.   Concluding Remarks

There are two ways to understand the Economics of Art: as the economic forces determining art and the economic consequences of art on the one hand, and the application of the economic analysis to the arts on the other hand. It is argued that the latter concept focusing on the methodological approach should be used because only there do economists enjoy a relative advantage. This does, of course, not mean that the former aspects should be neglected, but that the economic causes and consequences should be analyzed from the rational choice perspective in order to differentiate it from other approaches such as the sociology, psychology, or law of art.

The economic approach is characterized by its individualistic focus and its acceptance of individual preferences. "Art" is defined to be what people think art is, and economists do not judge whether art is "good" or "bad". The concept of "art" changes over time as a result of changing constraints, in particular changes in income, prices and the value of time. These constraints are in turn shaped by the institutional conditions existing on both the demand and supply sides of art. In equilibrium, the economic concept of art is defined as a consequence of the preferences and constraints of all the actors involved.

Disequilibrium situations, in which supply exceeds demand, or demand exceeds supply, help us to better understand the process by which art is produced and demanded, and therewith how the economist's concept of art evolves.

Chapter 3 -
For Art's Sake – Open Up the Vaults*

1. Why Is So Little Shown?

Museums keep a substantial share of their holdings hidden in storage rooms. Why is that so, and what can be done to overcome this situation? New possibilities can only be suggested in a useful way after having analyzed why the situation is as it is.

Many paintings belonging to art museums (the following discussion is focusing on these) are never exhibited to the public and are at best available to art historians, who are on good terms with the directorate. But quite often nobody may see these paintings because they are stored in such a way as to be inaccessible. Some of them are sometimes exhibited in the museum itself or loaned to other museums for special exhibitions, or they go on the road for travelling exhibitions. However, the percentage of paintings rarely or never shown is substantial. While – for reasons to be subsequently discussed – exact data are difficult to get, it is safe to say that most museums exhibit at best half of their total holdings, and often not more than one quarter of their stock. The Prado in

---

*   This chapter is based on Bruno S. Frey (1994), "Cultural Economics and Museum Behaviour", previously published in the *Scottish Journal of Political Economy* 41 (3), pp. 325-335, used by permission of Blackwell Publishers.

Madrid is a good illustration of this phenomenon. Only 1781 out of the 19056 objects the museum listed within its holdings in summer 1992 – i.e. not even 10 percent – were on permanent display (The Economist, May 1, 1993, p. 97). What is kept in storage rooms therefore constitutes a significant part of a museum's holdings.

To an economist analyzing art and, in particular, museums[1], the question immediately arises as to why the stock rarely or never displayed is not sold and the receipts used for buying paintings more suitable for the existing collection or for other important purposes of the museum such as: restoring dilapidated paintings, extending the showroom capacity, increasing visiting hours or improving security and fire precautions. Such an alternative use of museum holdings would be to the benefit of all art lovers. These issues are discussed in section 2: after analyzing why the museums rarely sell paintings, propositions are brought forward, in which the possibility of monetizing the existing stock of art is considered.

A wider aspect of museum behavior is also to be considered. Museum behavior is influenced by many different legal, administrative and financial constraints, but also by the way the museum people (such as the curators and art administrators) think and act. More flexibility, dynamism and new ideas should be introduced, resulting in a better fulfillment of the preferences of the people with respect to art. These aspects are discussed in section 3.

2.   Museums and Storage

2.1   Storage as a Capital Stock

In most art museums of the world, a considerable part of the holdings of paintings is not exhibited and not accessible, except possibly to specialists. Moreover, what constitutes the major part of the wealth of an institution, such as an art museum, does not even

---

[1]   Other aspects of the economics of museums are analyzed in the special issue of the *Journal of Cultural Economics,* edited by Johnson and Thomas (1998).

appear in the balance sheet; the bookkeeping procedure of art museums does not mention that the paintings collected are of any value, although at today's art market prices collections of even minor museums are likely to be worth dozens of millions of Euros, and in the case of major museums many billions of Euros.

To economists (as well as to practical people), a museum's holdings are part of the capital, which yields benefits in various forms, in particular for the enjoyment of the viewers. The value of this capital is the price at which the paintings could be sold on the market. This evaluation serves the purpose of explicitly showing the *opportunity cost* of a museum's holdings. At a (real) rate of interest of 5 percent per year for instance, a painting held by a museum and worth one million Euros means a steady flow of income of 50.000 Euros forgone each year, i.e. which could have been used in a different way. Thus, the painting under consideration could be "transformed" into a permanent flow of 50.000 Euros, which could be spent on hiring more guards, providing more security against theft and fire, undertaking conservation and necessary repairs, organizing exhibitions, conducting art historic research or improving the working conditions for the staff and the viewing pleasure of the visitors. As an art museum's total holdings are typically worth many tens or hundreds of millions of Euros, the corresponding opportunity cost of forgone income flows amount to many millions of Euros per year. Alternatively, the capital sum of one million Euros could be used to buy one or more paintings, or to extend the existing buildings.

The dramatic rise over the last decades in the general price level for paintings of old masters, of impressionists and of modern classics, is reflected in a strong increase in the overall value of art museums, but also in the steady flow of income forgone each year. Obviously, these opportunity costs are particularly acute for those paintings which are kept in storage rooms and never or rarely shown to anybody. The failure to consider opportunity cost throws up the question why such behavior happens. The museum managers know of course that their holdings have a great value, and they cannot be assumed to act in an irrational way. But why do rational, well-informed people systematically fail to account for these large sums of money?

2.2   Explanations

Six reasons will be discussed regarding the question of why the museum directorate keeps such large storage without exploiting the opportunities available by selling at least part of the storage and putting the receipts to better use.

1. *Low value.* Paintings kept in storage rooms are often claimed to have little or no monetary value, so that a sale is not worthwhile. This is implausible when considering the huge increase in the price of paintings which are not first rate (e.g. Pontormo's *Cosimo I dei Medici*, which in 1989 fetched $ 35 million) or of which there exist several, almost identical versions (e.g. van Gogh's *Sunflowers*, which was auctioned for $ 39.9 million). Obviously, the idea is not to immediately sell all the paintings stored by all museums – which would, of course, depress market prices – but to slowly de-access. Selling would not necessarily have to be restricted to the paintings in storage but could also extend to the art objects exhibited; relevant is only whether the revenue gained by selling could be put to better use, e.g. by buying a painting which fits better into that particular collection. In this context it might be argued that the museum decision makers are art historians who put a value on the paintings which differs from the market price. This is only relevant if the value attributed exceeds the market price (otherwise they would willingly sell). Two aspects should be distinguished here:

   (a) It is difficult to see why the *market evaluation* should deviate from the *art historic evaluation* because a large part of the demand exerted for paintings either comes from art historians themselves or directors of private galleries, art houses or art museums, an example being the Getty Museum which employs a large number of highly rated art historians among its staff or its advisers. If a particular art historian is confident that the market price currently underrates a painting's "intrinsic" value, he or she can buy the painting at the low price and can later sell it at a higher price, an activity by which art dealers indeed make a good living. The result of such art speculation is that the two evaluations come near each other. It is certainly true that an art historian holds adifferent evaluation from all the other buyers and sellers on the art market, but whether he or she is "right" in the sense that all the others later follow his or her view is a matter of good or bad luck, and basically the same as on a market for financial assets, say the stock market. Art historians are not *in general* better speculators on the art market than other actors, because what determines a painting's "value" depends on many factors, including fashions, which art historians find as hard to predict as other people.

(b) An art historian as museum director may value the funds gained from selling systematically lower than the market because the revenue received by selling cannot be used freely. This is exactly the aspect discussed in the following subsections; it should be clearly distinguished from aspect (a).

2. *Sale is forbidden.* In many countries, governments impose *legal constraints* to selling. Many, or even most, public museums in Europe are prohibited from de-accessing. The government has an incentive to restrict the museum directorate in order to maintain its dependence.

Quite a different matter are the voluntary contracts between the museum directorate and donors, who often want to keep the collection they give as a whole and often require it to be put into particular rooms. The directorate is faced with a trade-off between receiving additional paintings and having to accept certain restrictions. If it decides to accept the gift, its value must be higher than the cost of the restrictions involved, i.e. the museum people's evaluation of having the paintings exceeds their opportunity cost.

3. *Asymmetric mental accounting.* This explanation resorts to a psychological anomaly[2]. A painting that leaves the museum's holdings is considered a loss, but the potential income from selling it is not considered a gain of equal value. This may be due to lesser visibility of gains compared to costs because the latter are not dealt with in monetary terms but in terms of opportunities forgone. The perception of loss may also exceed that of the gain due to the endowment effect, a phenomenon well established in experimental research[3]. Asymmetric mental accounting is likely to exist in art, but the fact that private museums (especially in the United States) do sometimes sell part of their holdings suggests that it is not very common.

4. *Potential loss.* Museum directorates fear that the paintings sold may be looked at as a *loss* to the art community. This holds in particular when a painting *leaves the country.* However, there is no reason why art should not be traded internationally (see the arguments in Frey and Pommerehne 1989a, chapter 8).

Museum people may also resent it when paintings in their holdings move into a *private* collection. To an economist, this concern is difficult to understand because what matters is the willingness to pay (or marginal utility), which by definition in the case of selling is higher for the private buyer than for the public seller. Moreover, paintings in private collections are also often exhibited (e.g. van Gogh's *Sunflowers* by the insurance company Yasudo in Japan) and/or are loaned for special exhibitions and for travelling exhibitions.

In most cases, de-accessioning by one museum means that the painting is acquired by *another museum*, so that it is even more difficult to understand why a loss should be involved. On the contrary, the museum acquiring the painting is more likely to prominently exhibit the painting bought than to abscond it to its storage rooms, so that the public's exposure to art increases.

---

2   Surveys are given by Dawes 1988, Frey and Eichenberger 1989a,b; collections of readings are Kahneman, Slovic and Tversky 1982, Hogarth and Reder 1987, Arkes and Hammond 1986.

3   See the surveys by Butler and Hey 1987, Roth 1988, Smith 1989.

Museums do indeed quite often make such transactions, but on the basis of an exchange rather than a sale. To an economist, such barter is inefficient and should be substituted by explicit monetary exchange.

5. *Commercialization.* Museums do not sell the holdings in their vaults because such action would siphon off the museum's *administration energy* into commercial activities. The purpose of museums would therefore be endangered. Art historians feel that they should pursue the conservation and exhibition of art, but not meddle in monetary dealings.

However, such a view is idealistic and incompatible with reality. Museum directors today spend a large part of their energy and time on monetary affairs; in particular they have to lobby with politicians and public administrations to secure their budget and to attract private and corporate sponsors. This "rent seeking" activity involves a negative sum game, i.e. in the end the actors as a whole are worse off than at the outset. The museum directors, who in Europe are usually part of the public administration, have to observe a large number of legal restrictions, which also takes away energy from their art historic task. Empirically speaking, the charge that selling and buying holdings reduces the artistic quality of museums is difficult to maintain, considering the fact that some of the leading museums in the United States engaged in commercial dealings rank among the best art institutions. One example among many is the Museum of Modern Art (MOMA) in New York.

The five answers so far provided for the question why museums keep such a large share of their holdings inaccessible in storage rooms and do not sell are only partly convincing. The real reason for the disregard of opportunity costs lies in the particular *incentives* faced by the museum administration, to be discussed in the following.

6. *Lack of Incentives.* The decisive explanation of the behavior observed is that the directorate of public museums has no advantage in selling its holdings held in storage. It is rational for it not to de-access for two major reasons:

(a) When a painting is sold, the revenue gained is not added to the museum's disposable income but, according to the rules of the public administration in most countries, goes into the general public treasury. Even if this is not the case, the budget allocated to the museum is most likely to be correspondingly reduced. The politicians and the ministry of finance argue that the museum can (partly) fund itself, so that less needs to be given by the government. The museum directorate's effort to sell paintings not exhibited thus results in an implicit "tax" of one hundred percent. Such confiscatory taxation kills all incentive to de-access. Corporate sponsors are likely to react in the same way when approached by the museum directors. A similar undesired effect of selling part of the stock is that prospective donors are discouraged. When they give a particular painting to a museum, they want it to be kept, and have their name attached to the gift. If the painting is sold, the gift becomes anonymous and is no longer attributed to the particular donor.

(b) Selling paintings means that the existing stock of art is at least partly monetized, which eases outside interference by politicians and parliamentarians in the museum's business. The museum directorate's "performance" becomes easier to evaluate. Specifically, the buying and selling prices of particular paintings can be compared. As long as the criteria for evaluation are exclusively of an art historic kind, the museum community is to a substantial extent able to define its performance itself. Such isolation is a useful and successful survival strategy for museum administrators, which they want to preserve.

2.3   Proposals

On the basis of the six explanations offered, it is now possible to suggest measures to overcome the reluctance of museums to de-access their holdings. The museum directorate's behavior can be changed only if the *institutional arrangements,* which distort their incentives in the direction of accumulating, but not selling, paintings are rectified. Two proposals serve this purpose.

(a) *Greater freedom.* Museums should be made into administratively *more independent* bodies. They need not be fully privatized[4], but should be subject to only very general governmental supervision. At least they should be given complete budget sovereignty, so that they can sell paintings *and* use the corresponding receipts freely for buying other art stocks, for restoration, for exhibitions etc., i.e. for any other purpose the directorate sees fit.

Private American art museums are indeed active in selling and buying art in order to suit their purposes. In the period 1988-89, 88 museums sold 1284 lots worth $ 29.6 million, and 93 museums bought 142 lots worth $ 37.5 million (Cantor 1991, Table I.I, p. 21). The director of the Getty Museum states that "this practice . . . (is) the key to shaping the collections by the staffs of many major big city museums with large collections, and others too" (Walsh 1991, p. 26).

(b) *Internalization of externalities.* The government subsidy given to art museums is based on the "social value", or (in economic terms) on the "external effects", produced in terms of option, existence and prestige values. The museum is not – or only partly – able to internalize these externalities. The subsidy should *not* be based on the (projected) difference between expenditures and income – as is the case today – but on the external effects generated. Art museums, as well as other cultural institutions, have a good case for receiving public subsidies, in particular if compared to the many other subsidized institutions, such as sports clubs and other forms of leisure.

The two proposals result in a dramatic change in incentives for the museum directorate. The income earned by selling paintings from

---

[4]   Museums then have a mixed form of governance incorporating both public and private governing authorities. Such "hybridization" is under way both in the United States and Europe (see Schuster 1998 and, for the aspect of communication, Hutter 1998a).

their stocks is no longer fully taxed away and *the museum directorate* can spend the money for those activities it thinks most important.

3.   More Enterprising Museums

The two proposals made also set incentives in order to overcome the closed and restricted sphere in which most European museums operate today. The many administrative restrictions imposed on the management of the museums are removed when art museums become quasi-independent or fully independent institutions. This allows them to be more enterprising and to test new concepts and ideas, to the benefit of the art-loving public.

A museum directorate, which benefits from raising the museum's revenue, will want greater flexibility with respect to the admission of visitors' and additional income sources.

3.1   More Flexible Admission Policy

All over Europe, visitors are faced with the very restrictive opening hours of public museums. In many cities, for example, all museums are closed on the same day. Normally it is Monday, exactly a day when many weekend tourists are still in the various cities, as this substantially lowers the transport (flight) costs. A visitor thus cannot substitute one museum for another. Moreover, the *visiting hours* are short. A museum directorate interested in gaining revenue will make the effort to attract visitors by offering attractive opening hours, thus following the example of (private) service industries such as restaurants or leisure parks.

Even more possibilities exist with respect to *entrance fees*. The present inflexible pricing rules (essentially a single level entrance fee) could be adjusted to varying demand, thus allowing for the diversion of a larger part of the visitors' expenditure for the benefit of the museum they intend to visit (instead of for the suppliers of other goods). The principle (well known from optimal pricing theory) is that the more inelastic the demand is, the higher the price has to be. A museum can set about *price differentiation* in two ways:

(a) In times of high demand, i.e. during those hours of the day, days of the week and weeks of the year when a lot of people want to visit a particular museum, a higher entrance fee is asked than in periods of low demand. In particular, when large numbers oftourists decide to visit the museums in the summer, prices could be raised. The increase in revenue can be used to pay the additional cost of extending the opening hours e.g. into the late evening, or to open additional wings.

(b) Prices can also be differentiated between different types of visitors. For economic as well as for political reasons it can make sense to charge higher entrance fees to foreign visitors than to local visitors. The latter can, for example, be sold a ticket which allows them to visit the museums at all times when their capacity is not fully used, i.e. when the marginal cost of a visit is (practically) zero. On the other hand, the museum can offer guided tours through its exhibition which will be especially attractive for foreign visitors because of the suitable hours, the interesting setting and well-known guides (e.g. a film or TV celebrity showing a collection in the late evening with beautifully illuminated rooms). Such tours could, at least in the case of famous museums, be sold for a good price to tourist enterprises, which would then look after all the necessary advertising.

Prices can also be differentiated between visitors who want to spend little time on the visit to a museum and those who are prepared to spend ample time. In periods of high demand, when the art museum's capacity is fully used, two entrance prices can be set, a high and a low one. The high priced entrance will have a correspondingly shorter waiting queue and will be used by the first category of visitors. The low price entry option will be used by the second category of visitors, among them students and other young people who don't want to spend too much money, but who have plenty of time available. Price differentiation is advantageous for both categories of visitors (one gets in more quickly, the other pays less) as well as for the museum administration, which can therewith raise its revenue.

3.2   Other Income Sources

A museum directorate which can independently determine its budget, and therefore has an incentive to increase its revenue, has various possibilities to do so. Only three of the many options possible will be mentioned here. They suffice to show that an art museum which can make free use of its holdings may set about activities which under today's constraints are not, or only insufficiently, used.

1. *Improve amenities.* The museum can raise substantial revenue by establishing a good *café* and *restaurant* as well as a *museum shop* offering a broad range of artistic goods. For example, New York's Museum of Modern Art (MOMA), a first rate institution, covers as much as 30 percent of its total revenue from "publications and similar activities" (Parkhurst 1975, p. 85). In the period 1986-88, museums of art in the United States had total earnings of $ 301 million, which amounts to 17.5 percent of total revenue. Stock revenues were $ 84 million, revenues from restaurants $ 5 million, and other earnings (e.g. tuition charges, fees for the use of facilities) $ 130 million. The remaining $ 82 million were earned by admission fees (Rosett 1991, tables 6.3, 6.8, pp. 144-147). Clearly, such commercial enterprises are much to the benefit of the visitors, as any museum addict knows.

2. *Attract funds.* Special exhibitions, events and extensions of the museum can be financed by *sponsoring* from private individuals and firms. This source of revenue has, over the last years, been increasingly used. From 1986-88, private donations in the United States amounted to $ 465 million, or 27 percent of total revenue, corporate donations to $ 112 million or 6.5 percent of total revenue (Rosett 1991, tables 6.2 and 6.3).

3. *Increase art exchange.* Paintings, which the museum administration for one reason or another does not want to sell although it does not exhibit them, can be loaned for a fee. Of course, much care must be taken, but this can be guaranteed by

appropriate insurance. For example, New York's Metropolitan Museum of Art has, at any given time, between five and ten thousand works of art on loan (Feldstein 1991, p. 33).

4.   Concluding Remarks

The present analysis, as well as some of the proposals made, are likely to meet with heated opposition from the "museum community" and the "world of art". The high realms of "art" will be set against a lowly "commercialization". It has been made clear that such opposition is not surprising because any change in the existing situation threatens existing interests.

Artists, however, are not necessarily against the viewpoints submitted here. Painters, especially, are often well aware of the crucial role of the art market and particularly of private galleries for the propagation of their products. Indeed, from the economic perspective, private galleries are "speculators" in the sense that they invest in unknown artists in order to profit when they get famous. As only a very small share of them *will* become successful, private art galleries are engaged in extremely risky speculations, which explains why there is such a high turnover among them, with many galleries closing down each year. In a recent contribution to a monograph on public museums (Reder 1988, pp. 25-34), the well-known Austrian artist Arnulf Rainer argued that such museums can only become lively and dynamic with respect to opening hours, amenities for visitors and also exhibition policy, if they are privatized and if competition is introduced rather than suppressed. In Rainer's view, public museums should become similar to private art galleries. Expositions to "market processes in art would guarantee a better choice than any public institution" (p. 32, my translation).

In this chapter, it has *not* been proposed that all museums should become private. The question of legal ownership is not decisive, but what matters is that the persons responsible for public museums be given the necessary *incentives* and *independence* to employ the resources and possibilities at their disposition more freely.

Chapter 4 -
Superstar Museums:
An Economic Analysis*

1. What is a Superstar Museum?

There are thousands of museums of many different kinds in all
countries of the world. This paper deals with a select few among
those museums, namely the generally well-known and world famous
museums of art, particularly those focusing on paintings. I shall call
these institutions *"superstar museums"* because they have a special
status, which sets them apart from other museums.

Superstar museums are characterized by five aspects:

1. *A "must for tourists"*. Superstar museums are featured
   prominently in guide-books. The readers are told that a visit is not
   to be missed. Some travel guides and books on art use similar
   symbols to the Guide Michelin stars for restaurants. The superstar
   museums certainly "vaut un voyage". Such advice by tourist
   guides, though helpful, is not really necessary. Superstar
   museums have achieved cult status, which almost everyone is

* This chapter is based on Bruno S. Frey (1998), "Superstar Museums: An
Economic Analysis", previously published in the *Journal of Cultural
Economics* 22, pp. 113-125, used by permission of Kluwer Academic
Publishers.

aware of. There are not many tourists who, for example, go to Leningrad without visiting the Hermitage, Rome without the Vatican Museums, Florence without the Uffizi, Madrid without the Prado, London without the National Gallery, Vienna without the Kunsthistorische Museum, Amsterdam without the Rijksmuseum, or Paris without the Louvre. The same holds for the many tourists visiting the United States; there are certainly only a few who would not visit the Metropolitan Museum of Art and/or the Museum of Modern Art when in New York, the National Gallery of Art when in Washington, or the Art Institute when in Chicago and, more recently, the Getty Museum when in Los Angeles. In contrast, people often tour other major cities (e.g. Moscow, Copenhagen, Lisbon, Budapest or Prague) without entering a museum of art.

Tour operators exploit this demand to visit superstar museums by making corresponding offers. Art publishers also take advantage of this interest in superstar museums, which in turn increases their prominence, leading to what may be called a "virtuous circle". What has been said refers to the knowledge of the average person and not to readers of this book who can certainly point out dozens of further "important" museums in any of these and other cities. There are, of course, hundreds of additional art museums well known among art lovers and the *cognoscenti*. But they do not have the mass appeal which, I argue, has a strong influence on all museums.

2. *A large number of visitors*. Superstar museums have experienced a dramatic increase in the number of visitors and are now an integral part of mass tourism. In the nineties, millions of people visited the important art museums each year: for example, the Metropolitan Museum of Art in New York: 4 million; the National Gallery in London: 3 million; the Louvre in Paris: 6 million (see Bayart and Benghozi 1993). About 50 percent of the visitors to the British Museum or the National Gallery are foreigners, mainly tourists (National Audit Office 1993).

The superstar museums attract a growing share of visitors, while the other museums tend to have fewer visitors. In 1998, for example, the Louvre augmented its number of visitors by 11 percent over the previous year, to 5.7 million. For important French museums with more than 100,000 visitors, the growth rate in 1998 was 5 percent. In contrast, small museums with less than 100,000 visitors experienced a decline in the number of visitors by 3 percent.

3. *World famous painters and world famous paintings.* Superstar museums feature painters and paintings that are known to (almost) everybody. The superstar idea was originally developed to account for the high income of specific persons, emphasizing that the differences to other persons in income far exceed the differences in talent and performance. This also applies in the case of artists and painters. The great disparity among artists is a striking feature of all the studies on their income distribution (see e.g. Filer 1986 or chapter 9 in Frey and Pommerehne 1989a). The collections in large museums comprise works by thousands of artists; only a fraction of them are known to art lovers, let alone to the general public. Museums, which want to attract a large crowd, have to concentrate on the few renowned artists. This applies, in particular, to the superstar museums. They have no choice but to exhibit the superstar artists in their collection and, moreover, have to organize special exhibitions with superstar artists. While this leads to an unequivocal competitive advantage over the minor museums because the superstar museums can offer superior works, i.e. paintings by well-known artists, they are at the same time heavily constrained by the superstar status. Thus, it would be quite inconceivable that the Rijksmuseum in Amsterdam decides not to show Rembrandt any more, or the Prado to no longer show Velasquez. In consonance with the need to concentrate on major artists, the majority of newly established museums are devoted to one such artist only. Examples would be the Picasso Museum in Paris, the van Gogh Museum in Amsterdam, or the Miró Museum in Barcelona.

Some paintings are virtually known to everyone in the western world (and far beyond) but the number is rather small. A museum which owns one of them has no choice but to exhibit it most prominently, if possible in a hall by itself. Examples are the (so-called) "Nightwatch" in Amsterdam's Rijksmuseum, or "Las Meninas" in the Prado. The quintessential superstar painting is Leonardo's "Mona Lisa". The Louvre has responded by sign-posting, right at the entrance, the most direct route to the Mona Lisa. There are also plans to establish a special room dedicated to this one picture – including an entrance separate from the rest of the museum – in order to cater for the wishes of that segment of visitors only wanting to see the Mona Lisa. Even the Vatican Museum now posts the (more or less) direct way to another world famous painting, Michelangelo's frescos in the Capella Sistina.

Superstar museums, of course, have not yet become "one picture shows". However, what is argued here is that over the last decades they have moved in that direction. From the visitors' point of view, even very large museums are closely associated with, or defined by, very few (often one or two) paintings – the superstar phenomenon. Museums are not only the proud owners of these masterpieces but at the same time their captives. They are not only forced to exhibit them but this also means that, in comparison, their other paintings lose prominence. There may be a slight spillover of interest to less renowned pieces in the collection. The main effect is, however, to draw the attention away from the rest of the collection.

Museums without such major pictures are faced with problems. This even holds true when they have some paintings by world famous artists in their collection. A good example is the Kunstmuseum in Basle, which has an excellent collection of works by Picasso, van Gogh and other expressionists and impressionists, as well as by Holbein, but does not feature a painting which is known all over the world. The Getty Museum in Los Angeles can attract huge crowds due to its location and architecture. But until recently, it has lacked a superstar painting. Interestingly, the directorate has made a huge effort to acquire a world famous painting. It paid the enormous sum of $ 35.2 million to buy Pontormo's *Cosimo I*, one of the top ten prices ever paid at an auction. But selling price alone did not make it really prominent, probably because Pontormo does not measure up in popularity to Leonardo, not even among art lovers. Perhaps as a result, Getty has now (for an undisclosed price) acquired van Gogh's "Irises", which is far better known to the general public.

4. *Architecture.* Superstar museums are often located in buildings which themselves constitute a world famous artistic feature. Examples are Frank Lloyd Wright's Guggenheim Museum in New York; the Centre Pompidou in Paris; Mario Botta's San Francisco Museum of Modern Art; Frank Gehry's Guggenheim Museum in Bilbao, and Richard Meier's Getty Center in Los Angeles.

5. *Commercialization.* Superstar museums can be said to be commercialized in two respects:

   (a) A significant part of their income derives from the revenue from the museum bookshops and museum restaurants.

   (b) Superstar museums have a major impact on the local economy because the museum visitors spend money on many additional goods and services that are unrelated to the museum, such as hotel rooms or shopping.

Superstar museums differ with respect to the importance of these five characteristics. Ideally they fully meet all of them; the Musée du Louvre is an example, the architectural feature mainly being Ming Pei's pyramid in the special courtyard. Other superstar museums are very strong with respect to some characteristics while barely meeting other characteristics. An example is Amsterdam's Rijksmuseum, which is not particularly noted for its architecture – at least compared to, say, the Centre Pompidou in Paris or the Guggenheim Museum in Bilbao.

The superstar phenomenon is analyzed in the next section. Section 3 applies the phenomenon to the case of museums. Section 4 discusses the consequences for museum organization and museum policy.

2.   What Are "Superstars" in Art?

The superstar effect states that small differences in innate ability and quality may result in very large differences in outcome and particularly in income (Rosen 1981). The very best artists, the superstars, gain much higher income than those artists who are almost, but not quite as talented[1], Frank and Cook (1995) have applied this phenomenon to a great number of professions, including, for instance, lawyers. If a firm is engaged in a lawsuit of millions or even billions of dollars, it normally pays to hire the very best in order to maximize the probability of winning. The same holds for the best managers who also demand very high compensation but who may increase the value of the firm by billions of dollars.

The superstar phenomenon in art has been related to the demand and the supply side of the market.

2.1   Demand

On the *demand* side, consumers are *unwilling to substitute* lower for higher talent even for a cheaper price. They tend not to be satisfied with the performance of a less gifted but cheaper artist when they are able to enjoy the performance of a top artist, even if the cost is somewhat higher. Most of them buy, for example, opera recordings by Maria Callas or Placido Domingo at a higher price than the somewhat less expensive recordings by unknown tenors. This behavioral trait of individuals can also be transferred to painters. Most people, for example, choose not to spend time looking at lesser known Cubists when they can enjoy Picasso's paintings.

This unwillingness to substitute lesser for greater talent can be attributed to three different factors:

1. *An economic reason.* The cost of comparing the performance of artists has dramatically decreased over the last decades due to lower travel costs and the modern media. Centuries ago, an artist who dominated a city or region, could be a star because only a very few persons were able to compare his or her performance with those located elsewhere. This was the time when local opera

---

[1]   The very high income of top artists compared to other artists is documented in Frey and Pommerehne (1989a, ch. 9 on "Artists' Incomes"). For movie stars, see e.g. Albert (1998).

singers, for example, were highly appreciated and even worshipped. Today it is different. Radio, film, television, discs, video and internet make it possible for everyone to compare local and foreign talents. The frame of reference has completely shifted. As a consequence, local artists now have a very difficult time, even though their talents may be only slightly lower than those of the world superstars.

2. *Cognitive problems.* It is difficult to remember more than two or three top performers in any specific class. Virtually hundreds of millions recognize the names of tenor superstars Pavarotti and Domingo (and perhaps Carreras) but only very few remember the names of other tenors who are nearly as talented (if not more talented). A factor contributing to this focus of recognition on a few persons is the widening of general or superficial knowledge acquired by many people through watching television.

3. *Sharing knowledge.* Superstars also emerge because art consumption is not an isolated activity, but is socially shared (Adler 1985). Much of the pleasure derived from consuming art consists in the possibility of discussing it with other people, especially friends and acquaintances. Such exchanges of views and experiences require that the other participants share some common prior knowledge, which makes it much easier. As a consequence, discussion focuses on widely known persons, the superstars.

These reasons produce a concentration of demand on a select few artists[2], the superstars. It is reflected in differences in income and fame, which far exceed any differences in talent and performance.

---

[2]   The selection process of the development of these select few is not the topic of this chapter. I am simply trying to explain why the concentration exists today and to analyze what consequences it has for museum policy.

2.2   Supply

On the *supply* side, the modern media produce significant economies of scale (see e.g. Horowitz 1983). With nearly the same cost, it is possible today to reach an audience of 100, 10.000, 10 million, or one billion people. This means that the marginal cost of another consumer is extremely low. Technical progress, which has led to these huge economies of scale in production and distribution, has basically changed the supply of art. *In situ* attendance at a performance (e.g. of the three tenors Pavarotti, Domingo and Carreras at the Thermes of Carracalla) has become negligible compared to the real-time attendance via TV. Canned performances on CDs and videos are another technical means to make artistic productions available to a very large audience at very low marginal cost. A similar change has taken place in the visual arts. The number of people visiting a museum and actually viewing a work of art is small compared to those who have seen it in reproductions, on the Internet, or on TV.

This chapter generalizes the idea of "superstars' beyond people and thus beyond the labor market. It is argued that the same processes working on the demand and supply side that make *persons* into superstars also make *institutions* – in our case museums – into superstars. Even cities may qualify as superstars (see Towse 1991 and Mossetto 1992, who apply this term to Venice).

The following section discusses the character of museums as superstars.

3.   How Do Superstar Museums Function?

Some art museums have reached the status of superstars and have become household names to hundreds of millions of people. Only a few museums are of this rank; they are mostly associated with major tourist cities, which in turn owe part of their prominence to the superstar museums. Most cities have, at best, one art museum of that type (e.g. Los Angeles with the Getty Museum). Rather rarely, some cities have more than one superstar museum such as Paris with the

Musée du Louvre, Musée d'Orsay and the Centre Pompidou, or Madrid with the Prado, the Reina Sofia and the Thyssen-Bornemisza.

The emergence of superstar museums can be associated with the factors sketched above, where superstar persons were discussed.

People today are unwilling to substitute a museum of lesser quality for one of higher quality. With respect also to the arts, the world has become a global village. Due to low cost tourism, the media and internet, a large number of persons are now able to compare museums with one another. Such comparisons between museums in the old days were the privilege of a small group of art experts. But this knowledge in the general population is restricted to a few really prominent museums, because only they can be well remembered and discussed with other people.

Superstar art museums are able to fully exploit the economies of scale in reaching out to a large number of people. These museums are not only featured in newspapers, on radio and TV, but can raise enough money to produce their own videos and virtual museums. These costs are essentially independent of the number of consumers, and therefore favor the major museums, because the set-up costs are normally too large for smaller institutions. While the latter will certainly catch up (a homepage will soon be a matter of course for all museums), the major museums will have the funds to improve their scope and quality so as to keep their lead. Superstar museums have started to reach out by establishing museum networks. Thus, for example, the London Tate Gallery has spawned satellite museums at Liverpool and St. Ives, and the Prado has started to lend out about one third of its holdings to museums in the provinces. Such moves have the additional advantage of reducing criticism of the capital city that it monopolizes art and is given too large a share of the financial support provided by the government.

Those museums, which establish themselves as superstars, find themselves in a new competitive situation. Their reference point shifts from other museums in the city or region to *other* superstar museums. While there has always been a feeling of tacit competition between the directors and administrators of major museums with respect to art, there is now direct competition between the superstars extending over a much broader area, including visitors, commercial activities and sponsors.

The superstar museums must make great efforts to stay in that category. Frantic activities are therefore often undertaken: special exhibitions are organized in the hope that they turn out to be blockbusters, visitors' amenities are improved (e.g. a larger variety and fancier restaurants) and new buildings with stunning architectural designs are added (e.g. in the case of New York's Museum of Modern Art). The superstar status of a select group of museums inescapably leads, so it seems, to museums as providers of *"total experience"*. This new role stands in stark contrast to the traditional notion of museums as preservers of the past.

The "total experience" offered by the superstar museums, and demanded by the huge crowds of visitors, must meet two conditions:

1. *Establish contexts.* The first is that art must be related to history, technology and well-known events in politics and entertainment such as motion pictures. Thus, for example, a museum of natural history may do well to relate to Spielberg's vastly successful "Jurassic Park". Blockbuster exhibitions such as Tut Ank Amun (see e.g. Gavin 1981) have paved the way in this direction. They have often been devoted to superstar artists (e.g. Cézanne in Tuebingen), to well-known themes (e.g. El Oro de Mexico, the Imperial Tombs of China) or superstar personalities in history (e.g. Catherine the Great, Napoleon). But instead of relying solely on special exhibitions, superstar museums are always forced to be "special", i.e. to also embed the permanent collection in a context attractive to large numbers of visitors.

2. *Provide a large scope of entertainment.* In order to satisfy, "total experience" museums must offer a broad range of activities, not unlike entertainment parks. The entertainment offered extends beyond cafés, restaurants and museum shops. Many superstar museums have already gone far in this direction. The Louvre, for example, opened a commercial precinct called "Le Carrousel du Louvre". The floor space below Pei's pyramid extends without interruption into a large underground shopping mall. But the Carrousel offers more services than an average shopping mall; it also functions as a modern convention center with modular rooms

which can be hired by the general public for symposia, product launches, conferences, fashion shows and other events (see Eichberger 1996). Activities of superstar museums comprise all sorts of educational activities (not only for children but also for adults), and most importantly, plain entertainment. In particular, the relationship of the art exhibited with popular TV series and films is likely to be exploited much further in the future than is the case today. An exhibition of van Gogh's paintings, for example, would also provide the opportunity to see the various films on his life, or in which he plays a role.

It would be premature to argue that such "total experience" offered by the superstar museums would lead to superficiality. Clearly, it is not designed for the (few) real connoisseurs. But for the large number of visitors not educated in the arts, it would probably lead to a deeper understanding of art than is normal today. The experience may be narrowly focused on one painting and artist, but it is at the same time broader because it goes beyond art history to include more fully related social and scientific aspects. Such knowledge may even provide a stepping stone for greater involvement in art, including visits to more traditional museums.

4.   What Are the Consequences for Museum Policy?

The discussion so far has argued that superstar museums are mainly in competition with other superstar museums, as well as with other suppliers of "total experience". Superstar museums are also characterized by very large flows of visitors, often reaching millions per year. They constitute a sizable economic factor in the local economy because of the visitors' expenditures on hotel accommodation, meals in restaurants, shopping and so on. The superstar museums are therefore faced with new challenges which did not previously exist, at least not on the present scale. In the following, management, in particular organization theory, is used to discuss the consequences for museum policy. Some of the aspects traced out apply to museums in general (or for that matter, to any organization catering to customers), but they are of much larger and pressing importance to superstar museums. Based on the considerations discussed in the previous sections of this chapter, the policy conclusions spelled out are difficult, if not impossible, for superstar museums to evade.

The discussion proceeds in three steps, starting with the most general aspect of the strategic orientation, moving on to organization and finally to human resources.

4.1   Strategic Orientation

Superstar museums must use their historically acquired core competence in order to survive. They have to consider what they are uniquely qualified to undertake. To identify and establish the sustainable competitive advantage is one of the most important tasks of museum management.

Clearly, the need for superstar museums to provide "total experience" to its often millions of visitors per year requires major attention to the demands and expectations of these visitors. A superstar museum is simply forced to shift to a *visitor orientation*. In contrast, pure preservation, conservation, and art historic research become less central. This does not mean that these activities are declining in absolute terms, e.g. measured by the funds allocated or the number of employees engaged. Indeed, they may well become bigger because the concentration on the services for the visitors makes more resources available, which can also be used to bolster preservation, conservation and research. Nevertheless, activities that are directly devoted to meeting the demands of the visitors play a dominant role within superstar museums and do not simply play a small ancillary role in museum management.

4.2   Organization

A crucial decision of museum policy concerns the degree of *centralization* appropriate for the problems at hand. In Europe especially, where most of the major museums formed part of the public administration, the organizational form was highly centralized, as was government bureaucracy in general. A centralized bureaucracy organized along a functional division of tasks is ill suited to provide a "total experience" for the visitors. It is difficult or impossible to efficiently co-ordinate functions such as the classic curatorial activities, renovation of paintings, upkeep of the buildings or ticketing by a central directorate.

A more adequate organizational form for superstar museums is *process oriented*. The tasks are no longer defined according to classical functions but rather according to processes, thereby minimizing the interfaces within the organization. One could also speak of minimizing spillovers between the various employees and work groups within the museum. The processes relevant for a superstar museum are not exogenously given. Rather, the management has the crucial task of determining what these processes are for a particular superstar museum. The basic idea is to make certain people responsible for specific activities that cater to museum visitors. These persons are sometimes called "process owners" to emphasize that it is their task to act such that the customers (in the case of superstar museums, the visitors) are satisfied. This includes aspects which so far have often been considered to be outside the scope of museum activities such as travel arrangements to the museum, provision of sufficient and secure parking spaces, adequate ticketing procedures including entrance fees, and also amenities such as restrooms, restaurants and shops. While the directorate of a superstar museum must determine the most appropriate processes for its own case, for purposes of illustration, some practical examples of how such processes might be defined are given in the following:

1. *Processes relating to groups of visitors.* There may be process owners whose task is to care for organized groups such as school children or tour groups of national or foreign visitors. Other process owners may be charged with looking into the demands of individuals who are tourists or local visitors. In each case, the requirements for, say, travel and parking space are quite different. For instance, tourist groups often come in buses, individual national visitors by car, and local visitors by public transport. In each case, the person responsible for the respective process has to ensure that, as far as possible, adequate provisions are made. This

means that a service owner has to consider the requirements of his or her "customers". In particular, these requirements often concern aspects which, in the traditional understanding, have little or nothing to do with a museum, such as, for example, securing adequate parking space for visitors coming by car.

Another process could be social functions taking place in the museum premises such as receptions held by firms or individuals, or for various conferences. Yet another process might be defined according to particular interests in art. There may be groups of visitors who are mainly interested in particular epochs or styles; in portraits, landscapes or animals; or in paintings relating to historical events.

Such processes are only well defined if they take into account the competitive advantage or core competence of the superstar museum in question. Thus, for example, organized tours of foreign visitors normally only want to see the "superstar artist" which the museum is famous for. They are often quite satisfied if they can just see the "superstar painting", provided it is presented well. The reason is that such tourists often visit a substantial number of superstar museums during their trip: the Louvre in Paris, the National Gallery in London, the Prado in Madrid, the Vatican Museums in Rome and the Kunsthistorische Museum in Vienna. As such trips are often undertaken in a short period of time, these tourists cannot possibly appreciate more than a very, very small part of the treasures of a particular museum. Thus, the corresponding process is well organized if the "superstar" paintings are easily accessible (i.e. without endlessly going through rooms where the paintings are of little interest to certain visitors), the paintings are clearly visible (i.e. no hordes of visitors rushing to get a good view), and if the painting and its author are put into a historical and artistic context.

In contrast, the process owner for a group of art historians meeting for a congress has to obviously care for the widely different interests of normal visitors. Thus, for example, it is important for the group to view the collection undisturbed by throngs of visitors, and the holdings that are not accessible to the public could be opened to the group.

2. *Special exhibitions.* Another process which is useful for a superstar museum may be the organization of temporary exhibitions involving the conception, loan, transport and insurance, display of paintings, opening hours and entrance fees, advertising, as well as access. What matters is that all the elements of this process are designed with the prospective visitors in mind, and that the process owner has to look at the process as a whole.

3. *Support processes.* Particular services that are important for superstar museums such as museum restaurants, museum shops or amenities for infants and young children as well as facility management (i.e. activities such as air conditioning, security, building maintenance) can be defined as sub-processes. However, care must be taken that they do not become detached from the main goal, namely to care for the demands of the various types of visitors. The process owner responsible for foreign groups of tourists should ensure that these sub-processes care for the demands of this particular process. For instance, the restaurant must have sufficient capacity to cater for the sudden influx of a large number of hungry and thirsty visitors, and to consider their special tastes, as in the case of Japanese groups.

In some respects, these processes are already taken care of *in superstar museums*, whose organizational structure is decentralized. In many cases, the most adequate organizational form includes profit centers (e.g. parking, restaurants and shops). Museums also resort to outsourcing to an independent firm in order to profit from their core competencies. An example is provided by the newly founded Tinguely-Museum and the Beyeler Foundation in Basle, which have outsourced ticket sales, museum shops, security and cleaning, as well as other aspects of the facility management. The gains in cost amount to at least 20 percent.

The adequate extent of decentralization of museums depends strongly on the amount of *tacit knowledge*[3] which has to flow

---

[3]   Tacit knowledge cannot be encoded in symbols, letters or words: "we can know more than we can tell" (Polanyi 1966, p.4). Tacit knowledge is

between the various activities of a superstar museum. Tacit knowledge in various forms include atmosphere and mutually shared history. As such knowledge has to flow within a museum, there are limits to the creation of independent units such as profit centers and to outsourcing. Activities which depend strongly on such tacit knowledge (such as the organization of special exhibitions) should therefore be kept within the organizational structure, while activities where the transfer of tacit knowledge is less important (such as the museum restaurant) can well be decentralized in the form of a profit center, or can be outsourced to an independent firm.

4.3   Human Resource Management

As in any other large organization, personnel aspects cover a vast area in superstar museums. One such aspect is the relationship to the trade unions. In many countries, in particular where the museums are part of the public sector, trade unions often impose strong restrictions on management. Only two aspects of special relevance to superstar museums will be briefly mentioned here.

1. *Flexibility.* A superstar museum organized along processes must exhibit a special degree of flexibility with respect to how *labor* is deployed. Consider, for instance, the processes discussed above centering on different types of visitors. Each process requires different opening hours and diverse activities. Thus, when accompanying groups, well-educated guides are needed who implicitly perform the task of protecting the paintings. In that case, no guards are needed in the exhibition rooms, which are, moreover, under electronic surveillance. This means that the employees have to be flexible enough to undertake these new tasks. This, of course, does not mean that the previous guards are now lecturing to an expert audience but they could be trained to

---

acquired and stored within individuals and cannot be transferred as a separate entity. In particular, it is not easily transferred between independent units of an organization. Individuals working in profit centers, and even more in outsourced entities, have no incentive to share tacit knowledge with other members of the organization as a whole (see, more extensively, Osterloh and Frey 1998).

guide, for instance, groups of children or tourist groups who are solely interested in viewing the one "superstar painting".

2. *Staff Composition.* In superstar museums, *volunteers* play a substantial role. There is at least latent, if not open, tension between the paid staff and the volunteers. Many volunteers work based on their intrinsic motivation, i.e. because they enjoy the activity as such while a large part of the paid staff are extrinsically motivated, i.e. they do their job because of the money received. Accordingly, within limits, paid staff can be told what to do. This is much more difficult in the case of volunteers. Exactly because they do the work for intrinsic reasons, they have a rather clear conception of *what* work they wish to do and *how* they want to do it. If they are asked to perform a task which they do not like, they could easily discontinue working for the museum. As a consequence, " . . . paid staff . . . may be more productive and provide higher quality service" (Duncombe and Brudney 1995, p. 359-360; see more generally Weisbrod 1988). In superstar museums, an important task of the museum directorate is to find an adequate mixture and treatment of these two types of staff.

The discussion on the consequences for museum policy of the superstar phenomenon has so far been undertaken in a normative way. However, it is also necessary to consider the *incentives* for the directorate to pursue such policies. This leads us into the more general political economy of museums. As a substantial literature exists on this topic (e.g. Feldstein 1991, or ch. 5 in Frey and Pommerehne 1989a); there is no need to repeat it here. Suffice it to point out that the directorate has little incentive to follow the consequences outlined if it has no discretionary room but to follow the orders given by the higher echelons of bureaucracy in the Ministry of Culture. In contrast, if the museums are not part of the public sector and, in particular, if they can keep the revenue earned through their activities, the museum management would have an inherent interest to embark on the policies suggested here.

Chapter 5 -
Special Exhibitions and Festivals:
Culture's Booming Path to Glory*

(with Isabelle Vautravers-Busenhart)

1. An Artistic Boom

1.1 Special Exhibitions

There is hardly an art museum not running, or at least preparing, a special exhibition of some sort. Such an exhibition may feature one particular artist (often in commemoration of his or her birth or death), or a group of artists, may focus on a period or a genre of paintings, or may establish a connection to some historical event (see Belcher 1991, p. 49).

Table 5-1 shows how more than 1,100 exhibitions of various types are distributed among European museums.

* This chapter is based on Bruno S. Frey and Isabelle Busenhart (1996), "Special Exhibitions and Festivals", previously published in Ginsburgh and Menger (eds.), *Economics of the Arts. Selected Essays*, pp. 275-302, used by permission of Elsevier Science.

Table 5-1: **Exhibitions according to Theme**
300 Museums in Europe, 1994/95

Regional, Religious and Archeological

African Art	11
Archeology	11
Asian Art	19
Egyptian and Oriental Art	4
Greek and Roman Art	12
Islamic Art	1
Latin American Art	2

Other Art

Architecture	32
Cinema, Video, New Techn.	19
Photography	71
Design	22
Fashion	17
Graphic Arts	13
Jewelry, Ceramics, etc.	20

Visual Arts (Modern and Contemporary)

Solo Exhibitions	352
Exhibitions featuring two or more Artists	15
Thematic Exhibitions	153

Ethnology and History

Ethnology	22
History	33
Literature and Music	18
Society Museum	34

Decorative and Fine Arts

Art Object, Decorative Art	38
Fine Arts	169

Nature

Natural Sciences	13
Technology	23

Total: **1124 Exhibitions.**
Source: International Exhibition Guide, Grunfeld (1994); own calculations.

The data presented refer to 1994/5 and has been collected by the *International Exhibition Guide*. The structure has remained similar since then but, if anything, the number of exhibitions has increased. Dominant are exhibitions devoted to one particular artist (solo exhibitions), modern and contemporary thematic and classical fine arts exhibitions. The *International Exhibition Guide* only takes into account a rather limited number of museums and exhibitions (it is based on a voluntary survey, with a substantial number of non-respondents). For instance, where Zurich is concerned, only two museums are listed (the Rietberg Museum and the Schweizerisches Landesmuseum, each with two exhibitions in 1994/95) but, in actual fact, there were at least 38 museums with 34 exhibitions in August 1994[1].

Table 5-2 shows the distribution of art exhibitions organized by museums in various countries, based on the *Calendrier des Arts* of the *Journal des Arts* (July/August 1994). This enumeration is probably incomplete, especially for France, where many exhibitions by private galleries are included.

Some special exhibitions are composed solely of paintings from the holdings of the organizing museum, but most such special shows bring together works of art from different museums and private collections. Once put together, large temporary exhibitions frequently travel to other museums cooperating with the organizer. Some exhibitions, indeed, are already designed to be sent to various countries. Not rarely, important museums simultaneously display several shows, which they have either mounted themselves or taken over from other organizers.

Due to problems of definition, it is impossible to determine precisely how many special exhibitions museums run, but it is unquestionably a *booming industry*[2]. The example of Germany shows that the

---

[1]   The same applies to other countries. The "International Exhibition Guide" lists 231 exhibitions in Germany for the years 1994/95, whereas alone in 1991 as many as 1600 exhibitions took place, according to data from the German Institut für Museumskunde (1992).

[2]   Our analysis is restricted to temporary special exhibitions at art museums, neglecting similar events taking place in other types of museums. It must be

phenomenon is not only due to the increasing number of museums: while the number of art museums has grown by 35 percent between 1982 and 1991, the exhibitions held by these museums have almost doubled (Institut für Museumskunde 1992). A similar picture is presented in Feldstein (1991, p.80), where five major urban museums are considered: the number of large scale exhibitions no less than doubled in the seven years from 1980 to 1987.

Table 5-2: **Art Exhibitions July-August 1994** according to Countries

	July:	August:		July:	August:
Austria	26	23	Argentina	2	3
Belgium	48	36	Brazil	2	1
Czech Republic	12	13	Chile	1	2
Denmark	5	6			
Finland	5	5	Canada	15	14
France	629	476	USA	167	148
Germany	102	92			
Great Britain	56	51	South Africa	2	2
Hungary	2	2			
Italy	63	50	Japan	7	6
Netherlands	23	20	Singapore	1	1
Portugal	16	13			
Slovakia	1	1	Australia	9	9
Spain	22	11	New Zealand	3	5
Switzerland	103	107			
			Total:	**1322**	**1097**

Note: The same exhibition may figure both as of July and August.
Source: Le Calendrier des Arts, publication of Le Journal des Arts, August 1994.

---

noted that exhibitions come in many different forms and are therefore ill-defined (see Velardo 1988 and Belcher 1991, who develop an extensive classification of modes and types of special exhibitions).

Most noticeable are the "blockbuster exhibitions", attracting huge crowds and enjoying great media attention. Examples are the "Emperor's Warriors" in Edinburgh, 1985 with 220,000 visitors; "Monet in the 90s" in the Royal Academy in London, 1990 with 650,000 visitors; the Cézanne-Retrospective in Tübingen, 1993 with 430,000 visitors; Matisse in New York, 1993 with 900,000 visitors and the Klimt Exhibition in Zurich, 1993 with 250,000 visitors[3] – just to name a few such shows.

Museum exhibitions do not, however, always meet with enthusiasm. Thus, the director of the Metropolitan Museum of Art, Philippe de Montebello, complained that whenever he meets people, they ask him what show he is presently preparing, to which he retorts that he is the director of the Metropolitan *art museum* and not the Metropolitan Opera (Montebello 1981).

1.2   Festivals

A similar development can be observed for the *performing arts* as for art exhibitions. Virtually every city, or at least region, in Europe has its own musical or operatic festival. While the festivals at Bayreuth, Salzburg, Glyndebourne, or Spoleto may be older and more in the limelight than others, there are many thousands of festivals today[4]. Due to the problem of how to define a music

---

[3]   Attendance figures are quite important, though this is often disputed by the art people involved. According to one museum expert "Attendance figures still constitute an index of the popularity of museums and exhibitions . . . " (Belcher 1991, p. 197).

[4]   Only festivals devoted to serious music and operas are considered here. But even so, exactly what a music festival is, is ill-defined. There are, of course, many other types of "festivals", ranging from country music to jazz, theatre, circus or films. A classification is e.g. provided in Getz and Frisby (1988). Economists have tended to ignore art festivals as a *general* phenomenon; they have confined their attention to the local and regional multiplier effects of festivals (see, e.g., Vaughan 1980 for the Edinburgh Festival, Mitchell and Wall 1989 for the Stratford (Ontario) Festival, or O'Hagan 1992 for the Wexford Opera Festival), to the welfare theoretic implications of subsidization (e.g., O'Hagan and Duffy 1987; Pommerehne 1992), or to

festival, no precise count exists; rough estimates range from one thousand (Pahlen 1978, Dümling 1992) to at least two thousand (Galeotti 1992). Merin and Burdick (1979) list not less than 83 musical festivals for former Yugoslavia, 46 for West Germany, 42 for Spain, 38 for Portugal, 25 for Austria, 22 for Italy and 16 for Switzerland. This list is certainly not exhaustive because, for instance, for the United Kingdom, Merin and Burdick name 70 festivals, while the more detailed study by Rolfe (1992, p. 2) lists not less than 529. Even in tiny Denmark, roughly 45 festivals take place every year. An enumeration for France counts 864 festivals, of which 40 percent are devoted to serious music (Maillard 1994, p. 65). Another source lists 600 festivals, of which 450 are devoted to serious art (L'Expansion 1994, p. 32). An official publication by the French Ministère de la Culture comes up with 245 festivals of serious music and opera for 1994.

Festivals became a significant part of the *serious music* and opera scene in the 1920s but the real boom took place within the last 20 years. When the official "Association Européenne des Festivals" was founded in 1952, there were 15 members as opposed to 58 now. Clearly, this Association is very restrictive and limited to the most prestigious festivals. In its special issue on musical events, *L'Expansion* (1994, p. 32) estimates, for example, that 6 out of 10 festivals in France have been founded in the 80s. Festivals usually take place in summer and are often very popular. Some festivals are permanently sold out and entrance tickets can then only be acquired by good connections, or on the black market. The most famous example is the Bayreuth Wagner festival, where ordinary visitors have to apply several times before they are able to purchase (a restricted number of) tickets.

1.3   A Paradox

The boom in special exhibitions and music festivals poses a challenge to art economists because of the glaring contrast to the

---

specific festivals (see, e.g., Frey 1986 for the Salzburg Festival; Galeotti 1992 for the Spoleto Festival).

financial depression in which opera houses, orchestras and art museums find themselves. Many opera and concert houses are under such intense financial strain that they are forced to cut down their activities, dismiss artists, stage hands and other employees (if they are legally allowed to do so), or risk closing down completely. Unit labor costs of production in the live performing arts (or more generally in the service sector) steadily increase because the wage rates in this sector are rising at a rate similar to that in the economy as a whole, while labor productivity in the arts is more or less constant. This is the essence of the so-called Cost Disease. As a result, the live performing arts of opera, concert and theatre are faced with a secular threat of survival because of continually increasing cost relative to other consumption activities[5]. The relevance of the Cost Disease has been challenged for various reasons. In particular, if demand rises more quickly than that for other outputs (the income elasticity is larger than one), and the price elasticity of demand is larger than minus one, prices and revenues can possibly be raised sufficiently to keep pace with rising costs. In addition, labor productivity may to some extent be increased by switching to different art forms, for instance the use of chamber rather than symphony orchestras (Peacock 1984; Baumol and Baumol 1984), or by reducing the travel time of itinerant performers (Baumol 1993). The basic idea has, however, been accepted and provides one of the major building blocks of the economics of the arts. It provides a convincing explanation for why live performing arts suppliers are in perennial financial difficulties, and why many of them have not been able to survive.

Art Museums are also confronted with serious financial difficulties. In many of the world's leading museums, some wings are temporarily closed, and opening hours are reduced in order to save

---

[5]   The analysis of the Cost Disease is due to Baumol and Bowen 1966, and is sometimes also called Baumol's law. Major contributions to the large subsequent literature on the topic are included in Towse (1997b). Further contributions can be found in the special issue of the *Journal of Cultural Economics* (Vol. 20, No. 3, 1996) devoted to the topic, with contributions by Baumol, Cowen, Peacock and Throsby.

money. Curators are concerned that they have less and less money available for the restoration and conservation of their collection. The museum people's complaints about dwindling financial resources are not immediately obvious, at least not to economists. Over the last decades, the value of their holdings has greatly increased in real terms (see chapter 9 "Art Investment Returns"). In this sense, art museums are richer than ever. As was argued in chapter 3, the financial position of many museums would dramatically improve if they were to sell part of their holdings, in particular that share stacked in their cellars which is rarely if ever exhibited. However, most European art museums are public and are not allowed, nor willing, to sell any part of their holdings.

As things are today, both art performed and art exhibited in the traditional venues are faced with grave financial problems. At the same time, musical festivals and special exhibitions are thriving. This is a surprising paradox, which calls for an explanation.

2.   Special Exhibitions and Festivals: Similar Features

Special exhibitions and festivals are closely related in various important respects. This section first discusses similarities in demand and then in supply.

2.1   Demand

The similarities between special exhibitions and festivals are particularly strong with respect to seven features.

1. *High income effect.* Consumers tend to spend an increasing share of rising income on visiting musical performances and art exhibitions. Scattered empirical evidence exists, suggesting that econometrically estimated income elasticities of demand are greater than one, for both types of art. Throsby and Withers (1979, p. 113), for example, find an income elasticity for performing arts services of 1.55 for the United States 1949-73,

and of 1.4 for Australia 1964-74 (full income). This means that the expenditures for the performing arts rise by 15.5 percent, and 14 percent, respectively, when the population's disposable income rises by 10 percent. Brosio and Santagata (1992, p.11) find for Italy that the share of expenditures for visiting the opera, ballet and concerts in total expenditures has risen from 1.1 percent in 1970 to 2.6 percent in 1988. The rise in attendance for performing art events is also documented in Baumol and Baumol (1984). In a survey on cultural audiences in the Netherlands, Ganzeboom (1987) finds a positive and slightly increasing influence of income on museum visits for the period of 1962-83. Special exhibitions and festivals thus find themselves in the comfortable position of being in a growing market. This does not, however, explain the growth in the number of special events, as opposed to regular arts venues.

2. *Attracting new groups of visitors.* As has been well documented in cultural sociology[6], social factors may lead to a feeling of uneasiness in some groups towards attending certain cultural events. A large share of the population rarely, if ever, attends cultural events in opera and concert houses, or visits art museums[7]. Many people are overawed by the "temples of culture", feel insecure and unwelcome, and therefore do not even consider attending an opera performance or visiting the local art museum. This applies, in particular, to population groups with little formal education, which are also short of cultural tradition (see Blau 1989, and DiMaggio and Useem 1989).

---

[6]   Klein (1990) provides extensive empirical evidence on the socio-demographic background of the "museum visitor". Data refer mainly to the Federal Republic of Germany.

[7]   The situation is quite different for museums of technology or transport. Automobile and railway museums, especially, are very popular. In Switzerland, for instance, which boasts many fine museums of art, the museum with by far the largest attendance is the Verkehrshaus, the museum of transport, in Lucerne. In 1998, it attracted over 480,000 visitors (and 510,000 for the affiliated IMAX theatre) while the (famous) Basle Kunstmuseum was visited by a total of only 176,000 persons.

The situation clearly differs for special cultural events which are broadly advertised, and which are made attractive to new groups. This holds in particular for music festivals taking place in "public spaces", thus being more amenable to the great mass of the population, and less prohibitive than the established temples of culture (see e.g. Rolfe 1992, p. 82). Indeed, many festivals make a big effort to "go to the people" by e.g. playing in sport stadiums or popular meeting places (such as inner-city parks)[8]. As special exhibitions normally take place on museum premises – exceptions are at least partly the Biennale in Venice or the Documenta in Kassel – they still face the difficulty of attracting new groups. This is partly overcome by "dressing-up the museum" (see also Elsen 1986): special exhibitions are without exception marked by huge banners and other advertising gags, and even the museum entrances (which normally look menacing to non-museum goers) are virtually opened up and made welcoming. Extensive promotion also plays a role. Coutts (1986) relates the success story of a particular "blockbuster" exhibition, the "Emperor's Warriors" in Edinburgh in 1985. It attracted over 200,000 visitors. When questioned, a considerable share (15 percent) reported that they do not normally visit museums.

3. *Focusing attention.* A festival or an exhibition seek to attract consumers by presenting some extraordinary cultural experience. They specialize on some particular artist (e.g. Bach with festivals, Rembrandt with exhibitions), some period (e.g. renaissance music or renaissance paintings), some topic (e.g. courtly music or courtly paintings), some genre (e.g. mannerist music or mannerist paintings), or some type of presentation (e.g. original musical instruments or portrait paintings). As a result, the visitors interested in such particular forms of art come together, often from far away locations. This development is, of course,

---

[8]   A good example is the "Opera Spectacular" which tours the whole world. Its production of Aida is normally performed in sports stadiums, and has so far attracted many millions of visitors. Open air performances have attendances of up to 45,000 people (in Montreal), which can be attributed to its concrete visual elements (e.g. a sphinx 15 meters high, live elephants and camels), a large number of performers (roughly 600 supernumeraries) as well as the extraordinary emphasis on acoustic quality.

supported by low and secularly falling travel costs. Special exhibitions, in particular the "blockbusters", are in this respect not different from festivals, and may even be compared with major sports events such as Olympic games or world championships. In both cases, public attention is drawn away from the regular activity – showing the permanent collection and pursuing the normal sport schedule – towards a special and unique (or at least rare) event. Special exhibitions and festivals may even be compared to pilgrimages (Börsch-Supan 1993, p. 73) which also have an aura of mysticism, and are surrounded by much commercial activity.

4. *Newsworthiness*. Festivals and special exhibitions are *news*, and attract the attention of television, radio and the print media, which is otherwise impossible to get to the same degree, and especially free of charge. It is easy to get media people to report on a special exhibition, while the permanent collection hardly makes any news (see e.g. Bayart and Benghozi 1993, p. 210). Large exhibitions devoted to mystified artists, such as Rembrandt, van Gogh or Picasso, or to a far away, magic culture, mobilize the press and throw the organizing museum people into the limelight (see also Elsen 1986, p. 20). The publicity not only attracts larger crowds of viewers but also improves the museum directorate's position vis à vis politicians, sponsors and donors.

Operatic and musical performers get some media attention on opening nights but with few exceptions, i.e. short of a scandal, the respective reports are digested by only a small percentage of the population while the rest does not bother. Festivals offer much better opportunities to get media attention because they present themselves every year as a special occasion. This holds true even if they continually repeat performances, such as the Verona Festival does with "Aida".

Closely connected to novelty is the limited duration of both festivals and special exhibitions. The restricted time raises prospective visitors' incentives to really attend, while a visit to the local opera house, concert hall or museum is easily put off in the expectation that nothing is lost thereby.

5. *Low cost to visitors.* Festivals and special exhibitions are closely connected to tourism (see e.g. Getz 1989, O'Hagan 1992, p. 65). The French characteristically like to name them "estivals", in order to indicate that they normally take place in the summer tourist season. It has been econometrically estimated that as tourists have their income situation improve back home, they increase their vacation expenditure and correspondingly demand more cultural experiences during their stay abroad (Gapinski 1988a). A considerable share of visitors comes from out of town, from another region, and often from a foreign country.

Special exhibitions also strongly rely on tourists, but as they are mostly organized by major museums, which are located in large cities, the period outside summer holidays is more attractive. Winter is a good season for special art exhibitions as the prospective visitors are prepared to travel to these centers, thus combining holidays with a cultural experience (for the Basle Holbein exhibition, see Schenker 1988).

The combination of a cultural event with tourism lowers the individuals' cost of attending in various respects. In the case of the increasingly popular package tours, the consumers only have to take the initial decision and all the rest is taken care of by the travel agent. In the case of culture, where it is often burdensome to acquire the tickets, this reduction in decision and transaction costs is substantial. Festivals and special exhibitions should thus be considered one input into a consumption production function (Becker 1976). The total cost of the output consumed is made up of the cost of the various inputs which comprise, among other expenditures, the travel costs which have been secularly declining (especially if one takes into account the reduced time input required). This argument, however, also holds to some extent for a combination of tourism with regular art venues.

6. *Low price elasticity of demand.* The strong attraction of special exhibitions and festivals to tourists and people from out of town paying day-visits also affects the price elasticity of demand. Tourists tend to compare the ticket price to expenditures for the trip as a whole. A given price rise then appears small only and

does not have much impact on demand (Thaler 1980; for museum admission fees Blattberg and Broderick 1991). This effect is supported by empirical evidence. Attendance figures at the Museum of the Palazzo Ducale in Venice, for example, have been fairly stable, although admission fees for the exhibitions presented in the last years have increased by more than 10 percent on average. In fact, the number of visitors to the Palazzo Ducale seems to be in direct proportion to the number of people visiting the center of Venice (ICARE 1994).

The low price elasticity of demand, compared to the permanent venues, gives the managers of festivals and special exhibitions more leeway to increase their revenue by increasing entrance fees. It may indeed be commonly observed that the entrance prices for special exhibitions are often much higher than for the permanent collection (even if they are located in the same house). The same is true for many festivals compared to traditional performances. This suggests that entrance fees are more fully used as an income source when tourist demand is higher.

7. *High demand by business.* Festivals and special exhibitions offer many opportunities to make money. Indeed, there is a large literature documenting the monetary profitability of such cultural events[9]. Not only do they extend to the tourist industry but also to firms catering for the production of festivals and exhibitions. In the case of festivals, there is also a benefit to the recording industry. CDs and videos of classical music have become a huge commercial enterprise, with correspondingly high profits. Festivals provide an excellent opportunity to hire superstars for often very large crowds of spectators. This effect is greatly magnified if the performances are televised and propagated by CDs and videos. The recording companies also use festivals to launch the careers of their future stars. As festivals are less regulated than concert and opera houses, these companies can more easily influence the program to favor the artists they have under contract (this has been particularly noted at the Salzburg

---

[9]   For art exhibitions, see Börsch-Supan (1993), Feldstein (1991), Fronville (1985), DiMaggio (1985); for festivals, Frey (1986) and O'Hagan (1992).

Festival, Frey 1986). The same applies to the sponsoring activity of companies producing goods unrelated to the arts. At festivals, they can appear more prominently and can therefore expect more publicity from a performance for a given sum of money.

In the case of special exhibitions, book publishers tend to benefit not only by selling the catalogue, but also books related to the exhibition's theme. They thus profit from the interest raised by glamorous cultural events.

2.2   Supply

There are five major determinants of supply which are similar, if not identical, for music festivals and special exhibitions. They contrast with the conditions faced by the permanent venues and contribute to the boom of festivals and special exhibitions.

1. *Low production cost.* The absolute cost of many festivals and special exhibitions is certainly high. But it is low *compared* to the sum of money they would require if all the resource inputs used were attributed to them. In the case of both art forms, important resources are taken from the permanent venues and only marginal (additional) costs are covered by the special artistic events.

   Museum employees are taken to organize and run special exhibitions, but the corresponding cost is not attributed to the special events (Montebello 1981). In real terms, the costs are substantial but often appear in disguised and long-term form only. One such cost is the neglect of cataloguing and keeping-up the permanent collection (see Börsch-Supan 1993 for several pertinent examples). But also the museum rooms, where the special exhibitions take place, do not enter the accounted-for costs as the forgone opportunities are not part of book-keeping.

   The costs of mounting a special exhibition are also significantly lowered because the art works shown do not have to be rented at market price. Extensive inquiries with museum administrators, private collectors and a variety of art experts have revealed that a rental market for art objects only exists under very exceptional conditions, and is of little importance (see also Frey and Eichenberger 1995). Rather, the exhibits are lent free of charge; the organizing museum at best has to cover the insurance and transport costs (which may be substantial). The cost of this lending "free of charge" shows up in a non-monetary form. The whole system of special exhibitions is built on mutual exchange or on the principle of reciprocity. Only those museum directors who are prepared to also lend art objects from their own permanent collection are able to participate in this exchange system. The (indirect) cost of being able to show the treasures of other museums at one's own special exhibitions consists in the temporary loss of treasures of one's own collection. But again, these are opportunity costs, which are nowhere accounted for, at least not in monetary form. The production costs can be further lessened by arranging travelling, circulating or touring exhibitions, where they can be shared by those museums who are to show the exhibition (see more fully Belcher 1991, p. 51-55).

Festivals taking place outside the permanent venue have to carry a higher share of total cost in monetary form than museums. However, as festivals are predominantly organized during the summer holidays, they can hire much of the artistic and technical staff at marginal cost, as these persons are otherwise not employed[10]. They can also to a considerable extent draw on volunteers. In the United Kingdom, for instance, almost 40 percent of the over 500 arts festivals are run by unpaid staff (Rolfe 1992, p. 1), but that source of labor is also important in virtually all festivals (see e.g. Curtis 1990, p. 4; O'Hagan and Purdy 1993, p. 161). The locations at which the festivals play are often "public" (they belong to the state or the church) and can be rented at a nominal charge, and are frequently free (Rolfe 1992, p. 62; Galeotti 1992, p. 133). This makes sense, as many of these

---

[10]   At the festival of La Roque-d'Anthéron (France), for example, artists accept to perform for half the fee they get on other occasions (L'Expansion 1994, p. 35).

venues are otherwise unused, as for example the Roman theatres in which some festivals (Verona and Orange are well-known cases in point) take place.

2. *More scope for artistic creativity.* Permanent opera houses and orchestras are strongly bound by the clientele they have to cater for. They often find it impossible to interpret classical plays in a new form, and even more to perform modern and/or unknown plays, because they risk losing their regular customers[11]. The holders of season tickets with mostly conservative taste are, moreover, strongly interested in what is presented and form a powerful lobby, which can exert considerable pressure on the managers and the subsidy-giving politicians if they are dissatisfied with "their" opera house or orchestras. As a consequence, the directors have little possibility of fulfilling their artistic conceptions of originality.

In contrast, independently organized festivals provide a possibility of exhibiting artistic creativity. Festivals may well specialize in an audience honoring unorthodoxy, excellence and special tastes. While a permanent opera house or orchestra only performing contemporary plays and music comes under heavy pressure from their established clientele, and is quickly forced by the subsidizing politicians to conform to broader tastes, a festival exclusively devoted to such contemporary art may well prosper, as the festivals at Donaueschingen and Lockenhaus demonstrate.

Museum directors are similarly bound by artistic conventions. The particular hanging of pictures at many museums has become part of the cultural heritage, and it is next to impossible to rearrange the permanent collection to any significant extent. Special exhibitions offer a chance of avoiding such historical restrictions. One of the major tasks and potentials of an art exhibition is to arrange the art object in a way which creates new insights and effects. In addition, the assembly of art objects

---

11   As Baumol and Baumol (1994, p. 178) point out, this was not always so. In Mozart's time " . . . audiences generally were prepared to listen only to *new* music, usually to works written no more than a decade earlier".

coming from many different permanent collections provides a much-sought challenge to the museum directors, curators, exhibition and graphic designers, conservators, editors and managing officers, to exert their artistic creativity and sense of innovation, and possibly to raise controversy – aspects which are highly valued by museum people, not only for their own sake, but also because it is beneficial for their career.

3. *Evading government and trade union regulations.* Cultural institutions' freedom to act is restricted by two major institutions, the government and the trade unions[12].

(a) *Administrative restrictions.* In continental Europe, establishments of classical music and operas, as well as of art museums, are to a large extent either directly part of the public administration, or at least have to follow the administrative rules of the public sector as they are heavily subsidized by it. In particular, they are subject to the "non-affectation principle", according to which all expenditures are covered by the public budget, and in return all the revenue goes to the public treasury. All revenue thereby gained is "taxed" by the public treasury at one hundred percent as the subsidy is correspondingly reduced. Indeed, the effort to gain own revenues is taxed at more than one hundred percent in the long run, because the budgetary authorities become aware of the money-earning potential and correspondingly tend to reduce future subsidies. As a result, arts institutions (as well as all other governmental units) have no incentive to gain revenue by their own efforts, e.g. by ticket sales or income from auxiliary activities, such as selling goods in the museum store or recordings of operatic and musical performances. The director of the highly subsidized Wiener Burgtheater, for instance, categorically refuses to include advertisements in the theatre program "for

---

12 This argument especially applies to Europe. In the United States, where generally less regulations are imposed on cultural institutions (at least compared to other institutions), the incentive to evade regulations is lower. In the case of festivals, the empirical picture is consistent with that observation: fewer festivals take place in the U.S. than in Europe (see Frey 1994).

esthetic and artistic reasons" (Österreichischer Rechnungshof 1994, p. 28) without mentioning that this is routinely done at equally renowned theatres elsewhere. A major reason why museums do not charge for loaning out works to special exhibitions, but rather rely on exchanges, is that non-monetary activities are extra-budgetary, and are therefore more likely to escape intervention by the ministry in charge of museums.

Government restrictions go much beyond budgetary affairs. They hinder the art institutions' way of acting and performing in a myriad of ways. Thus, pricing policy is very restricted, as well as opening and performing days and hours (for many examples, see e.g. Börsch-Supan 1993, pp. 11, 15). In view of the strong hand of the government, and its persistence due to a long tradition, the major possibility of avoiding these regulations is to engage in special events.

Festivals are, with very few exceptions, organized as private enterprises, in which public bodies are at best one of several members. As a consequence, the directors of music festivals do not have to conform to administrative regulations, and in particular do not have to transfer surpluses to the public treasury, but can use them in a way they find sensible, above all to invest them in innovative features of their festival[13]. The directors risk losing their degree of freedom to the extent they accept, and become dependent on, public subsidies, in which case the festival's possibility of engaging in artistic originality is reduced to the low level corresponding to established opera houses and orchestras.

---

[13]   Abundant evidence exists, showing that festivals enjoy greater financial freedom than normal music establishments. A good example is the Schleswig-Holstein Musikfestspiele, where the originator and promoter, Justus Frantz, enjoyed more leeway than he would ever have had at an established venue. While receiving public subsidies, he kept his independence by relying on financial support from many different sponsors. However, he perhaps went too far, and was subsequently dismissed.

Special exhibitions provide a good opportunity for directors of art museums to appropriate at least part of the extra revenue generated. Being an extraordinary event, the museum directors are in a good bargaining position vis-à-vis the public budgetary authorities to use some discretion where these funds are concerned, and not be fully "punished" by a reduction in future budget allocations. A pertinent example is the Cézanne exhibition in Tübingen, held in 1993. Being as the organizing museum (Kunsthalle) is public, its expenditures and revenues form part of the budget of the town of Tübingen. Eventual profits are normally absorbed by the public budget. However, things looked different in the case of the Cézanne-Retrospective, which unexpectedly accounted for a profit of 4.5 million DM. This surprisingly good result made it possible for the museum director to bargain with the town authorities. In the end, the museum was exceptionally allowed to keep more than a million of the profits for the purpose of organizing more such special exhibitions[14].

A few art exhibitions are at least formally outside the public sector, such as the Documenta in Kassel or the Biennale in Venice, but the organizers are in constant danger of being subjected to government regulations. Of course, financial independence strengthens the organizer's position vis-à-vis the state.

(b) *Employment restrictions.* One of the most stringent public regulations imposed on art institutions pertains to government sector employment. The virtual impossibility of dismissing inefficient or downright destructive employees, promoting and paying employees according to performance, and adjusting working hours to needs, are major factors reducing creative endeavors, and turning art institutions into mere bureaucracies. Additional regulations have been pushed

---

[14]   Personal communication by the director of the Kunsthalle Tübingen, Professor Götz Adriani, to the authors, 20 June 1994.

through by the trade unions, and are often fully supported by the government. Festivals and special exhibitions make it possible to evade at least some employment restrictions, especially as most of the respective employees are only part-time and temporary[15], not union members, and therefore not legally bound by trade union regulations.

In the case of both government and trade union restrictions, festivals and special exhibitions only provide relief as long as they do not occur in a too regular sequence. A museum which organizes yearly exhibitions with a large surplus risks losing the special status relative to other governmental units. One therefore observes that museum directorates stress the extraordinary nature of each exhibition. They moreover purposely feature exhibitions meeting their own criteria of a "good" exception (and therewith attract the attention and admiration of their reference group i.e. art critics and other museum directors), but which are due to produce a substantial deficit. That festivals are on average more independently organized than special exhibitions may be attributed to the fact that as (mostly) yearly events they are under greater danger of being subjected to outside regulations.

4 . *More sponsoring*. Politicians and public officials have a pronounced interest in festivals and special grand exhibitions. They not only respond to the respective demands of the arts world and the local business community, but it gives them an excellent opportunity of appearing in the media as "patrons of the arts" (with tax payers' money). The fact that some festivals initially make a profit, until the politicians seize the chance of intervening, suggests a causality which is reverse to the accepted one: subsidies are not offered because deficits must be covered, but deficits appear because politicians offer subsidies[16].

---

[15]   Many museums employ part of their personnel only temporarily when they have an exhibition on display (Bayart and Benghozi 1993, p. 199). For an analysis of temporary work contracts in the performing arts, see Menger 1991.

[16]   DiMaggio (1985) confirms that it is possible in the U.S. to get government subsidies to cover the cost of mounting an exhibition. See also Frey (1986) for the reverse causality of deficits in the case of the Salzburg Festival.

Business is also more prepared to sponsor festivals and special exhibitions than regular activities[17], where legal provisions often hinder sponsoring. The most important reason is certainly not only the higher media attention of these events and their particular contribution, but also that an individual firm has more control over the funds contributed, and sees less of it wasted by an inefficient bureaucracy than in opera houses or art museums. Sponsors "want a well-defined, high-quality event aimed at specific audience" (The Economist, 5 Aug. 1989). For the reasons given above, the corporate sponsors also feel that their contributions add to cultural output, and do not simply induce the government to provide less subsidies.

5. *Career enhancement.* As a result of increased internationalization, particularly with European unification, many of the top positions in opera houses, orchestras and art museums are open to foreign competition. The normal career pattern has thus changed from staying all one's life in one house, and reaching a senior position by internal promotion. The change has been especially marked in the case of art museums (see Schouten 1989).

In order to successfully compete in this changed setting, the (potential) curators and directors have to make themselves internationally known. An excellent means is to actively participate in festivals and, even more, to mount a special exhibition. Such an event also opens the possibility of editing an exhibition catalogue, whose scientific value is often quite limited (see Börsch-Supan 1993, pp. 56-60), but which receives outside attention. Newspapers are much more likely to review, or at least prominently mention a catalogue of a special exhibition than a documentation of the museum's holdings.

---

[17] Data from the Ifo-Institute Munich suggest that enterprises do more often sponsor special art events than regular art institutions (Hummel 1992). For examples of business sponsorship in the arts, see Tweedy (1991) and Perrot (1992).

The art museum directors are increasingly chosen from, and transform themselves into, exhibition organizers ("Ausstellungsmacher" is the apt German expression), and move further and further away from just being respected scientists. This change in the museums' career system may run into problems in the long run. Some museum specialists argue that special exhibitions will experience diminishing returns because most attractive topics have been exploited, and repeating them only brings little prestige and recognition to the organizers[18]. Moreover, there is a rising perception that travel tends to reduce, and sometimes outrightly damages, the quality of art works, which makes it increasingly difficult to collect the objects necessary to mount an attractive exhibition.

3.   Difference between Festivals and Special Exhibitions

The chapter has so far focused on the similarities between festivals and special exhibitions. It is instructive to also discuss the dissimilarities between the two. They refer to location, the relationship to normal activities, and to exchange.

3.1   Location

Festivals typically take place in locations outside established opera and concert houses. As most of them play during the summer season, they are often outdoors. The most famous and oldest festivals have succeeded in having their own houses, examples being Bayreuth, Salzburg and Glyndebourne.

In contrast, special exhibitions normally take place in the premises of the organizing museum. Rooms outside the museum must meet

---

[18]   An example is the Cranach exhibition in Kronach in 1994 which, according to the Neue Zürcher Zeitung (25/26 June 1994, pp. 65-6), is less interesting and of a lower standard than the Cranach exhibition in Basle in 1974.

specific security and climatic requirements, and are expensive to rent as they can also be used for other purposes, in particular for commercial exhibitions of all sorts. Rooms in the museum are used free of charge; the opportunity costs of not being able to show part of the museum collection do exist but do not have a monetary equivalent. They thus do not show up in the museum's budget. To hold an exhibition on the museum premises has the further advantage of being able to use the museum staff, including the guardians, for the special exhibition. It is simply considered a part of the museum activities.

3.2   Relationship to Regular Activities

As festivals tend to take place outside the stationary venues and outside the regular playing season, the two art forms are quite separate. In particular, festivals are unlikely to draw visitors away from the performances of the established opera and orchestra companies. If anything, a glamorous and highly advertised festival raises people's interest in serious music and may even induce them to attend local art performances[19]. As a side effect, visitors may start to entertain higher expectations concerning the quality and professionality of the local performers. They may realize that they are sometimes far from top class, which tends to reduce attendance[20].

---

[19]   A similar complementary relationship exists with special sports events. A world football championship makes many people interested in this sport who would otherwise not care. Empirical evidence suggests that TV-reporting of football games raises, rather than reduces, attendance in subsequent games, i.e. complementarity outweighs the substitution effect (Gärtner and Pommerehne 1978).

[20]   High expectations are also produced by audio and TV recordings, or radio broadcasts, and are therefore difficult to distinguish from the effect produced by a local festival. In any case, raised expectations enhance the "superstar effect" discussed in chapter 4.

Special exhibitions, in contrast, tend to reduce visits to the museum's collection. People flock to the extraordinary event and often disregard the masterpieces of the permanent collection, probably because they find that they can visit it at some unspecified later date (see Montebello 1981 for the Metropolitan Museum of Art).

In the long run, however, blockbuster and other grand exhibitions are likely to raise interest in the arts (see Conforti 1986). Again, media publicity plays a significant role. Another contributing factor is that persons far away from culture lose their fear of entering a museum, i.e. the social barriers are reduced by the more welcoming special exhibitions. Again, the special event may have raised visitors' expectations to such an extent that the quality of the local permanent collection is a disappointment to them. This is not necessarily to the organizers' disadvantage because it may serve as an argument to get additional funds for purchases from the government.

3.3   Exchange

Music festivals are able to get their administrative and technical staff as well as the artists from the open market, and can therefore organize themselves quite independent of the stationary venues. The organizers of special exhibitions, on the other hand, must for the reasons given above be embedded in a system of exchange. This is a major reason why special exhibitions must be closely attached to art museums because the latter's collection is needed to offer art works in exchange. If a special exhibition were arranged independent of an art museum, it would be impossible to get the exhibits from other museums, as they do not lend their treasures on an open market. The only source for exhibits would be from private collectors, who are generally averse to such "commercialization", or would ask high renting prices. Private collectors are, in contrast, prepared to rent to special exhibitions arranged by major museums because the art objects lent take part in the museum's prestige, and their authenticity is raised, both of which make them more valuable.

4.   Concluding Remarks

This chapter endeavors to explain the boom in the number of music festivals and special exhibitions to a common set of factors based on an economic analysis. On the demand side, the major factors identified are the rising interest in cultural events in general (a positive and sizeable income elasticity of demand); the opening up of such events to groups of persons so far not patronizing the arts; caring for specialized cultural tastes (i.e. exploiting niches of demand); newsworthiness and publicity – going with rising importance of the electronic and print media; lowering of consumption costs due to an efficient combination of art with tourism; the possibility of raising revenue by asking higher entrance prices because of the low price elasticity of demand due to tourists; and the increasing awareness of local business that festivals and special exhibitions can be commercially exploited. On the supply side, major factors supporting the rise in festivals and special exhibitions are the possibility of staging these events at lower cost than in the established venues (essentially no fixed costs have to be carried); larger scope for artistic creativity; increased possibilities of avoiding conventions of taste as well as government and trade union restrictions; the increasing role of corporate sponsoring, and the change in the career patterns in art institutions favoring cultural events receiving outside attention and publicity.

Does this mean that festivals and special exhibitions are going to dominate cultural events completely in the future? There are various reasons why this is not to be expected. Certainly, these special cultural events are here to stay, but they will become less and less "special". As a result, the gap now existing between the traditional venues and festivals and special exhibitions is due to narrow down in the future. The brunt of the demand for festivals and special exhibitions will be carried by an increasing share of the population attending such events, which were earlier the province of a selected few. Closely related, the cost of attending special cultural occasions will be further lowered by an increasingly efficient merging of tourism and art consumption. There will also be some leeway to care for niches of special tastes, but it will be increasingly difficult to mount original new art exhibitions – especially large ones – and music festivals. However, it is to be expected that new, so far unknown, forms of art presentation will be invented, not least as a result of the changed career patterns of art producers.

The major factors curbing the rapid future growth of festivals and special exhibitions is likely to come from the supply side. The advantage of comparatively low production costs is lost the larger the number of such special cultural events is. They are no longer able to draw on the resources of the traditional venues at low or even nominal costs because an increasing share of artistic performers have become freelance as a result of the great opportunities offered by festivals and special events. Even more importantly, as these special events become a regular feature, the supervisors of established opera houses, concert halls and art museums react and will force the organizers of "special" cultural events to participate in the fixed costs. Many of the best known and most prestigious festivals have become fully established: they often have buildings of their own and an increasing number of permanent staff. They have many features of the conventional opera and concert houses: they have to cope with increasing government and trade union regulations and interference and they rely ever more on a fixed set of visitors, with expectations shaped by the respective festival's traditions. As a result, many of the "old" festivals have become victims of their own success, and find it difficult or impossible to engage in new artistic endeavors. Not surprisingly, some of the "old" festivals have given birth to new festivals, trying to evade the conventions and bureaucratic restrictions, and to break new artistic ground. Examples are the "incontri musicali fuori programma" existing since 1978 in the context of the Spoleto festival (Galeotti 1992, p. 128), or the various "Fringes" at the Edinburgh festival. However, it seems that even part of the Fringe in Edinburgh has already become established again.

The situation is similar with art museums. As special exhibitions become the rule rather than the exception, there is pressure to have them carry the whole cost, and to subject them to the same govern ment and trade union regulations as the other museum activities. The supervising ministries have already started to interfere in the exchange lending of art objects and have restricted it. Corporate sponsoring, which in the past has been one of the major supporters of festivals and special exhibitions, is also due to lessen in importance. With the great increase in the number of special cultural events, each particular effort is less likely to receive substantial sums of money. Moreover, the more regular the special events become, the smaller the media attention. The influence of sponsors will be reduced the more government and trade union regulations intrude, so that prospective sponsors have an incentive to look for new ways to gain publicity. This may be the new, yet unknown, forms of art presentation, but also other activities such as (most recently) the support of minority events (often called "festivals"), such as meetings of homosexuals or other minorities.

Even if the rapid rise in festivals and special exhibitions cannot be expected to persist, they have had a strong and lasting impact on the art world. On the demand side, it has opened up art to an increasing share of the population. This "popularization" may not be in the interest of some art suppliers and art lovers, but from the point of view of caring for individual preferences it is a considerable achievement. On the supply side, the increased competition between producers of art has transformed career patterns at (European) opera houses, orchestras and art museums, and has led to a new relationship to potential as well as actual art consumers. By subjecting art producers at least partly to the market, it has also favored more efficient forms of organization and production in the world of art.

Chapter 6 -
How Can the Arts Be Publicly Promoted?*

(with Werner W. Pommerehne)

1.   The Economist's Role

Many politicians, journalists and artists, and a large part of the
general public, regard art as something outside economic reasoning
and calculation. They express reservations regarding an economic
analysis of artistic and cultural creation, or call for the economic
consideration at least to be based on an aesthetic analysis of supply
of and demand for art[1]. But art – like beauty, freedom or justice – is
an abstract concept and therefore cannot be grasped directly. If the
product cannot be accurately described, how is the economist then
able to say something leading to a better understanding of art and
culture, and, on that basis, about the way to finance them?

Regarding this point of view, Boulding (1977) has objected that a
precise distinction between goods and services, and also between

---

*   This chapter is based on Bruno S. Frey Werner and W. Pommerehne (1990),
    "Public Promotion of the Arts: A Survey of Means", previously published in
    the *Journal of Cultural Economics* 14, pp. 73-95, used by permission of
    Kluwer Academic Publishers.
[1]   Sometimes even economists assert that "to properly study the market for
    artistic goods, it is necessary to deal with the aesthetic nature of the art"
    (Shanahan, 1978, p. 13).

firms that produce goods and those that provide services, is often not possible at all. Therefore, an economic analysis of art (as with education, health or sport) leads to no greater problem of definition than the analysis of most other goods and services in an economy. It may be that the number of factors influencing artistic creation and artistic consumption is particularly large, and that the relationships between them are essentially more complex than in the case of, for instance, the production and consumption of bread. But art and culture are subject to scarcity, as are any other goods or services, i.e. they are not free. Culture goods provide benefits to the individual who demands them, and resources are necessary for their creation. As soon as there are observable expressions of preferences by individuals, such as a willingness to pay for a theatre ticket, to produce a painting for sale or even to play the piano for one's own pleasure, it becomes possible for the economist to analyze the behavior of suppliers and demanders of art and culture. Then it also becomes possible for him or her to investigate the important and popular question how the government can best promote art.

This last question is not, however, necessarily the most important one for the economist. As will be discussed in the following section, this question sometimes does not arise at all, since the market in particular areas of art is thoroughly effective. Section 3 describes areas of art and culture where the market functions less well, though it is not easy to justify government promotion and financing through public funds on this basis. In section 4, the question is raised of the approaches and instruments available to government, provided art and culture are (for whatever reason) to be publicly supported.

The procedure is deliberately using such customary categories as performing art (theatre, concerts, ballet) and visual art (art museums, galleries), since it is the common features and not the peculiarities of the individual areas that are stressed. The effect of official subsidies on artistic creation is similar, whether they be for opera, ballet or concerts, visual arts, cinema or literature. Similarly, the problem of creators' rights arises in the areas of the visual, literary and performing arts, given the possibilities of inexpensive reproduction. The concluding section summarizes the insights that economists have reached with respect to the promotion of art and culture.

2.   Art Support via the Market

In discussions on art and culture, art produced for the market is often pooh-poohed as "commercial". Poor taste is allegedly unavoidable with this form of supply. The conclusion is drawn that government must intervene in order to guarantee the dignity and quality of the art.

In many areas of art, however, the market is quite capable of producing art graded by experts as high quality. Above all, mention should be made here of industrial art (for instance the products of Citroen or Ghia)[2], including advertising and poster art. More subject to popular taste are department store art, popular theatre performances and cinema, and also cabaret and circus. It is indisputable that much of this is considered art of high quality: jazz or films of Fellini or Bergman are pertinent examples.

Private galleries constitute a market for the visual arts characterized in part by very high quality and by provision for *avant garde* artists. New unconventional art quite often makes its way via this market, with "cultural entrepreneurs" in Joseph Schumpeter's sense supporting progressive developments – in the expectation of demand rising in the future. A well-known example is art dealer Kahnweiler. Among other artists, he took Picasso under contract, who soon became extremely successful[3]. Pecuniary participation in the proceeds from the successful artists allows this kind of policy of risk to spread which, on the whole, brings new, creative impulses into art. The hope that a hitherto unknown artist will make the grade, and the price for his work rises, represents a major reason for the

---

[2]   The New York Museum of Modern Art's department of architecture and design displays a 1945 Bell-47 DL helicopter.

[3]   See Moulin (1967, p. 109ff). Another example is the recently deceased New York gallery owner Leo Castelli. He became famous for promoting, among others, the work of Robert Rauschenberg, the later internationally leading pre-pop-artist, against the then prevailing taste and against massive opposition by the artistic profession (see Pommerehne and Schneider 1983). Castelli also discovered and helped draw attention to the works of Jasper Johns, whose *False Start*, sold for over 17 million dollars in 1998, which is the most expensive work of art by a living artist to date (*Economist*, September 4, 1999).

(speculative) demand for paintings. In particular, it results in an economic interest in the discovery and the promotion of unknown painters and sculptors.

In other areas of art and culture too, "production and financing" through the market cannot be *a priori* ruled out. In the case of theatres or art museums on the "free market", whose ticket receipts exclusively cover the costs, performance is – in line with the fundamental premise of economics – evaluated by those who attend. If an institution doesn't attract customers, it can close its doors. At least in one respect, the prerequisites for meeting with a response from potential demanders are not bad for a private business enterprise. The enterprise is flexible, since it is subject to few administrative constraints, and there are no governmental adjudicators or bureaucratic bodies making evaluations of the art's content.

Of course, the market also considerably narrows down the room for maneuver of the suppliers of art and may – though need not – be an obstacle for innovation. This seems to be the case, for instance, with the big, privately administered American opera houses (like the New York Metropolitan Opera House or the Chicago Lyric Opera). They can survive only if performances are nearly sold out (the Met, for instance, budgets for seat occupancy of 96 percent). Therefore, risky and modern pieces are excluded, and the repertoire concentrates on works by Verdi, Puccini, Rossini and Wagner[4].

However, it is interesting that precisely the same applies to the highly government-subsidized opera houses in the Federal Republic of Germany. Of the almost 300 different compositions performed on German stages in the post-war period, 200 were written in this century. But these 200 works together scarcely account for 18,000 out of a total of 200,000 performance evenings, i.e. not even one tenth of all performances.

---

[4]   In the 1971-72 season, about 53 percent (1974/75 as much as 62 percent) of the productions at the Metropolitan Opera House were by these four composers. In several seasons, no works by contemporary composers were performed at all at the Met; see Martorella (1977).

Table 6-1: **The Leading Opera Composers in Germany**
(by number of performances)

Composer	Number of performances: 1947-75		1901-10
Verdi	30,059	(21)	6,798
Mozart	24,490	(18)	5,129
Puccini	17,997	(9)	2,981
Wagner	12,997	(13)	17,365
Lortzing	12,317	(6)	6,714
Strauss	6,036	(15)	n.a.

Note: Figures in brackets are the number of different operas performed.
n. a. = not available.
Source: Honolka (1986)

The operas of the "iron six" composers listed in Table 6-1, along with other individual "classics" such as *Carmen, The Barber of Seville, The Freischütz, Fidelio and The Bartered Bride*, have dominated the programs of the government-subsidized opera houses over the recent decades, as they were in fact already doing before the end of the German empire. Modernity, even moderate modernity, has not been able to break through[5]. Modern operas have no chance as far as the number of performances or spectators are concerned. As a consequence, they are shunted off to studio theatres in many places. The question then arises whether performances of the standard repertoire ought to be publicly subsidized at all and not rather – as is the case in the United States – financed largely through the market. As various studies have shown[6], the price elasticity of demand seems to be low enough for this type of opera performance. Would it not be sufficient to support only studio theatres from public

---

[5]   On the contrary, the weight has clearly shifted in favor of the tried and true: while in 1907 the average "age" of the performed opera pieces was still 42 years, nowadays it is more than a hundred years.

[6]   Thus, for example, Touchstone (1980) calculated values of around –0.11 for the long-term price elasticity of demand for opera performances in the United States. According to her simulations, an abrogation of all (private and state) subsidies would imply raising entrance prices by 125 percent, which would however lead to a decline in attendance of only 14 percent.

funds, allowing the creation of *avant garde* plays that can be put on stage in major houses when they become accepted by a large number of opera visitors (such as Alban Berg is today)?

3.   Why Government Support of Art?

3.1   Theoretical Arguments

The market solution does, to be sure, also have some serious drawbacks, which on the whole would tend to favor public support in the area of art and culture. In the popular discussion concerning the support of the arts, the following three arguments are often adduced, but hard to reconcile with economic reasoning:

1. The arts have a stimulating effect on the economy;

2. The arts encourage tourism and thereby induce desired effects on the regional economy (so-called spillover effects);

3. Only government support of the arts can allow artists to remain in their usual occupation.

These arguments are not convincing for several reasons. First, these and similar arguments, brought forward for instance by Myerscough (1988) and Hummel and Berger (1988), could be analogously adduced for many other areas beyond culture, in particular amusement parks or sport events. Second, it remains to be shown that interventions in favor of the arts are more suited than other instruments to achieve the goals desired, i.e. stimulating the economy, promoting the regional economy or guaranteeing employment. Moreover, these goals must constitute important economic policy goals (see also Hughes 1989). The same requirements should, of course, be made the basis for assessing other categories of government intervention, such as government subsidies to the agriculture and shipbuilding sectors.

In contrast to these popular arguments, the economic literature has dealt exhaustively with the various reasons for "market failure" in the area of art[7]. The essential argument against purely market-financed art is that – due to the public-good component of parts of their "product" – the suppliers of art cannot get the whole profit via the market. As a consequence, the provision of art can be lower than the social optimum. Such public-good components, or "non-user values" consist in the following:

1. *Option Value.* The individual may already draw considerable benefit from the existence of cultural supply, even though he or she may not at present make use of it. Since this option value does not take the form of effective demand, it cannot be expressed on the market. The option value may, however, become visible in private donations and in the membership of supporting associations of private cultural institutions. But at the same time, the "free rider" problem arises. Therefore, one may at best interpret them as a lower boundary of positive evaluation. The option value may even be negative, e.g. when the intervention interferes with a more highly valued alternative of the same sphere (e.g. appearance as film actor instead of theatre actor).

2. *Existence Value.* This non-market value goes one step further still: people derive individual benefits from knowing that a cultural good or activity exists. This holds in particular for historic buildings, which – once destroyed – could hardly be rebuilt in the original state on pure market considerations.

3. *Bequest Value.* Individuals may value a cultural good or activity not for themselves but for future generations. This bequest value matters because the future generations are not in a position to express their preferences via today's markets. Valuable traditions of artistic creation may be irretrievably lost if those arts are not practiced and passed on to the next generation. This argument has

---

7   See the already "classical" treatments in Baumol and Bowen (1966, chapter 16) and Peacock (1969), also Netzer (1978, part 2), Wahl-Zieger (1978, part 4), Cwi (1979), Throsby and Withers (1979, chapter 10), Leroy (1980, chapter 4), Austen-Smith (1980), Withers (1981), Horlacher (1984, part 1), Sagot-Duvauroux (1985, part 4), Grampp (1983, 1986-7) and O'Hagan (1998).

been emphasized by Baumol and Bowen (1966) in their defense of public support for the arts.

4. *Prestige Value*. Artistic and cultural institutions often have a positive prestige value attributed to them by non-users and, in individual cases, like the Paris Opera and La Scala in Milan. This applies even to people not interested in art at all and who never exert any respective consumption activity themselves. Hence this demand does not become effective on the economic market. The reason is that such institutions preserve and promote the feeling of regional or national identity.

5. *Innovative Value*. The practice of the arts makes an essential contribution to the development of *creative thinking* in a society, to improvements in the capacity for critical evaluation and to the creation of aesthetic standards that ultimately affect most individuals positively. To be sure, these flows of benefits can only be partly internalized via the market. To a lesser extent, this is true also for external effects of production, e.g. when the media and other industries derive considerable profits from the arts without the artists' training being paid for through the market.

These at first sight purely "qualitative" arguments for market failure are accepted by most economists as far as art and culture are concerned (exceptions are Grampp 1989a and Cowen 1998). But this says little about the extent and nature of any possible government intervention.

There is another argument often adduced to justify government intervention: the *meritorious* nature of art and culture. A good or service has this characteristic if in the eye of the decision-maker – in this case the government – it *ought* to be used more than it would be used if the decision was left to consumers. From the economic viewpoint, this concept is not convincing, since it is very hard to justify why in a world with sovereign consumers, such goods and services should exist at all. If the argument of the meritorious good was to apply, then it would still be of slight analytical value. For then art and culture would by definition be worth just as much as politicians are prepared to spend from public money on their support. Instead, it should also be shown "quantitatively" that sufficient positive external effects arise that cannot be internalized in any other way, and that the benefit of government intervention in favor of art exceeds the costs arising therefrom.

3.2   Empirical Evidence

There are many statistical studies supporting the importance of non-user values.

1. *Survey* results show that the majority of those questioned are in favor of government support to art and culture[8]. But it is hard to take these as evidence for the thesis of market failure. It is quite possible that a large part of those questioned, at any rate the suppliers of art and its demanders, advocate increased government support to art and culture for strategic reasons based on self-interest and not because of the alleged positive external effects. This is supported by the evaluation of 250 American studies on attendance during the period 1960-77 by DiMaggio, Useem and Brown (1978). Active demanders of performing and visual arts constitute a very small part of the population with, among other things, above average incomes and, in particular, above average education. They are also those who particularly advocate art support by public funds. Other representative surveys for the United States (ACC 1980, Hendon, Costa and Rosenberg 1989) arrive at the same findings, as do similar representative surveys for Australia (Throsby and Withers 1979, p. 116). There are now some initial studies that seek to pick out and quantify some of the above-mentioned positive external effects. Thus Bohm (1979, 1984) has developed a special method of questioning individuals without giving them significant inducement to act strategically. Throsby and Withers (1983, 1986) applied this procedure to a representative sample of Australian taxpayers and found out that 70 percent of those surveyed support higher public expenditure for art and culture, and that 80 percent of them would prefer a reduction in other government expenditure to a tax increase. Morrison and West

---

[8]   As seen for example in the Federal Republic of Germany in various representative surveys on the theatre (cf. among others Marplan 1968, Biermann and Krenker 1974).

(1986) carried out a still more refined survey in Canada. They asked those who defined themselves as non-frequenters of artistic events and cultural institutions but nevertheless were in favor of financing existing state support to art from taxation, about the kind of benefit they received in return for their tax payments. The main answers were: feeling of national pride, possibility of future use, welfare of future generations and so on, i.e. exactly the prestige, option and bequest values mentioned above. The findings suggested on the whole that the existing extent of official support to the arts should be maintained. In other words, the positive marginal external effects seem to correspond to the marginal costs in the form of the tax burden. The total perceived benefit evidently exceeds the total costs of the public provision of art.

2. Another approach of measuring the public good aspects of cultural amenities consists in using *actual behavior* (as opposed to stated behavior in a hypothetical situation). Therefore, Clark and Kahn (1988) applied a hedonic wage approach to derive the private and public good benefits from improving a number of cultural amenities (museum, ballet, opera, theatre, symphony orchestra) in U.S. metropolitan areas. The empirical estimates of willingnesss to pay – in the form of a, *ceteris paribus*, lower wage rate – suggest significant marginal benefits for a representative city, ranging from nearly $1 million for an additional theatre to $31 million in the case of an additional symphony orchestra.

Finally, an econometric analysis of a referendum in the Swiss Canton of Basle City on the purchase of two Picasso paintings from tax funds (it is more fully discussed in chapter 7) shows that the acceptance rate of 54 percent yes votes is hard to explain (in a statistical sense) if narrowly defined motives of self-interest are taken as a basis. It was, instead, necessary to consider such aspects as bequest, prestige and option values in order to provide a satisfactory explanation for this particular public expenditure of the art. The same result was reached in a study analyzing the support for opera in the Canton of Zurich in a more recent referendum (Schulze and Ursprung, 2000).

4.   How Can the Government Provide Support?

If the public – including the majority of those who are not effective demanders of art – experiences positive external effects to a significant extent, this can be seen as a necessary prerequisite for government intervention and support measures. But what is the most efficient way to support art and culture? After all, there are numerous conceivable approaches to promoting culture on the one hand and an extremely vague concept of "artistic output" on the other hand. It is perhaps more important to clear up the question of whether the "most efficient" support measure – however defined – is still to be preferred when the self-interests of the institutions and individuals that provide or receive the support are taken into account. By analogy with market failure, one must also reckon with "political failure".

4.1   Approaches of Government Support to Art and Culture

There are many approaches and measures calling for differing amounts of financial resources from the government and requiring differing levels and degrees of examination and assessment of "artistic production".

1. *Making art more marketable.* No financial resources, or only minor ones, are required by an approach which can be called market facilitating measures. At the same time, they have the advantage that there is no need for government bodies to undertake an assessment of the artistic "output". They are aimed at improving production and sales conditions for artistic creators, and at facilitating access by demanders of art. Among these are copyrights, which have to be specified and protected, taking care to avoid excessive (too long-lasting) "incomes". The same is true for publication rights, which should inter alia protect against piracy, but not guarantee permanent protection. Generally, the government may provide institutional assistance in the creation and assertion of property rights that make the internalization of external effects possible. Educational institutions like theatre,

television, radio or even record firms, which are places for both experimentation, new ideas and presentations, should be able to obtain payments from the recipients of beneficial externalities, where necessary under threat of exclusion.

Also, many regulations and requirements promulgated by public authorities (whatever the reason may be in each individual case) for artistic and cultural institutions should be examined in the light of the overall goal being pursued and, where necessary, abolished. In particular, such regulations ought not to be imposed on private cultural institutions and suppliers of art. In many museums, for instance, inflexible and in part dubious regulations are to be found: starting with the opening times, often inconvenient to potential visitors; the frequently unfortunate mode of presentation (including total lack of consideration for user comfort) up to the exclusion of a more flexible price policy for such things as the theatre, concerts and ballet. Thus, entrance prices could differentiate between premieres and non-premieres; weekdays and weekends; on and off-season; artistic genres; or star performers. Existing public cultural institutions (particularly in Europe) could reap additional income from the box office by applying a differentiated price policy and by raising attractiveness and flexibility in what's offered and when.

In the case of museums, government subsidies are often justified by pointing out the positive external effects on education and training (see Smolensky 1986). However, education and culture policy advocates should seriously take into account a suggestion made by Banfield (1984). He asks whether well-produced copies for purely informational purposes should not be preferred to expensive originals that have to be carefully displayed, conserved and guarded[9]. Or would it injure the sense of national prestige if copies were used? Additionally, many exhibits are gifts or long-term loans by private donors, not infrequently given on particular conditions. When, for instance, gifts are given, they often include

---

9   Interestingly, some American towns have actually refused public support for purchases of art on the grounds that only connoisseurs need the original. It was argued that to use tax money would only benefit those few who derive high aesthetic enjoyment from an original (see again Smolensky 1986).

secondary works, but the gift must be exhibited as a whole. This may severely constrain museum policy.

But even when there are no such restrictions, and gifts go into stock and not on display, considerable overhead costs arise for storage and conservation. Montias (1973) has therefore questioned whether the regulation that publicly-owned museums are not allowed to sell works of art is rational in terms of efficient performance of the essential tasks of a museum director. It leads to opportunity costs which, though not directly visible, are nevertheless of considerable economic importance (see chapter 3). The stock could be reduced and used to finance "visitor-oriented" presentations.

2. *Indirect government support.* There are also indirect means of government contributions. Tax rebates to private individuals and firms[10] in return for contributions and gifts to non-profit institutions are more oriented towards an active expansion of the range of possibilities open to suppliers of art and culture. Individuals may deduct up to 50 percent of gross income, firms up to 10 percent of taxable earnings. The resulting support for the arts is hard to measure. In the case of the United States, this indirect government financial assistance is known to constitute a quite significant support. According to calculations by Feld, O'Hare and Schuster (1983), in 1973 these almost "invisible" contributions amounted to more than one third of all government expenditure on art and culture.

With this type of support through "uncollected" taxes, also called "tax expenditure", the recipient has little incentive to make profits and therefore pursue a differentiated price policy. It would then lose the status of non-profit undertaking (and therefore its own tax privileges), with the consequence that gifts to it would not (any longer) be tax-deductible. But that does not necessarily mean that "potential" surpluses are made to disappear in the form of costs being pushed up, for the recipient has to show (potential) givers that the gift will be used "efficiently", i.e. that "first-class"

---

[10]   Schuster (1999) discussed tax-based indirect aid schemes for a variety of national contexts and tax regimes.

theatre performances with well-known actors and opera stars will be produced, or that "outstanding" museum purchases will be made and "exceptional" exhibitions put on. Obviously, this type of art support may be associated with conditions that lead to restrictions on the decision-making power of the directors of cultural institutions. However, in the United States the existing competition among (numerous) donors seems to work against this tendency. Nevertheless, for these reasons, Feld, O'Hare and Schuster (1983) advocate exclusively monetary contributions and, in the case of gifts in kind, the abolition of restrictions by donors of an artistic work, or at least a limitation on their duration.

3. *Direct public support.* The requirements for examining the detailed effects of support measures become greater when it comes to direct government financial aid, the third form of aid here discussed. Government subsidies may take various forms and have very diverse effects on the extent and quality of the results secured, on price and other receipts policies, on internal organization and on the chosen "production technique" of the artistic and cultural institutions[11].

The provision of a *fixed subsidy* per person attending (irrespective of entrance fee charged), or of a public subsidy on *total ticket revenue,* is rarely practiced. The opposite case, purchase tax on entrance tickets, is more frequent.

However, economists advocate a specific form of subsidization according to the number of visitors[12]. Potential demanders should receive a *voucher,* i.e. a coupon that entitles them to reduced entrance tickets at competing cultural suppliers. The main idea in

---

[11]   For a formal analysis of the effects of direct subsidies (and of the tax expenditure mentioned above) on extent and quality of artistic production and on social welfare (measured by consumer surplus), see Hansmann (1981) and Le Pen (1982). Dupuis (1983, 1985) and Austen-Smith and Jenkins (1985) further discuss the questions on how far subsidies influence the target function of recipients, affect the nature of their demand for support and affect the choice of further instruments of artistic production.

[12]   See e.g. Peacock (1969), but the idea can be found earlier with respect to the American school system. For more recent discussions, see Horlacher (1984), West (1985) and Peacock (1988).

this user-controlled system of subsidy payments lies in introducing an element of competition with, as a consequence, a comparatively stronger orientation of artistic and cultural supply to the wishes of those who demand and finance it. Above all, this considerably lowers the enormous demands on the government bodies that otherwise have to distribute the subsidies. It moreover reduces the danger of bureaucratic assessors arriving at discriminatory decisions that cannot be implemented. Baumol (1979, p. 50) argues in favor of the experimental experience with the voucher system applied to the New York off-Broadway theatres: "The main conclusion to be drawn from the evidence of the voucher program . . . is that it works. It has brought support to a large and diverse group of organizations and seems to have contributed somewhat to the influence of audiences upon the performing groups. The evidence indicates most strongly that it has made life easy for the dispensing organization whose administrative costs have been kept low and which has been spared the distasteful job of arriving at aesthetic judgments it does not care to make and, worse still, of translating those judgments into specific pecuniary figures."

It should be added that the authorities broke off this experiment, as well as another one, in Canada (West 1985), without providing any convincing rationale.

In contrast, *lump sum subsidies,* linked only with the existence and not with the output, input or prices, are much more common in reality. They allow (at least in the short run) the survival of artistic creators and cultural institutions that would otherwise have to terminate their activities for commercial reasons. Especially for newly formed theatre groups with younger artists, they make it easier to overcome initial financial difficulties. If they are granted for longer periods and accompanied by a repayment clause (should a surplus be achieved), they may cause considerable undesired incentives. To make profits then imposes an additional burden because government support is reduced and part of, or all, profit has to be transferred to the government. Profits are therefore avoided and hidden as far as possible. The consequence is a pursuit of an exclusively art-centered policy, aiming at a quality that by far exceeds the level desired by demanders (performance excellence). Moreover, this results in rents being paid to actors and other employees.

European artistic and cultural institutions are, to a considerable extent, a part of the general public administration. Accordingly, they need to recover only a part of the costs from their own activities; the rest, the deficit, is covered by government subsidies. As part of the general administration, public museums, theatres, etc. are subject to the budget principles applied to these institutions, including the principle of non-earmarking, which means that surpluses cannot be retained by the institution concerned and used as it likes, but must be paid back to the general public budget. Therefore, there is little incentive to produce surpluses. The government subsidies are not "given", but are set on the basis of a "projected" deficit and are then the result of a bargaining process between the individual cultural institution and the responsible cultural bureaucrats. The negotiating process takes place in a context of asymmetrical information; the institution asking for the subsidy in general has a considerable information advantage: it can easily document cost increases, while the cultural bureaucracy is scarcely in a position to prove that the projected deficit might be kept smaller (public bureaucrats are not accepted as competent judges on artistic quality by the cultural institutions). Again, there is little incentive on the part of cultural bureaucrats for genuine intervention. They prefer having a friendly relationship with the artistic and cultural institutions, which in turn introduce them to the "world of art".

In view of the existing asymmetrical information and the incentives provided, negotiating rules are set up in order to facilitate the decision-making process. Deficits and subsidies of the past are taken as a starting point for forecasts of future deficits. Foreseeable cost increases are added. One direct consequence of this kind of linkage between current subsidies and former deficits is that the directors of a cultural institution have a twofold incentive to avoid reducing the deficit. If a surplus or deficit reduction is achieved, the benefits will not affect the institution concerned: in other words the implicit tax is 100 percent. Moreover, future subsidies are reduced.

Deficit coverage from the public purse has considerable effects on the management of publicly-owned artistic and cultural institutions. There is no incentive for any orientation towards market efficiency. On the contrary, other goals may be pursued, such as reputation within the world of art, the production of excess quality, increase in personal monetary income[13] and the creation of a good atmosphere (above the efficient level), in order to have contented, loyal workers.

4.2 Policy Failure

As the arguments so far have shown, government support of art and culture is not without problems. The more levels and institutions of government are involved, the more difficulties arise. A good example is the Salzburg Festival (Frey 1986; see Gapinski 1984, 1988b for a similar study of the Shakespeare Festival in Britain). There, the total deficit is covered jointly by the Austrian government, the Salzburg province and the city of Salzburg. The budget restrictions on the Salzburg Festival fund (with four directors and a president) are therefore extremely weak. Effective restrictions on deficit coverage could only arise if the financing possibilities of all the bodies subsidizing the festival were no longer adequate, and the law was correspondingly amended.

As a consequence of these extremely favorable conditions for the festival fund, its directorate pursues a remarkable redistributive policy. The Austrian taxpayer is burdened with financing the subsidies, while the benefits are divided among the directorate, the employees, the artists and a selected group of visitors. The wide discretionary room of the directors is reflected in the typical rent-seeking activities of the festival: entrance tickets are sold at prices lying substantially below the equilibrium price, with the

---

13   For empirical evidence, see the reports of the Bavarian Supreme Court of Auditors (B.O.R. 1984, p. 52 ff) on such behavior by the public radio orchestras, and of the Austrian Court of Auditors (RH 1988) for the national theatres in Vienna.

consequence that demand constantly exceeds supply. For example, in 1981/2, when the number of persons attending amounted to 175,000, a total of 35,000 requests for tickets were rejected. In this way, the directorate can claim to be charging "socially appropriate" prices, which in turn is good for their prestige. But the resulting costs have to be borne by the anonymous taxpayer. The directorate is, moreover, able to hand out tickets, which are otherwise hard, or impossible, to obtain for interested demanders, in a discriminatory fashion. The main recipients of these tickets are festival administration workers, press-persons and individuals from whom political support to the festival may be expected. The emergence of a black market in tickets, moreover, provides a fair-sized group (including hotel employees) with an opportunity to make money by selling the tickets at a higher price than the official price.

The almost automatic coverage of deficits allows artists and administration workers to receive considerably higher wages than elsewhere, i.e. pure rents are paid. This is evident from Table 2, which gives a comparison of wages for administrative staff of the Salzburg Festival and the Bundestheater in Vienna. It should be noted that the wages have been made comparable by the Austrian Court of Accounts (Oesterreichischer Rechnungshof 1984, 1988) – except that the Salzburg Festival plays only for a fraction of the time the Bundestheater does. The rents are not only paid in the form of excessively high current monetary incomes, but also in the form of additional retirement pension entitlements and a number of fringe benefits (gifts, subsidized travel, etc.).

Table 6-2: **Wages of Administrative Staff** of the Salzburg Festival and the Vienna Bundestheater (with functionally equivalent duties); 1981-82, in Austrian Schillings.

Administrative area	Salzburg	Bundestheater
Ticket sales	814,000	314,000
Buildings	821,000	467,000
Press Office	775,000	434,000
Technical section	797,000	679,000

Note: The Salzburg Festival lasts five weeks, while the Bundestheater plays for ten months. The wages indicated have not been adjusted accordingly.
Source: Oesterreichischer Rechnungshof 1984, section 1.31.1.

As the example shown in Table 2 makes clear, there may be spectacular failures of subsidization policy. But this does not mean that less important cases, such as the support to the individual artist, should be neglected. The danger is that mainly those artists receive government support who meet the requirements and conceptions of the public bodies in charge. In such cases, the cultural bureaucracy will not refrain from evaluating the content of art, since that means it can exercise power and influence.

However, the danger of "benevolent elitist" decisions also exists with private organizations, which receive funds by the government for distribution to individual artists and art institutions, according to their own criteria. With this variant of public support of culture, art is given some freedom vis-a-vis government patronage. However, the public money can be given only to "official" private organizations, otherwise any association whatsoever could claim it. Thus, government assessment is simply replaced by an elite assessment of an art association. In art, private groups of this kind have not infrequently sought to obstruct innovation. This is quite understandable since, as recipients of government money, they have an interest in preventing competition from new kinds and variants of art and the respective new art institutions.

5.   What Can Economists Say About Art Support?

As pointed out in chapter 2, economists cannot by themselves determine what art and culture is or is not. They may, however, contribute to a better understanding of how individuals and institutions deal with art, whether as creators, mediators or demanders of art. Economists can show that artists, art and cultural institutions and cultural bureaucracies each pursue goals of their own within the set of possibilities open to them. And these possibilities differ strongly, according to the particular instruments of government support used. As a consequence, expected and actual modes of behavior of all the actors involved also differ.

The approaches and instruments of support available to the government have been discussed, but not what is the best possible government support and financing scheme. On the contrary, it has instead analyzed from what kind of support the government should abstain – at least as long as individual preferences are to constitute the essential reference for collective action. But a selection of negative points may often provide useful insights and valuable suggestions. Increased government support to art and culture is not necessarily identical with additional public money. While this statement looks obvious after what has been analyzed, this principle is often violated in practice; too often the support of the arts is identified with handing out public money to the arts. Examining and loosening up restrictive regulations, and removing bureaucratic restrictions, often provide a more effective support of art and culture.

Private markets should not be underestimated. Especially as far as innovation is concerned, the market represents an excellent decision-making system (see chapter 8 for a fuller description). By creating property rights and making them usable for the general public, government may contribute to a strengthening of that decision-making system. In many cases, more indirect government financial aid in the form of tax expenditure should be considered. On the whole, private donors have a stronger incentive to benefit artistic and cultural institutions caring for the preferences of a large proportion of demanders of art. Moreover, the transaction costs can be kept relatively low, especially if tax deductibility is restricted to monetary gifts. Finally, one may expect that this decentralized support instrument contributes to a better regional provision in the supply of art and culture. Direct government financial aid in the form of vouchers to potential demanders brings a broader share of the population in touch with art and culture. This instrument can again be applied to promote the regional spread of art and culture.

Direct government financial aid, which is not linked to performance, is in general the least advantageous support instrument. This holds, in particular, if it is given as a deficit guarantee to big and regionally concentrated cultural institutions, such as theatres, opera houses and museums of capital cities like Paris and Vienna. The opportunity costs of striving for performance excellence and obstructing a better provision to other regions, as well as supporting other types of art, are likely to be considerable.

Chapter 7 -
Public Support for the Arts
in a Direct Democracy*

(with Werner W. Pommerehne)

1. Can Voters Judge on Art?

One of the most controversial areas of the arts is its relationship to democracy. Most people are fully convinced that artistic choices cannot be left to the citizens. A popular referendum on an art issue must be decided by a cultural élite. This judgement is shared by most economists, even by those who in other areas of life unquestionably accept consumer sovereignty as the guiding norm for resource allocation (a typical example is Scitovsky 1972). These persons argue that if art issues were subject to (direct) democratic decisions, public support for the arts would drop to an abominably low level, and to the extent art is still supported, would be of terrible quality.

---

* This chapter is based on Bruno S. Frey and Werner W. Pommerehne (1995), "Public Support for the Arts in a Direct Democracy", previously published in the *International Journal of Cultural Policy*, pp. 55-65, used by permission of Gordon and Breach Publishers.

This chapter argues that this view is largely mistaken, at least in a well-structured democracy. An extreme case of democratic interference with art, namely by *popular referenda,* is empirically analyzed. Two questions are studied:

1. Do voters in direct democracies discriminate against art as such by supporting lower levels of public spending on the arts than for other public purposes?

2. Are popular referenda on art inconsistent with a high quality of art?

The empirical analysis uses Swiss data since Switzerland is the country with the most established system of direct democracy in the world (Cronin 1989, Butler and Ranney 1994).

Section 2 examines referenda on art expenditures in a large number of Swiss municipalities for the period 1950-1983 and seeks to answer the first question. This section also serves as descriptive background for the case study in section 3[1], which focuses on a particular referendum concerning paintings by Pablo Picasso, the embodiment of modern, abstract and high quality art, seeking to answer the second question. The following section 4 provides a tentative explanation for our observations, and section 5 draws conclusions.

2.   Public Support for the Arts and Direct Democracy

In Switzerland, public spending on cultural issues has been submitted to referenda in a large number of municipalities. Table 7-1 presents the outcomes of such referenda on cultural expenditures, compared to the outcomes of referenda on all other public spending.

The city of Basle has the lowest rate of successful cultural propositions brought before the electorate, but even so, more than half were clearly accepted. In other cities, such as Zurich and Berne, roughly nine out of ten propositions by the respective municipal

---

[1]   The case discussed stems from the year 1967, i. e. in middle of the period treated in section 2.

governments were favored by a majority of voters. In total, out of 108 cultural expenditure referenda, 89 (i.e. 82 percent) were approved by the electorate. Of the more than 1700 expenditure referenda on other issues, a somewhat higher share (90 percent) found a majority. However, the proportion of accepted referenda between cultural and non-cultural issues does not differ significantly for the various municipalities (with the exception of Lucerne and Biel). In view of these results, the often-stated claim, that culture would suffer once the population were accorded a direct say, comes into question. Although this may at least partly be attributed to specific conditions in Switzerland, it is difficult to see why this country should be that much of an exception. If anything, many people would think that the Swiss are a rather materialistic and egoistic breed, who do not specially favor spending money for the arts.

Table 7-1a:
Voting outcome of popular referenda on public expenditure for culture

municipality	no.	Voting participation in %	% yes votes	% of referenda accepted by a majority of voters
Basle	9	37.2	55.2	55.6
Biel	3	36.2	58.9	60.0
Lucerne	6	35.3	63.3	66.7
Chur	7	53.0	54.9	71.4
Zurich	24	46.6	62.9	83.3
St. Gallen	17	46.7	63.8	88.2
Winterthur	20	65.2	56.5	90.0
Berne	15	35.0	74.4	93.3
Thun	5	46.6	58.6	100
Total	108	47.2	61.2	82.4

Note: Those municipalities were selected which had at least five expenditure referenda on culture in the period indicated.
Source: Computed from official electoral statistics and collected by Frey and Pommerehne from the unpublished data made available by the statistical offices of the various municipalities.

Table 7-1b: **Voting outcome of popular referenda for all others.**

municipality	no.	Voting participation in %	% yes votes	% of referenda accepted by a majority of voters
Basle	54	32.9	53.0	57.4
Biel	132	31.5	75.1	90.2
Lucerne	143	40.0	70.7	88.8
Chur	74	52.2	64.9	79.7
Zurich	415	47.9	76.4	91.6
St. Gallen	145	46.4	71.7	86.9
Winterthur	311	66.7	86.7	84.6
Berne	280	38.7	78.8	96.8
Thun	147	36.8	77.3	95.2
Total	1701	47.2	46.5	89.5

Note: Those municipalities were selected which had at least five expenditure referenda on culture in the period indicated.
Source: Computed from official electoral statistics and collected by Frey and Pommerehne from the unpublished data made available by the statistical offices of the various municipalities.

Also revealing is the development over time, as shown in table 7-2.

Table 7-2a:
Voting outcome of popular referenda on public expenditure for culture.
Major Swiss municipalities, 1950-1983.

subperiods	no.	Voting participation in %	% yes votes	% of referenda accepted by a majority of voters
1950-1964	50	49.4	55.9	80.0
1965-1973	30	36.2	59.8	83.3
1974-1983	29	44.3	57.4	79.3

Note: Same municipalities as in Table 7-1;
Source: see Table 7-1.

Table 7-2b: **Voting outcome of popular referenda on public expenditure for all other purposes.** Major Swiss municipalities, 1950-1983.

subperiods	no.	Voting participation in %	% yes votes	% of referenda accepted by a majority of voters
1950-1964	881	47.5	73.0	93.6
1965-1973	541	40.6	70.3	89.5
1974-1983	279	37.1	63.5	75.3

Note: Same municipalities as in Table 7-1;
Source: see Table 7-1.

Between 1950 and 1983, the electorate became increasingly less inclined to accept the public spending propositions brought forward by their governments: the proportion of non-cultural referenda passed fell from 94 percent (1950-64) to 90 percent (1965-73) and to 75 percent (1977-83). The situation is quite different in the case of expenditure propositions on the arts: while the percentage of accepted referenda amounted to 80 percent between 1950-64, this rate was up to 83 percent between 1965-73 and then fell slightly to 79 percent between 1974-83. This was not achieved by reducing the relative number of cultural to non-cultural issues; rather, the reverse is true.

This favorable attitude of the electorate towards cultural proposals is mirrored in the development of municipal expenditure, as shown in table 7-3.

Compared to the earlier period (1965-73), the share of public expenditure spent on culture rose from 3.3 to 4.9 percent in 1974-83, taking only the municipalities' own financial efforts into consideration. When the grants from other public authorities (mostly cantons) are included, the proportion of expenditures devoted to culture is lower in both periods. But the share of cultural expenditure again increases over time.

Table 7-3: **Proportion of cultural expenditure in total municipal expenditure, major Swiss municipalities.**

subperiods	Proportion of cultural expenditure, excl. grants from other public authorities (%)	Proportion of cultural expenditure, incl. grants from other public authorities (%)
1965-1973	3.3	2.6
1974-1983	4.9	3.6

Note: Municipal cultural expenditure outlays on libraries, museums, theatres and concerts, monuments, historic preservation, mass media and other cultural activities.
Data based on the same municipalities as in tables 1 and 2.
Source: Computed from unpublished official data collected by the authors from the statistical offices of the various municipalities; for the period 1950-1964, no data were available.

3.   High Quality of Art and Direct Democracy

Basle's Art Gallery is famous for its collection of old masters such as Hans Holbein the Younger. But its collection of Post-Impressionists and especially of Expressionists, such as Cézanne, van Gogh and Gaugin, is also impressive. Some of the most important paintings are not owned by the museum, however, but are on loan from a collection in possession of a patrician family of this town. Owing to the pressing financial needs of one of the members of this family, four of the 27 pictures on loan to the museum were to be sold in 1967. The family offered two Picasso paintings, *Les Deux Frères*, created in his "Rose Period" (1905/6), and *Arlequin Assis* (1920) to Basle's Art Gallery for purchase, at a price of CHF. 8.4 million. The government and the parliament of the canton Basle-City decided to donate CHF. 6 million in order to buy these paintings, provided the remaining CHF. 2.4 million were raised by individuals and private firms. This decision was subject to the obligatory popular referendum. The vote was taken in October 1967 after a lively discussion about the value of art for the community and, in particular, the role of modern art in the form of Picasso paintings.

In popular referenda such as this one on the Picasso paintings, citizens may be assumed to vote according to what they consider to suit their preferences the best. The larger his or her net benefit from the two paintings exhibited in the Basle Art Gallery, the more likely a citizen will cast a favorable vote. The following factors may be hypothesized to play a major role in this decision:

1. The higher a voter's income, the more likely he or she supports the proposal to spend public money to buy the Picassos. The major reason is that income is highly correlated with education, which in turn fosters interest in the arts.

2. The lower the physical cost of access to the museum (the lower the cost of transport due to geographical vicinity), the more positive the attitude towards the proposal.

3. On the other hand, the larger the expected increase in a person's tax burden resulting from the spending proposal, the less likely he or she will vote in favor of the proposal.

The hypotheses have been empirically analyzed, using data for each of the 21 voting districts in the canton Basle-City.

The outcome to be explained is the percentage of "yes" votes cast. This variable being constrained between 0 and 100 percent, expressing the dependent variable in terms of logits is the appropriate specification in order to carry out a least squares estimation. Consequently, the variable to be explained is the natural logarithm of the fraction of "yes" votes over the percentage of "no" votes.

The estimated voting equation is as follows:

$$\ln\left[\frac{\%' \ yes' \ votes}{\%' \ no' \ votes}\right] =$$

0.17		Constant term
0.01** (2.92)		Average per capita income
-0.10** (-2.78)		Expected increase in tax burden
-0.01* (-2.19)		Physical cost of access/transport cost

$$\overline{R}^2 = 0.47; \ F\text{-ratio}=11.4; \ \text{d.f.}=17$$

The figures in parentheses below the parameter estimates indicate the t-values, and thus show whether the corresponding estimated parameter differs in a statistically significant way from zero. Two asterisks indicate statistical significance at the 99 percent, and one asterisk indicates significance at the 95 percent confidence level, using a two-tailed test. Thus, all three variables contribute to explain the outcome in a statistically significant way. $\overline{R}^2$ is the coefficient of determination, corrected for the degrees of freedom (d. f.). It shows that the estimated equation accounts for 47 percent of the differences in voting outcomes among the 21 voting districts. The calculated value of the F-ratio in this case indicates that the independent variables as a whole have a statistically significant influence on the dependent variable.

The results are in line with the proposed influences: those districts with higher average per capita incomes and those with a lower cost of access to the Art Gallery were more in support of the purchase of the Picasso paintings; a higher expected tax burden tended, on the other hand, to depress the proportion of "yes" votes. As indicated, the empirical analysis was, however, able to account for only less than half of the differences in the proportion of "yes" to "no" votes in the 21 voting districts.

The limited explanatory power of our simple estimate is not too surprising. Our model so far assumes that voters look at the two proposals purely in terms of their direct private benefits, without considering broader issues. Art may, however, have considerable *bequest, prestige* and *option* value (see chapter 6), which should be taken into account.

These values cannot be directly observed nor can they be easily measured by surveys, as the persons interviewed tend to respond in a superficial way. In order to capture the influence of these evaluations on vote decisions, auxiliary variables are introduced. They serve to indirectly capture these influences, but are only approximations. The influence of the bequest value is indirectly captured by calculating the number of children (age 0-15) per citizen; it is thus proposed that the larger the number of children in a family, the more the parents take the interests of subsequent generations into account. The prestige value is important for voters born in Basle and therefore having a special attachment to the city's history and culture. The share of voters born in the city of Basle is therefore taken as one of the determinants of the voting decision. Finally, the importance attributed to the option value is captured by the proportion of citizens who are holders of season-tickets in the two public Basle theatres. This purchase indicates that they have an interest in maintaining the option of visiting art institutions.

All three factors are expected to contribute to a stronger support of the proposal to buy the two Picasso paintings. Moreover, the non-monetary cost of visiting the museum may be explicitly included by taking people's educational level into account. This level is measured as the proportion of those individuals with a secondary school or university degree in the electorate. Finally, the intensity of involvement for, and interest in, the quality of the Art Gallery may be expressed by including the proportion of voters belonging to the "Friends of the Art Gallery" among the explanatory factors.

The result of empirically estimating this more extended model is:

$$\ln\left[\frac{\%\ 'yes'\ votes}{\%\ 'no'\ votes}\right] =$$

-1.09	Constant term
0.02** (2.37)	Average per capita income
-0.10** (-2.69)	Expected increase in tax burden
-0.01 (-1.52)	Physical cost of access/transport cost
0.03* (2.02)	Bequest value
0.13* (2.52)	Prestige value
0.05* (2.34)	Option value
0.02* (2.02)	Psychological cost of access (education)
0.01* (2.14)	Intensity of involvement

$$\overline{R}^2 = 0.85;\ F\text{-ratio}=12.2;\ \text{d.f.}=12$$

Including the indicators for bequest, prestige and option values, as well as those for the level of education and preference intensity, drastically improves the performance of the empirical analysis. All five variables additionally introduced exert a statistically significant influence on the vote decision. The higher the bequest, prestige and option values are, the more the citizens are prepared to support buying the two Picasso paintings. Support also increases with the psychological accessibility of cultural institutions (measured by the level of education) and with the intensity of involvement with Basle's Art Gallery. The differences in support levels between the various districts in Basle are now accounted for to a much higher degree by the model; the share of explained variance rises from 47 to 85 percent. The results demonstrate the importance of factors going beyond the narrowly conceived private interest of the voters: 'non-use' values are of great importance.

These conclusions are supported by the overall result of the referendum. The proposition to acquire the two paintings by Picasso was supported by a majority of citizens of 53.9 percent. An (ex post) forecast on the basis of the first estimated equation predicts a support of 46.2 percent. It thus deviates considerably from the actual result and, moreover, suggests that no majority would be reached. Using the second estimation equation, which takes into account the non-user values, the forecast is much better. The second equation predicts a support level of 52.9 percent, which is very close to the actual support of 53.9 percent. The model now correctly predicts that the referendum was accepted. It is thus crucial to take voters' bequest, prestige and option values into account.

4.   A Tentative Explanation

The generally expected "bad" results, when average citizens are allowed to decide on art in a referendum, do not materialize in the case of Switzerland: there is no low support of public expenditures for the arts and high quality of art is not rejected. This is surprising in view of the popular prejudice that the average citizen is not as fond of the arts as the decision-makers in a representative democracy. There the decisions are in the hands of the cultural élite and the politicians, who clearly have above average education and income. The support for acquiring the Picasso paintings in the referendum analyzed, shows that people with above average education and income are indeed more favorably inclined towards the arts. The average voter certainly has a less developed "taste" (defined according to the prevailing standards of the art world) than the cultural élite. Hence, the expectation of "bad" results seems to be well grounded.

What may be the reasons for the empirical finding that those "bad" results do not materialize, at least not for the post-war experience in Switzerland? There are two countervailing effects which, under favorable circumstances, may outweigh the generally expected effects.

1. *Involving the Voters.* The first reason why the voters may favor art more strongly than expected is that a popular referendum vote is preceded by a *discussion* (see Frey 1994). This discourse changes the voters' perceived possibility set; they get to know new aspects and alternatives. Moreover, it affects their stated preferences. Sociological research, as well as everyday experience, suggests that new forms of art can only be evaluated and appreciated by being accustomed to it (see e.g. many articles in Foster and Blau 1989). Hence, particularly in the case of art, lively discussions at the pre-referendum stage are of crucial importance. Indeed, in the case of the Picasso referendum in Basle, the preceding discussion was extraordinarily intensive, and the same is true (though in general to a lesser extent) for other referenda on cultural matters. Under these conditions, the much debated "paradox of voting" (Downs 1957) is overcome. It proposes that citizens have little incentive to become informed and to participate in elections and referenda, due to the public good effect involved. The public good nature of political discussions is transformed into a *private* decision because a large number of citizens become personally engaged in the discussion. Their family members, friends, acquaintances and job colleagues expect them to take a position on the issues presented in a referendum. According to Hirschman (1989), "Having opinions is an element of well-being"[2].

The intensive discussion preceding the Picasso referendum, as well as other cultural referenda, performs an educational function. When they vote in a cultural referendum, many citizens are confronted for the first time with a specific work of art. They have never been concerned with art as private consumers, both for lack of interest and money. As a result of the discussion induced by impending referenda on culture, many voters' appreciation of art is raised. Therefore, they are prepared to support the corresponding public expenditures.

---

2   The argument is more fully developed in Bohnet and Frey (1994).

2. *Low Burden*. The second reason why the generally expected "bad" outcomes of using referenda on culture do not materialize is related to the *low cost situation* (see Kliemt 1986, Kirchgässner and Pommerehne 1993), in which those citizens who are not strongly engaged in the discussion process find themselves. As their voting decision (provided they participate at all) is of little or no importance to them, they cast their vote according to their ideological predisposition. They are influenced by the information and propaganda to which they are subjected. Typically, the information and propaganda provided is *asymmetric* in favor of the arts. The persons dominating the public discussion are in general of above average education and income. The few outsiders who are against art find it advantageous to conceal their point of view because they would be negatively censored by their colleagues, the art lovers.

Opponents are likely to oppose the referendum proposal in public primarily on financial grounds. In the case of the Picasso-referendum in Basle, the money argument was weakened because the public expenditure would only take place provided the private sector also carried a significant share of the cost. Sharing the burden may be of considerable importance in the case of public expenditures for particular art objects. As indicated by the empirical estimates, a lower tax burden significantly raises the willingness to vote in favor of such referenda.

5.   Conclusions

The popular objection to submit art to the judgement of the voters in referenda has been shown to be unwarranted in a mature democracy. While the body of voters has a lower preference for the arts than the political, social and cultural élite, the induced discussion favors the appreciation of art. Moreover, the information and propaganda offered in support of art dominates the pre-referendum discussion. As a result, in a direct democracy such as Switzerland, one may observe that referenda on cultural expenditures receive a higher level of support than other kinds of public expenditures. Even referenda on public outlays for modern art, such as for paintings by Picasso, have been accepted by the voters who, as private consumers, previously had little appreciation of this kind of art.

The referendum on the two Picasso paintings held in Switzerland seems to have been the first time that the population was asked to make a decision on (the then) modern art – and to incur part of the consequent cost. It is worth noting that, at that time (1967), such a referendum on art was not a matter of course. Rather, it was considered to be an extraordinary event. Many art lovers feared that the voters would reject the proposition. Picasso himself was aware of the importance of the event. He was so pleased about the positive outcome that he donated two paintings, *Vénus et l'amour* and *Le couple*, as well as two drawings, to the population of Basle.

It may further be added that the referendum decision was also fortunate from a purely financial point of view. In the following 20 years (1967-87), the auction prices for Picassos experienced a sharp increase. On average, the owners of Picassos reaped an average real rate of return of 13.2 percent per year. This is a substantial financial return (see chapter 9).

The results presented in this chapter refer to Switzerland. There is, however, no reason to suppose that referenda on art should not be possible in other countries. True, Switzerland has a long tradition of direct popular participation in politics, dating back to 1848. But in recent decades, many countries have resorted to initiatives and referenda to decide political issues. Thus, almost all countries concerned have held referenda on whether to enter the European Union. As a result, the voters of many countries have become accustomed to deciding on matters of content instead of only being able to elect their representatives.

To introduce referenda on art in countries without much tradition in direct democracy needs to be done with care. One possibility is to start with *local* art issues. But it is important that the citizens as voters also have to carry the corresponding financial consequences. This requires a certain extent of local autonomy. At the local level, most citizens are well aware of the issue at hand so that an informed discussion before the vote will take place.

However, art referenda can also be successfully undertaken at a higher federal level. But sufficient time must be given to enable an extensive discussion of the art issues involved. There is no sense in asking voters to precipitously decide on any issue by pushing a button. This is certainly not the kind of direct democracy envisaged here. Rather, the voters should hear the pros and cons, including the financial consequences. Obviously, in such a debate, the art experts play an important role. If they are able to bring good arguments in favor of the arts, no doubt the voters will consent.

Chapter 8 -
State Support and Creativity in the Arts*

1. Market Failure, Government Bashing, or Something More?

The case for state support of the arts has been based on market
failures, in particular the public goods or positive externalities that
culture provides for society (see chapter 6). This is the approach
normally used by economists.

This kind of analysis has the advantage of building on a well worked
out theory of welfare. A major shortcoming is that it leaves open
what these externalities might be. While they can be evaluated using
empirical methods, *why* they exist in the first place remains
unexplained. Clearly, they change over time. In particular, a work of
art may at first be considered to be a negative externality, but over
time people often start to enjoy it, so that it produces a positive
externality. Whether a piece of art or an artistic production generates
positive or negative externalities is the outcome of a social process.

---

* This chapter is based on Bruno S. Frey (1999), "State Support and Creativity
in the Arts: Some New Considerations", previously published in the *Journal
of Cultural Economics* 23, pp. 71-85, used by permission of Kluwer
Academic Publishers.

More recently, some economists have concluded that no such thing as an externality exists in the arts. Consequently, there is no need for governments to support the arts (e.g. Grampp 1989b). On the contrary: the state damages culture. This "government bashing" constitutes a rather extreme ideological view, and remains popular in some quarters.

This chapter endeavors to overcome these rather unsatisfactory approaches to the analysis of government support for the arts by considering aspects neglected so far. It does not deal with the categorical question of whether the state should support the arts at all. Rather, it asks: *"What state?"* It is argued that the answer to this question is crucial in determining the effects and desirability of government support. In particular, the differences between a centralized or federal state, and between a democratic or authoritarian state are analyzed (section 2). A second, equally neglected, question with respect to government support is: *"How is artistic creativity fostered?"* To answer this question, which is again crucial for the effects of state support on culture, Crowding Theory is used. It allows us to systematically analyze the relationship between government intervention and intrinsic motivation, which is an important source of artistic creativity (section 3). The final section discusses the far-reaching consequences of these new considerations for the public support of the arts.

2.   What Kind of State?

Most studies in cultural economics take the state as a welfare maximizing black box[1]. However, this assumption goes against the

---

[1]   In many cases, the analysis is, however, focussed on the *effects* of direct subsidies and other tax expenditures on artistic production and social welfare (e.g. Peacock 1969). Formal studies are provided e.g. by Hansmann 1981, Le Pen 1982, Dupuis 1983, Austen-Smith and Jenkins 1985. A survey of the instruments for the public promotion of the arts is provided in chapter 6, as well as in monographs, e.g. Throsby and Withers 1979, Trimarchi 1985a,b, 1994, O'Hagan and Duffy 1987, Heilbrun and Gray 1993, Benhamou 1996. See also the collection of articles in Towse 1997.

insight of modern political economy, showing that the government (politicians) pursue selfish aims. Social welfare is only maximized under highly restrictive and improbable conditions. It is therefore important to go more deeply into the political economy of art by using a comparative institutional perspective. Two crucial aspects, characterizing the state, are focussed on: whether it is centralized or decentralized (subsection 1), and whether it is democratic or authoritarian (subsection 2).

2.1   Centralized or Decentralized State

A centralized government, on the one hand, is a monopolistic supplier of publicly provided goods and services. In a decentralized system, on the other hand, there is a differentiated supply from which citizens and firms may choose. These institutional differences strongly affect the supply of art.

In a centralized monopoly state, an artist or art group in line with official art policy can receive much support from the concentrated funds at the government's disposal. Artists who ask for support must at least conform to the formal requirements set by the monopoly state. This reduces their artistic freedom and, in practice, the chance of getting support is clearly higher if the kind of artistic project submitted suits the tastes of the party and the politicians in power. As a result, such centralized nations are characterized by large, lump artistic expenditures. The establishment of the Centre Pompidou, the Opéra Bastille, the Arche de la Défense, or the Librairie Nationale, all located in Paris, or the huge subsidies to the Viennese Opera, the Burgtheater and the Wiener Philharmonie, all located in Vienna, provide examples in France and Austria.

Artists and art groups out of line with what is defined as "good art", or even as "art", by the government find it most difficult, and even impossible, to get public support. If their art is not, or not yet, marketable, they have to emigrate or to wait until a government comes to power with an arts policy that suits them better.

In a federal system of government, an artist has alternative sources of government support to turn to. The possibility of tapping funds by geographically moving enlarges artistic freedom. History provides many examples of this. The Holy Roman Empire of German Nations, consisting of hundreds of small units (see e.g. Volckart 1997), provided an institutional setting for flourishing arts because an artist found it very easy to move the few kilometers to another dukedom. A well-known case is Friedrich Schiller (1759-1805), who was severely suppressed by the duke, Karl Eugen, but who had outside opportunities. He took advantage of them by fleeing to Mannheim, and later to Weimar, where he found the freedom and the support to write his masterpieces. Another case is Wolfgang Amadeus Mozart, who was able to leave Fürsterzbischof Colloredo's intolerant rule in Salzburg, and found more welcoming conditions in Vienna and Prague (see Baumol and Baumol 1994).

The same supportive conditions for the lively arts was provided by the many independent city states in Medieval and Renaissance Italy. Artists, among them the geniuses Michelangelo Buonarroti and Leonardo da Vinci, frequently switched their patrons. They were not subservient to them because both sides knew that the artists had good opportunities elsewhere (see e.g. Warnke 1985).

This stimulating effect of decentralization (federalism) on the arts is often overlooked because historiography is still dominated by the view that the formation of unified nations (Germany, Italy) was a great achievement. While it has slowly been understood that it was – to say the least – a mixed blessing politically (viz. the two World Wars), the notion of a "national arts policy" is still very current. Some even dream of, and actively promote, a "European arts policy" within the European Union. The Political Economy of Culture would do well to study more deeply the conditions of the artists in the historical periods of a multitude of diverse competing states.

2.2   Democratic or Authoritarian State

It is commonly taken as evident that authoritarian systems produce bad art. One tends to think of dictators as often having bad taste and using whatever means at their disposal to impose it on their subjects. That is certainly sometimes true. But consider, for example, the autocratic popes of the Renaissance, such as Julius II (who ruled from 1503-1515), who employed artists such as Bramante, Bernini, Raffael or Michelangelo to build St. Peter's Cathedral and the Vatican, including the *stanze* and the *capella sistina*. Even in the case of Hitler, one of the most terrible dictators ever, views have somewhat changed. While he destroyed or drove expressionist and abstract art into exile, some art-work, films and especially architecture commissioned by him is today no longer considered to be so bad. In the case of Mussolini, it even tends to be favorably acknowledged (e.g. some buildings of the EUR, *Esposizione Universale Romana*).

Rather than simply identifying auto cratic rule with bad or good art, as the case may be, I wish to put forward two conjectures:

1. *Larger variance in quality between authoritarian rulers.* In democratic countries, governments are controlled by the citizens; in the pure model of two competing parties, or simple majority voting, their arts policy converges on the preferences of the median voter, i.e. on "average art taste". This means that extreme views don't carry much weight (in the median voter model, actually no weight), which produces a more stable art policy.

   In authoritarian states, on the other hand, the preferences of the ruler with respect to art are decisive. The art supported and produced therefore depends on what artistic tastes the ruler happens to have, resulting in large variances. The personal tastes of various authoritarian rulers may differ greatly and are sometimes too extreme to be directly translated into arts policy. If the ruler happens to have what art historians ex post consider a "good" taste in art, the respective policy is likely to produce high quality art. An example would be the Egyptian pharaohs erecting magnificent temples and pyramids. But if the ruler has a "bad" taste in art, the resulting cultural policy is likely to produce junk. Stalinist arts policy may be an appropriate example.

   A large majority of art lovers and, not surprisingly, politicians and public officials abhors the idea of letting citizens participate in decisions on art. They are absolutely convinced that an élite must decide. They believe, of course, that they themselves belong to the chosen few, and that the decisions taken by them are far better than if they were left to the population at large. The same argument is used by authoritarian rulers: they are also convinced that they possess *the* ultimate in good taste. To differentiate between art support favored by an élite in a democracy and by authoritarian rulers, one would have to argue that the latter represent an adverse selection with respect to artistic taste. This *may* well be so, but this proposition would have to be empirically established. What *is* known, on the other hand, is that decisions on art via popular referenda do not destroy art. As has been shown in chapter 7, the empirical evidence suggests that citizens in directly democratic institutions are quite prepared to financially support the arts (see also Vautravers-Busenhart 1998).

2. *Smaller variation with respect to the types of art supported and produced within authoritarian states.* Authoritarian rulers are forced to impose their influence upon the population in order to stay in power. To allow, or even support, artists and artistic groups and movements in opposition to the government is dangerous and therefore evaded[2]. Democratic states are committed to tolerating divergent views. This may be more an ideal than reality because artists and art groups conforming to "official" arts policy find it much easier to get financial support from government. Nevertheless, democracies typically allow more types of art.

According to a combination of the two propositions, the variety of types of art in authoritarian states is smaller, but the range in quality is larger. The prototypes of art supported by authoritarian states are dominant "monuments" (they need not be architectural, but may be virtual, e.g. orchestras or theatre groups) some of which are hideous, some of which are beautiful (according to an ex post art historic evaluation). In contrast, financial support to the arts in decentralized democracies benefits a broader set of cultural activities and shows less variance in quality.

---

2   One might argue that this policy leads to "underground art". This is quite true, but in most cases it is rather small in terms of art consumers reached, and confined to particular art forms suitable for clandestine presentation.

The purpose of the discussion in this section has been to demonstrate that it is a worthwhile endeavor to analyze *what type of state* supports the arts. In addition to the two dimensions discussed here – extent of centralization and authoritarianism – several others may also have a significant effect on the kind of art produced. Many of these aspects have so far received scant attention in Cultural Economics. Yet, they may constitute a rich source of insights, going beyond what has been studied by (art) historians.

3. How Does Government Support Affect Artistic Creativity?

Creativity is an elusive concept and most difficult to deal with in a way that provides useful insights into the typical problems with which the economics of art is faced. In particular, the effect of government intervention on artistic activity is complex, and does not lend itself to simple relationships and conclusions.

3.1 Institutional and Personal Creativity

For our purpose, it is useful to distinguish two types of creativity:

1. *"Institutional Creativity"*. This is the creativity produced by adequate institutional conditions, some of which have already been touched upon. An institution particularly supporting creativity is the price system. This also applies to the art market. Prices produce incentives to be innovative, and reward those who are successful in this endeavor. This feature of the market or price system has been neglected in traditional static economics (such as general equilibrium theory), but it has been the center of thinking of Schumpeter, Hayek, the New Austrians and Evolutionary Economics. It has also been appreciated in the economics of art. Voucher systems, which give more choice to the consumers than

direct government support, have been suggested, not least because they promise to foster variety and creativity[3].

The negative effects of some types of institutions on creativity have also been well studied in art economics. Thus, for example, a guaranteed public financing of the budget deficits of art organizations, prevalent in many European countries, discourages creativity. To receive funds largely independent of performance makes for a comfortable life. But it promotes conservatism rather than creativity. The recipients have an overwhelming urge to stick to the easy source of finance. Accordingly, they have a strong interest in not antagonizing the politicians and bureaucrats handing out the money with innovative art, which necessarily fosters conflict. The many government regulations and restrictions imposed on public art institutions are another way of inhibiting creativity, as it hampers or forbids change. The same holds true for union restrictions (particularly in the case of orchestras, theatres and opera houses), which are often supported by the government (see e.g. Frey and Pommerehne 1989a).

Interestingly enough, institutions damaging creativity may *indirectly* promote artistic innovation elsewhere. Provided there are persons with strong intrinsic motivation to be artistically innovative (which will be called Personal Creativity), they will seek ways to fulfil it outside established art manipulated by government intervention. As has been argued in chapter 5, the rise in the number of festivals can at least partly be interpreted as an effort to free oneself from the governmental and union restrictions existing in the traditional art institutions. However, this is only a short-term escape, because governments and unions are keen on regulating the new territories as well. Some of the famous old festivals (such as Bayreuth and Salzburg) have experienced that fate. Governments have increasingly stepped in with direct and indirect subsidies, which have been accompanied by ever-increasing regulations. As a result, they are in constant

---

3   This view is not generally accepted in cultural economics. Dolfsma (1997, p. 245), for instance, states: "Real art is innovative and thus has, almost by definition, no market on which it can be sold".

threat of becoming ossified and have partly succumbed to that danger.

2. *"Personal Creativity"*. This creativity is based on the intrinsic motivation to be artistically innovative given the institutional conditions. Intrinsically motivated persons pursue artistic activities for their own sake (in contrast, extrinsically motivated artists do so in order to get acknowledgements and rewards, including income). Personal Creativity may vary, even if the institutions governing the arts are the same. While Institutional

Creativity depends on the nature of the constraints on behavior, Personal Creativity is a feature of the individual's motivations, i.e. belongs to the set of preferences or tastes[4].

Personal creativity has been rather disregarded in cultural economics[5]. It will be studied in the remainder of this chapter.

3.2 Government Intervention and Personal Creativity

There are two opposing views on what incentives make artists creative (see also Tietzel 1995, p. 138-143).

1. *Intrinsic creativity.* The dominant view held by art historians[6], other art experts, and artists themselves is that creative art can

---

[4] But, as will be argued below, Personal Creativity is not independent of institutions, but is governed by different theoretical relationships than envisaged in orthodox economics.

[5] This includes my own book with Werner Pommerehne (Frey and Pommerehne 1989a), which does not even mention the terms "creativity", "innovation" or "invention". Exceptions are works by e.g. Heilbrun 1991, Hutter e.g. 1992, 1996b and Klamer e.g. 1996. Hutter and Klamer proceed in a quite different way than done here. To capture creativity, they give up traditional economic theory and turn to philosophical and sociological approaches. In contrast, this chapter endeavors to extend art economics by using *specific* and *empirically* tested theories from social psychology.

In disciplines going beyond economics, creativity is a central concept. See, for instance, the fascinating and encompassing book on "Greatness" by Simonton 1994, who also gives a large number of references. For a sociological approach see e.g. Kavolis 1964, and more generally Foster and Blau 1989.

only be produced by intrinsically motivated persons. George Bernard Shaw (1903, p. 22) states: "The true artist will let his wife starve, his children go barefoot, his mother drudge for her living at seventy, sooner than work at anything but his art". Most artists would emphatically deny that they produce art because of the monetary compensation thereby received. The fact that some artists state the opposite is a good attempt at "épater le bourgeois", but should not be taken seriously.

Such a view is not inconsistent with an economic analysis, provided one makes the additional assumption that creativity is possible only when the activity is undirected and time-consuming. This assumption is similar to, though not identical with, the intrinsic view of creativity. But the effect of outside intervention is the same. If an artist receives monetary compensation for producing art, either through public subsidies or through the market, the artist's opportunity cost of time rises. The cost of spending time with undirected activities then rises. The time-consuming creative activity is then reduced in favor of producing tried-out work for the artistic market. This opportunity cost of time being more expensive particularly affects the artists successful on markets. In contrast, young artists who do not fetch high prices for their art works have lower opportunity cost of time, and can therefore "afford" to spend more time with undirected, and thus potentially more creative activities. This opportunity cost argument helps to explain why young artists are often more creative than older artists. This holds in particular because there are fewer commercially unsuccessful older artists than younger artists, because when artists are still not making money with their products, they tend to choose another occupation.

2. *Extrinsically induced creativity.* Most economists, and other rational choice scholars, believe, however, that reality can be well explained by assuming that *only* extrinsic incentives matter. To assume income or wealth maximization is quite current but, of

---

6   An exception is, for instance, Alpers 1988, with her account of Rembrandt's life.

course, not necessary. What matters is that changes in extrinsic motivations, and therewith in behavior, can be attributed to changes in external intervention via constraints on behavior (McKenzie and Tullock 1975, Becker 1976, Hirshleifer 1985, Frey 1999). This relative price effect applies to all kinds of behavior and persons, i.e. also to creativity in the art world. Artists are thus taken to be the more creative, the higher the benefits, and the lower the costs are. In particular, when the government changes relative prices by handing net subsidies to artists, it becomes more profitable to work as an artist, and creativity is therewith increased. The same effect takes place when artists earn more money by selling their art on the market. If indeed the market actors are able to recognize creativity, *and* if there is a demand for artistic creativity (it is doubtful whether both assumptions normally hold), creative art reaches higher prices, and artists have an incentive to produce such art. The relative price approach, just sketched for the case of creativity of artists, is powerful, as it forbids attributing changes in behavior to haphazard and unexplained changes in preferences (Stigler and Becker 1977, Becker 1996). Moreover, it provides clear and empirically testable hypotheses.

Interestingly enough, among *psychologists* specialized in research on personal creativity, two similar camps may be identified.

The conventional and dominant view, the "intrinsic motivation hypothesis of creativity", states: "Intrinsic motivation is conducive to the idea-generation stage of creativity, but extrinsic motivation is detrimental" (Amabile 1988, p. 154). Rewards, in monetary or non-monetary form, reduce creativity. According to an extensively cited literature review (Condry 1977, pp. 470-471), individuals who are given rewards "seem to work harder and produce more activity, but the activity is of a lower quality, contains more errors, and is more stereotyped and less creative than the work of comparable non-rewarded subjects working on the same problems". The major reason is that rewards divert "attention from the task itself and non-obvious aspects of the environment that might be used in achieving a creative solution" (Amabile 1983, p. 120). These findings are directly applicable to artistic creativity (e.g. Loveland and Olley 1979, Amabile 1979, 1985, Hennessey and Amabile 1988).

The second camp in the psychology of creativity arrives at the opposite conclusion, also on the basis of laboratory experiments. Systematic rewards enhance creative performance (e.g. Torrence 1970, Winston and Baker 1985). "The use of periodic salient reward may provide an effective way to help individuals sustain their creative efforts when success comes slowly and with great difficulty" (Eisenberger and Armeli 1997, p. 661; also Eisenberger and Selbst 1994). However, psychologists have more in mind than economists' relative price effect. They assume that rewards create a *general* tendency to behave creatively, even when the reward is no longer active. They thus posit a "Motivational Spill-Over Effect" (see Frey 1997, chapter 5).

It is time to overcome the divergent views held by economists and non-economists about artists' personal motivation to be creative. For that purpose, a relationship called *Crowding Theory,* which systematically links intrinsic and extrinsic motivation, is called upon.

3.3   A More Balanced View: Crowding Theory

Crowding Theory analyzes the effect of external interventions on intrinsic motivation. It is thus applicable to Personal Creativity, which depends on a motivation for acting for its own sake rather than for external compensation. The external intervention may consist of monetary and non-monetary rewards, as well as regulations. It is based on a well-developed psychological effect known as "Hidden Cost of Rewards", stating that rewarding highly motivated persons for undertaking a task tends to reduce their intrinsic motivation. Due to the external incentive introduced, intrinsic motivation is no longer needed nor appreciated. This psychological relationship can be generalized as the *Crowding-Out Effect*. But there are also instances under which an external intervention raises intrinsic motivation, leading to the *Crowding-In Effect*. Psychologists have shown that Crowding-In takes place when the intervention is perceived to be supportive, and Crowding-Out when it is perceived to be controlling. Crowding Theory has been empirically analyzed under a large number of experimental conditions in the laboratory as well as in the field, and has most recently been subjected to econometric tests[7].

The Crowding-Out Effect contributes a new aspect to economic theory. It states the exact opposite of the relative price effect, which so far represented the core of economics. An increase in price (or monetary rewards) *decreases* effort (work input) when Crowding-Out dominates the relative price effect. Government support to the arts may now be analyzed from this perspective. According to traditional economics, granting money to an individual or organization should not reduce their artistic effort. The possibility space is extended, which benefits such activities, provided it is a normal good[8].

If government support is provided to cultural activities in an incentive compatible way (e.g. the higher the artistic output, the higher the support granted), the induced relative price change is expected to raise artistic effort. Crowding Theory questions this result. If government support is perceived to be controlling by the artists in question, their intrinsic motivation and Personal Creativity is undermined. Depending on the size of Crowding-Out and the relative price effects, government support might well lead to an unintended, perverse effect on artistic creativity.

As stated above, Crowding-Out occurs when the recipients of government support perceive it to be controlling. In the artistic field, such a reaction by the recipients appears to arise quite often, not least because the government, for bureaucratic reasons, does indeed

---

[7]   Crowding Theory is developed in Frey (1997). The experimental findings are discussed in Wiersma (1992), Cameron and Pierce (1994), Eisenberger and Cameron (1996), and Deci, Koestner and Ryan (1999), the econometric findings in Barkema (1995), Frey, Oberholzer-Gee and Eichenberger (1996), and Frey and Oberholzer-Gee (1997). The empirical evidence is summarized in Frey and Jegen (1999).

[8]   It is, of course, possible to construct *some* story so that artistic activities are reduced. One such possibility is provided by rent-seeking activities, which might consume more resources than are granted from outside. But such stories require many additional assumptions.

control the recipients to some extent. In the extreme case, we have the (so-called) "artist", whose artistic zeal has been completely destroyed by the funds received, who produces junk and is even aware of this.

Several geniuses are reported to have feared the corrupting or distracting effect of monetary rewards. It has been argued that this may even apply to the Nobel Prize. T.S. Eliot got depressed when he was awarded this most prestigious prize: "The Nobel is a ticket to one's own funeral. No one has ever done anything after he got it". And Oscar Wilde put it even more succinctly: "Genius is born, not paid" (see Simonton 1994, pp. 57-8 for the references).

On a more analytical level, motivational Crowding Theory suggests the following effects on creativity and intrinsic motivation are at work when the arts are supported e. g. by the government:

1. *Crowding-Out intrinsic motivation.* Conditions have been identified under which the controlling perception is particularly vivid, and therefore *Crowding-Out* is strong (see Frey 1997, chapter 4).

   (a) Government support *contingent on a particular performance* strongly reduces intrinsic motivation.

   Immediate feedback is inimical to intrinsic motivation, and even more so to artistic innovation. Personal Creativity needs time to develop, and is damaged if the support is closely connected with behavior.

   It is interesting to note that the same conditions strengthen the relative price effect: perfect incentive compatibility is best reached when the support is as closely contingent on performance as possible. The Crowding-Out Effect only takes place if the recipient has some amount of intrinsic motivation. But this means that an effective way of government subsidization – namely as contingent as possible on performance – tends to produce more, but rather mediocre, art because the artists concerned are not intrinsically motivated in producing original art. On the other hand, if the potential recipients of government support are highly intrinsically motivated, and hence potentially creative, this high motivation tends to be crowded-out by contingent rewards. In this case, it is better to grant subsidies leaving the artists considerable leeway so that they are able to engage in creative art.

(b) Uniform treatment of artists by the government strongly crowds-out intrinsic motivation.

A fundamental characteristic of artists certainly is that they are a varied lot which reacts most negatively to any effort to treat them uniformly. Government support of the arts does not account for this variety and is therefore inimical to creativity.

This should be compared to the relationship of artists with their gallerists and impresarios on the art market. In most cases, this relationship is intimate and far transcends the commercial aspects. A successful and creative co-operation only emerges if the gallerist is willing to tolerate, and perhaps even instigate, the idiosyncrasies of each one of the artists he or she represents.

2. *Crowding-In intrinsic motivation.* We can now turn to the conditions under which external interventions *raise intrinsic motivation*, i.e. where a strong *Crowding-In* Effect is expected.

(a) The more artistic creativity is fostered, the more each artist's intrinsic motivation is acknowledged and appreciated.

In order to meet this condition, government support must be given in a way which supports artists' autonomy and which make them feel that they are taken seriously. If, in contrast, governments hand out money to artists as if it were just one of the many interest groups claiming support, artists tend to lose their unique characteristic creativity. One way to maintain creativity is to give the support in an unconditional way, i.e. only preventing obvious embezzlement, for instance by granting stipends to cover the expenses of living in a challenging place for a particular period. Another way is to grant support indirectly by leaving the task to better equipped private persons who, in turn, are partly compensated by tax exemptions.

(b) Intrinsic motivation is also supported when the addressees of external intervention have a measure of participation.

Today, in the art world, this condition seems to be met to a higher degree than ever before in history. In former times, artists were often hired for very specific tasks. For instance, medieval monasteries used to commission painters to complete a picture of the Holy Mary, in which even the colors used for her coat were exactly laid down (Baxandall 1972). In the centuries thereafter, the artists were given more leeway, but they were nevertheless much constrained by the patron. This dependence of the artists applied also to public commissions.

In the 20th century, such constraints have become difficult to imagine. It would lead to an uproar in the art world and beyond if the government exactly specified how a commissioned painting or a piece of architecture commissioned has to look. Indeed, the artists today have considerable freedom in that respect, and may therefore imprint their particular understanding of aesthetics on publicly-funded works. Examples abound, but are particularly well seen in recent museum buildings, such as the Museums of Art in Stuttgart or in Mönchengladbach, where the respective architects had much leeway to do what they wanted. It may well be that the outbreak of creativity in the arts in the 19th, and especially in the 20th, century with its wide variety of, and rapid innovations in, artistic styles, is the result of strongly enhancing the participatory role of artists. This "grand" relationship is a conjecture which needs to be subjected to serious empirical analysis. But it is consistent with the psychological findings on which Crowding Theory is based.

The discussion has shown that government policy is, on the whole, not well-equipped to support and enhance Personal Creativity. Under many conditions, government support tends to undermine artistic innovation. Much would be gained if government support were at least neutral, i.e. would leave Personal Creativity unaffected. Private art supporters and art professionals (such as gallerists) are better prepared to meet the conditions for supporting artists' innovative capacity. Museum buildings are again a good example. Indirect public support, i.e. through the tax exemption of art foundations, has created stunning examples of artistic creativity, such as the Frank Lloyd Wright's Guggenheim Museum in New York, Frank O. Gehry's Guggenheim Museum in Bilbao, or Richard Meier's Getty Center in Los Angeles.

This does not mean at all that government support to the arts should be suspended or curtailed. But the politicians and bureaucrats should not believe that they can plan creativity, because "creativity always comes as a surprise" (Hirschman 1970, p. 80). Rather, the government should concentrate on setting the right conditions for *Institutional* Creativity. In particular, it must lay the rules that allow a flourishing art market, e.g. by setting adequate property rights for artists' output[9] and promoting the international exchange (trade) in art. Econometric cross-country research has established more generally that "open societies, which bind themselves to the rule of law, to private property and to the market allocation of resources, grow at three times (2.7 to 0.9 percent annually) the rate of . . . societies where these freedoms are circumscribed or proscribed" (Scully 1992, p. 183). The government can promote *Personal* Creativity by a hands-off policy, giving private actors incentives to take over the role of enhancing artists' intrinsic motivation to produce innovative art. Such a policy is not free of charge. Most importantly, it involves tax expenditures (i.e. income lost through tax exemptions).

---

[9]   See the special issue of the *Journal of Cultural Economics* 19 (1995) No 2 on "The Economics of Intellectual Property Rights", and chapter 11.

4.   Conclusions

An extensive literature in the economics of art deals with the categorical question of whether the state should support the arts. It is answered in two quite different ways. Those taking market failures to be an important phenomenon tend to answer positively. Proponents of the new right tend to answer negatively, because they reject the very notion of market failures and emphasize instead political failures.

There is also a large literature on the most efficient forms of public support, in particular of government subsidies. It concludes that support should be given in an incentive-compatible way, i.e. the subsidies given should be as closely related to the desired performance as possible.

This paper proceeds quite differently; it wants to explore neglected aspects of the public support of the arts. Two issues have been discussed:

One fundamental issue is *what kind of state* is supporting the arts. Once this issue is settled, the level and type of support is endogenous. At best, marginal changes are possible. The basic decisions are determined by a politico-economic equilibrium within a given constitutional setting.

Two constitutional aspects and their effect on the support of art are discussed. One is the extent of democratic participation rights of the citizens (autocracy or democracy), the other the extent of decentralization (unitary or federal state).

An authoritarian and centralized state tends to support larger "monuments" (including not only architectural, but also virtual objects, such as orchestras), has a smaller variance of types of art, but a larger variance in quality compared to decentralized democracies. Representative, but largely centralized, democracies, in which the political élite dominates the decisions on art, reveal a similar type of cultural support to authoritarian countries.

The second issue concerns the effect of government support on *artistic innovation*. Two kinds of creativity are distinguished. The first relates to *Institutional Creativity.* An institution beneficial to creativity is the market: it provides monetary (i.e. extrinsic) incentives for creativity. In contrast, fixed government subsidies – in particular an automatic coverage of budget deficits – leads to the maintenance of a comfortable life and artistic behavior inimical to innovation.

The second type of artistic innovation is called *Personal Creativity.* It is governed by the extent of intrinsic motivation of the artists. Crowding Theory allows an explicit analysis of the effects of external interventions (government support) on Personal Creativity. Government policies tend to undermine intrinsic artistic motivation, and therewith Personal Creativity. The contingency of the support on a particular artistic performance and a uniform treatment of aid recipients are major conditions contributing to crowding-out Personal Creativity.

The analysis undertaken leads to a more differentiated view of public support compared to received (cultural) economics. The difference is most clearly visible in the case of public subsidies relying on incentive compatibility. For orthodox economics (principal agency theory), a close relationship between artistic performance and support is required for efficient support. In sharp contrast, Crowding Theory, derived from a well-established and empirically supported psychological effect, points out that discretionary room is necessary for artists to experiment and to develop creative ideas. Contingency of support for artistic performance crowds-out artistic innovation.

It is also concluded that government support in general is ill-suited to support and enhance (crowd-in) intrinsic artistic inventiveness. Private persons as supporters and/or art managers (gallerists, impresarios) are better equipped to provide the supportive atmosphere needed for personal artistic creativity. The state can support it directly by granting tax exemptions to private persons or by non-monetary means, such as allowing for adequate property rights for artists' output.

Chapter 9 -
Art Investment Returns[*]

(with Reiner Eichenberger)

1.   The State of the Art

1.1   The Beginnings

"What are the returns on investments in art objects?" This question has attracted the attention of the public and of economists for a considerable number of years. One of the reasons for this interest certainly stems from lay people's belief that the art market yields huge profits in comparison to ordinary financial markets – at least when the investors are well-informed. This belief has been nourished by the media, which were all too ready to predict that the rapid increase in the general price level of auctioned art objects in the 80s, and in particular the ever higher record prices paid for paintings by van Gogh, Picasso and Renoir, would persist forever. Van Gogh's *Sunflowers* sold at an auction for $39.9 million in

---

[*]   This chapter is based on Bruno S. Frey and Reiner Eichenberger (1995), "On the Return of Art Investment Return Analyses", previously published in the *Journal of Cultural Economics* 19, pp. 207-220, used by permission of Kluwer Academic Publishers.

March 1987. This was very soon topped by the sale in November of the same year of his *Irises* for \$53.9 million. In May 1989, *Io Picasso* sold for \$47.8 million. In May 1990, van Gogh's *Portrait of Dr. Gachet* fetched \$82.5 million and Renoir's *At the Moulin de la Galette* sold for \$78.1 million. The simple expectation of ever exploding arts prices proved to be drastically false, considering the marked downfall of such prices after 1989. Thus, for example, as late as in May 1996, Picasso's *La Lecture* failed to sell (i.e. was "bought in") at \$4.8 million after having sold for \$6.3 million in May 1989. But the media, nevertheless, renew the story of the extraordinary financial returns in art markets whenever prices show any indication of rising again.

The two following figures show the development of the *Art Market Price Index* for the Italian Market of modern and contemporary paintings during the period 1983-1994, as an example (Canela and Scorcu 1997, p. 189-190). Other art markets have developed in a similar way as the comparison to other indices, such as Sotheby's Index, based on the auction house experts' personal judgments, suggests (ibid: 188). Figure 1 compares this art index to the Italian consumer price index. The art market boomed in the second half of the 1980s but, beginning 1992, the art market index is roughly back in line with the consumer price index. Thus, in *real* terms, art prices have not risen between 1983 and 1992-4.

Figure 2 compares the Art Market Price Index to investments in shares (index of stock prices traded in Milan) and in houses (index of house prices in the Milan market). The Art Market Price Index peaked sharply in 1990, but fell to a lower level than the two other investments thereafter. Stock values rose drastically in 1985-6, but then held more or less, albeit with considerable fluctuations. Housing values rose rather gradually over almost the whole period.

Figure 1: **Art Price Index and Consumer Price Index**

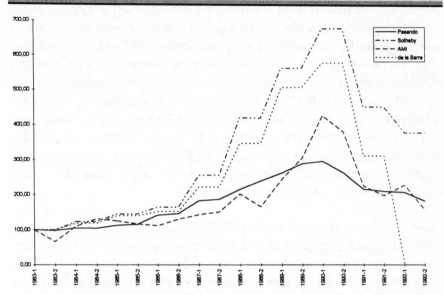

Source: Canela & Scorcu (1997), *Journal of Cultural Economics.*

Figure 2: **Assets Price Index**

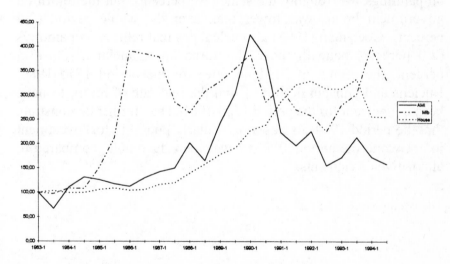

Source: Canela & Scorcu (1997), *Journal of Cultural Economics.*

One of the first professional economists to systematically study the development of art prices and rates of return was Wagenführ (1965), whose study has been overlooked in the academic literature, probably because it was written in German. Better known early works explicitly calculating financial rates of returns of auctioned paintings are by Anderson (1974) and Stein (1977). Both found that the rate of return in art is lower than for alternative investments. Anderson calculates a nominal return of 3.3 percent for paintings over the period 1810-1970. This compares to a return of 6.6 percent for stocks. Stein finds nominal returns of 10.5 percent for paintings for the period 1946-68, compared to stocks which yielded 14.3 percent. Ten years later, Baumol (1986) published a paper which started a boom in studies on the subject, not surprisingly coinciding with the boom in arts prices in the late 80s.

Baumol shows that, over the period 1652-1961, the real return on auctioned paintings averaged 0.55 percent, compared to 2.5 percent on British Government bonds. This study was extended and refined (e.g. by taking auction fees into account) by Frey and Pommerehne (1989b). They find that the real rate of return on paintings averages 1.5 percent for the period 1635-1987, compared to 3 percent on government bonds. For the post-war period 1950-87, the real return on paintings was roughly the same (1.6 percent), but the return on government bonds was lower than over the whole period (2.4 percent). Goetzman (1993) also calculates real returns on paintings (2.0 percent) beneath the real returns on financial assets (3.3 percent, the Bank of England rate) for the period 1715-1986. Buelens and Ginsburgh (1993) find the real rate of return to have been 0.9 percent for the period 1700-1961. They further demonstrate that the period 1914-50 was a particularly poor one for investment in art, while the period 1950-61 was more favorable, compared to alternative investments.

1.2   The Purpose of Art Return Studies

When calculating rates of returns on art, three goals may usefully be distinguished:

1. *Market equilibrium.* The art market is taken to be a *market as any other* and one endeavors to compare the financial returns attainable compared to alternative investments. Certainly, many art markets are characterized by particularly high transaction.

2. *Technical virtuosity.* Investigating art market returns is at least partly motivated by the internal dynamics of the economics profession (Frey and Eichenberger 1994): it is a new area in which to apply technical virtuosity. The art market provides a welcome opportunity for using the modern techniques of finance and econometrics. Accordingly, attention has been devoted to the question of whether the art market is efficient. Granger causality tests have been used to analyze price and return independencies between:
   - various types of markets for art, e.g., between Old Masters and Impressionists;
   - various locations, in particular between auction houses in New York, London and Paris;
   - the art market and various financial markets, especially the New York, London and Tokyo stock markets and government securities.

3. *Art and economists.* Art investments are analyzed by scholars who are themselves involved in the arts (William Baumol, Alan Peacock and Hans Abbing are prominent examples) and who are interested in knowing what is *specific* to the arts, and for whom the consumption aspect of owning art is central. At the same time, these researchers see the art market as an area where aspects otherwise treated lightly or negligently show themselves more clearly. One such aspect is the crucial importance of transaction costs in art dealings. Thus, for instance, the commissions due when buying or selling an art object at an auction are far larger than in financial markets. Another primary aspect of art markets

is the psychic benefit of owning art which, in contrast, is largely absent in the case of owning financial assets.

The following section provides a brief overview of major studies on the rate of return on art objects, presenting both the result of the calculations and the analytical approaches used. Section 3 pursues the question of what distinguishes the art market from other markets. We argue that art markets are characterized by a stronger prevalence of behavioral anomalies and asymmetric information between buyers and sellers, as well as by thin markets. Section 4 considers to what extent, and under what circumstances, art is more likely to be a consumption good (with traditional collectors prevailing) or an investment good (with financial speculations prevailing). Section 5 offers concluding remarks.

2.   An Overview of Results and Approaches

Table 9-1 provides a summary of major studies on financial returns on art investment. It documents that the research has gone far beyond paintings and has considered other pictures such as drawings or prints, antiques such as violins and American antique furniture, as well as various collectibles such as toy soldiers, old fire arms and even beer mugs. They also differ greatly with respect to the period covered and its duration, as well as many other attributes such as the (minimum) length of the holding period. The table reveals that most studies find that the financial return on art investments is lower than for investments in stocks, and even in government bonds. This result holds in particular for the general studies on paintings already mentioned above, including the calculations by Anderson, Stein, Baumol, Frey and Pommerehne, Goetzmann and Buelens and Ginsburgh (in chronological order). But it also holds for other art works such as antique furniture (Graeser 1993) and violins by Stradivari (which have a surprisingly low financial rate of return of 2.2 percent; Ross and Zondervan 1993). More curious collectibles, such as Mettlach beer steins and antique firearms (Kelly 1994, Avery and Colonna 1987), even have a negative financial rate of return.

Table 9-1: **Returns on investments in paintings, antiques and collectibles**

Object	Time period	Return (in percent)		Return on alternative investments[a] (in percent)	Authors
		real	nom.		
Paintings in general					
	1800-1970		3.3	6.6 (st)[b]	Anderson (1974)
	1652-1961	0.55		2.5 (gb)	Baumol (1986)
	1635-1987	1.5		3.0 (gb)	Frey (1989b)
	1716-1986	2.0		3.3 (BoEr)	Goetzmann (1993)
	1700-1961	0.9[c]			Buelens/ Ginsbergh (1993)
	1946-1968		10.5	14.3 (st)	Stein (1977)
	1950-1987	1.6		2.4 (gb)	Frey/ Pommerehne (1989b)
Specific paintings					
Impressionists	1951-1969		17.2		Anderson (1974)
-do-	1700-1961	3.0[c]			Buelens/ Ginsbergh (1993)
late Renaissance	1951-1969		7.8		Anderson (1974)
English paintings	1700-1961	0.6[c]			Buelens/ Ginsburgh (1993)
paint. From the 50s	1960-1990	5.9			Rouget et al. (1991)
paint. Of selected artists	1960-1988	6.7		Higher (Jap. st) lower (US st)	Chanel et al. (1994)
Modern Chinese p.	1980-1990		53		Mok et al. (1993)
Other pictures					
Drawings	1951-1969		27		Anderson (1974)
-do-	1950-1970	11.3[d]			Holub et al. (1993)
Watercolors	1950-1970	15.8			Holub et al. (1993)
Prints	1977-1992	1.5		2.5 US gb), 8.1 (st)	Pesando (1993)
Antiques					
violins by Stradivari	1803-1987	2.2			Ross and Zondervan (1993)
Am. Antiq. Furniture	1967-1986		7	7.3 (90-day Tb)	Graeser (1993)
Collectibles					
Mettlach beer steins	1983-1993	-1.1		3.3 (Tb)	Kelly (1994)
toy soldiers	1967-1982		19[e]		Wellington / Gallo (1984)
antique firearms	1978-1984	- 2.3		4.0 (90-day Tb)	Avery/ Colonna (1987)
Collections					
- H. Mettler:					Frey/ Serna (1990)
Impressionist paint.	1915-1979	2.8		1.2 (Swiss gb)	
- G. Guterman:					
old masterpieces	1981-1988	3.2		6.9 (US gb)	
- British rail pension fund: overall		6.9		7.5 (FTI)	
Asiatica, old	sold 1987	3			
masterp. Imp. paint.	sold 1989	9.9			

[a] gb = government bonds; st = stocks; BoEr = Bank of England rate; Tb = Treasury bills; FTI = Financial Times Index. [b] See Anderson (1974), p. 25. [c] See Buelens and Ginsburgh (1993, p. 1358, Tab. 5). [d] Paintings had about the same performance as drawings (see Holub et al. 1993, p. 65). [e] Own computation on the basis of Wellington and Gallo's (1984) data.

It is important to also consider collections, because they may exploit the possibility of hedging art works with countervailing price developments. Collectors, who are able to find an auction house taking their whole collection, may either be particularly lucky or may have been able to acquire a work of art, which thereafter appreciates in value. This tends to bias the financial returns upwards compared to a representative sample of collections. Many collections are not recognized as such when it comes to putting them on the market (normally by the heirs) because they are of little value. An upward bias is also introduced by the "celebrity" value of some famous collections, which results in many buyers being ready to pay much more for pieces from such an auction.

Table 9-1 shows that Guterman's collection of old masterpieces yielded a return lower than for US government bonds (3.2 percent compared to 6.9 percent). Interestingly enough, this collection was bought for the explicit purpose of financial benefit. The same holds for the British Rail Pension Fund, with an overall return of 6.9 percent for art investments compared to 7.5 percent for the Financial Times investment index. In contrast, the Mettler collection of impressionists yielded a somewhat higher return than for Swiss government bonds (2.8 percent compared to 1.2 percent).

The so far most extensive study on a collection is devoted to the 1997 Christie's auction of 20th century art works from the estate of Victor and Sally Ganz (Landes 1999). The auction brought more than $207 million, a record sum for a single-owner sale of art auction. More than 25,000 people visited Christie's to view the works, and more than 2,000 people attended the auction. The auction created enormous excitement and publicity, praising the couple as having had remarkable foresight and talent in choosing the "right" work. They had indeed spectacular successes: a Picasso painting purchased for $7000 in 1941 sold for $48.4 million (this is the second highest price ever paid for a Picasso at auction) and a Jasper Johns bought for $15000 in 1964 was sold for $7.9 million. The $7000 in 1941 would have been worth $47.8 if invested in small company stock. This is about the same as the Picasso painting; but the stock investment was worth more after deducting the buyer's premium and seller's commission. As the last entry in Table 9-1 shows, the real rates of return for the collection as a whole turned out to be higher than for US investments in stocks. This is particularly true for those parts sold before the breakdown of the art market (i.e. in 1986 and 1988). For that part of the Ganz collection sold in 1997, the real rate of return of 11.74 percent is only slightly higher than for investments in small company stocks (10.85 percent), but considerably larger than in large company stocks (7.81 percent).

The studies surveyed in Table 9-1 (as well as others) are subject to four major problems, which are briefly touched upon:

1. *Data.* Most analyses are based on auctions[1], because the data are easily available and reliable. Other sales, which may be quantitatively more important and may show different price movements, are disregarded. The reason is that such data are most difficult, if not impossible, to get: art dealers refrain from offering price data. Moreover, auction prices should be interpreted as wholesale prices referring mainly to dealers; private collectors usually buy at higher prices from, and sell at lower prices to, art dealing houses (see Guerzoni 1994). Thus, dealers enjoy a systematically higher, and collectors a systematically lower, rate of return than suggested by the studies reproduced in table 9-1.

2. *Transaction cost.* Most studies (exceptions are Frey and Pommerehne 1989b and Landes 1999) disregard the high auction fees, which range from about 10 to 30 percent and sometimes even more when buying and selling, as well as insurance and other handling costs because they vary considerably between countries, periods, auction houses and individual transactions (e.g., in the case of very high prices, auction fees are determined by bargaining and are likely to be lower; in other cases they may be even higher). At least in the past, such costs were often

---

[1]   General treatises of auctions from the economic point of view are in book form, e.g., Cassady (1967), and in articles, e.g., Riley and Samuelson (1981), Milgrom and Weber (1982), Ashenfelter (1989) and various contributions in the 1989 Summer issue of the *Journal of Economic Perspectives*; a pathbreaking contribution is Vickrey (1961). A sociological analysis (with many references) is provided by Smith (1989).

unknown or unreliable, but due to their size they significantly influence the calculated rates of return.

3. *Taxation.* No study seriously takes into account the taxes due when transacting and holding an art object, though it is widely known that in many countries investment in art is one of the major possibilities of escaping, or at least lowering, the tax burden. It is, however, practically impossible to calculate rates of return net of taxation because taxes vary greatly between countries and time-periods. Moreover, it is often unknown where an art object bought is finally located and thus unclear which country's taxes apply and, above all, what the differences between formal tax codes and actual taxation are. In view of the significant size of many of the taxes involved, this is a major, but perhaps inevitable, shortcoming.

4. *Comparison to financial assets.* Most studies only make a rather superficial comparison to the rates of return for alternative investment opportunities. The relevant alternative investments are unclear, and for past periods insufficiently known. Even a comparison to the rates of return in stocks is unsatisfactory, as they normally do not consider dividends (see, e.g., Goetzman 1993, p. 1374). For these reasons, most analyses make a comparison with interest rates on U.S. and British government bonds or with U.S. stocks. They thus neglect investments in other countries and in other assets, such as houses or land, which are often a closer substitute to art investments, not least because in many countries they also benefit from preferential taxation.

The various studies of the returns on art investment have focussed on various aspects and have therefore employed various analytical approaches. Table 9-2 provides an overview of some of these aspects.

Table 9-2: **Major analytical approaches to art price movements**

Analytical approaches	Authors
rate of return: repeated sales regression	Stein (1977)
	Baumol (1986)
	Frey and Pommerehne (1989b)
	Goetzmann (1993)
rate of return: price indices	Anderson (1974)
	Goetzmann (1993)
	Buelens and Ginsburgh (1993)
efficiency in the art market	Coffman (1991)
	Louargand and McDaniel (1991)
	Pesando (1993)
	Goetzmann (1994)
determinants of art price movements	Goetzmann (1993)
	Chanel (1995)
interdependence of art markets	Ginsburgh and Jeanfils (1995)
heterogeneity of actors	Beltratti and Siniscalco (1991)
psychic returns	Stein (1977)
	Frey and Pommerehne (1989b)

The rate of return of investments in paintings, in other art objects and in collectibles, has been studied intensively. Many studies are based on the Reitlinger (1961) data set but, more recently, the yearly edition of the Mayer International Auction Records on CD-Rom have been used. Essentially two different techniques have been applied. Some of the most important studies use the "double sale method", which applies the standard compound calculation to estimate the rate of return for paintings sold at least twice during the period studied, thus comparing the selling and buying prices of identical paintings at different points in time. This method has been refined by estimating a "repeat sale regression". The (log of) price of each painting is requested in a set of dummy variables. Other studies are based on art price indices. The "average price method" uses some a priori criteria to weight the various artists included in the sample. The "representative painting method" is a refinement estimating a price index for a representative painting, which can be used as a close substitute for all paintings in the market. This technique is faced with the arbitrariness in the identification of the a priori criteria and the representative painting. Some authors search for the underlying forces behind art price movements, such as income, inflation, stock price movement, but also dimensions of paintings, techniques and artistic medium, signature. Others look at the interdependencies between the markets for various types of paintings and various locations. The efficiency of the art market is theoretically and empirically analyzed. A small number of studies focus on the psychic return of art investments and look at the interaction of various types of actors (i.e. collectors and speculators) in the art market.

A *general shortcoming* of many art returns studies (especially those applying advanced techniques of analysis) is their undue focus on mechanistic calculations and their disregard of the underlying behavior of the various actors. One of the purposes of this chapter is to look at these missing *behavioral* foundations. In particular, we seek to analyze the *determinants* of the *psychic returns* from art. This aspect has been disregarded in the literature, though several studies suggest that the implied psychic return is at least as large as the financial return on art investments.

3.   What Distinguishes the Art Market?

We propose that a major distinguishing characteristic of art markets is the greater importance of *behavioral anomalies*, i.e. of systematic deviations of individuals' behavior from the von Neumann-Morgenstern axioms of rationality and, in particular, from subjective expected utility maximization (see, e.g., Schoemaker 1982, Machina 1987). It has been shown that irrationalities such as the January-, Holiday-, Christmas- and Small-Firm-effects persist in financial markets (Thaler 1992, 1993, Shiller 1989, 1990), i.e. that arbitrage does not wipe out supernormal profits in this most perfect market. Due to the data limitations and other problems mentioned, only some restricted aspects of efficiency in the art market can be tested. Louargand and McDaniel (1991) find, for example, that the estimated selling price ranges given by the auction houses are unbiased predictions of the hammer prices.

There are good reasons why particular anomalies are even larger and more widespread with respect to art than in financial markets:

1. Many *private collectors* are not profit-oriented and are therefore particularly prone to anomalies. Circumstantial evidence suggests that private collectors are strongly subject to the endowment effect (an art object owned is evaluated higher than one not owned), the opportunity cost effect (most collectors isolate themselves from considering the returns of alternative uses of the funds)[2] and the sunk cost effect (past efforts of building up a collection play a large role)[3]. A bequest aspect is also relevant: bequesters value art objects presented as gifts to their children more highly than the corresponding monetary value, because they therewith transfer also part of their own personality.

2. *Corporate collecting*, apparently undertaken in a profit oriented setting, is often in the hands of the firm's leading persons and is purposely managed outside the realm of profit thinking. Especially when firms start to collect art, this activity belongs to the top managers' discretionary room, and is used for consumption purposes. A good example is Hermann Abs, former CEO of the Deutsche Bank. It is also typical that the best-known institutional art investment was undertaken by the British Railway Pension Fund, i.e. an institution not under competitive pressure, which indeed made a lower return than it could have made with financial investments (see also Table 9-1).

3. *Public museums are relevant buyers of art.* The top administrators are subject to many severe constraints; thus they are (with few exceptions) neither able nor willing to sell art objects (see chapter 3), nor to change the specialty of their

---

2   Consider the case of persons owning a painting worth 1 million ECU. Few such owners would be prepared to spend 50,000 ECU per year (assuming that the interest rate is 5 percent per year) or roughly 4,000 ECU per month to have the benefit of looking at the painting hanging in their drawing room.

3   Some of these anomalies, especially the endowment effect, are also relevant for owners of private homes, which constitutes an additional reason why the rates of return on art should be compared to rates of return on houses.

collections, and thus prevent arbitrage. In order to buy a particular, expensive art object they have to lobby with the responsible ministry for funds budgeted for this specific purpose; usually, these funds cannot be used for any other purpose. Moreover, fundraising is easier during upturns in business (when prices tend to be high) and for acquisitions of the "latest hyped contemporaries" (Singer and Lynch 1994, p. 22). As a result, sellers to museums enjoy a systematically higher rate of return. Pommerehne and Feld (1997) carefully identify the various constraints which actors encounter on art auction markets. In particular, they show that the directors of public museums face substantially different conditions than do private museums and collectors. Public museums are prepared to pay higher prices because of the lower opportunity cost once the funds have been granted. With resale data covering the period 1820-1970, the authors are able to show that the owners of paintings sold to public museums earn a premium real rate of return (4.1 percent p.a.) compared to other sales (1.1 percent). A regression analysis keeping other influences constant (in particular business cycle movements) suggests that the difference in the rate of return caused by purchases by (European) public museums and all other buyers amounts to 2.7 percent p.a. This result strongly supports an approach emphasizing institutional differences.

In response to pointing out these anomalies in the art market, it could be argued that for a market to be efficient it suffices to have a limited number of persons buying and selling assets. However, art markets were only partly open in the past. Though the situation improved during the 20th century, arbitrage is still restricted. Short selling is impossible and supply is rather inelastic in the short term, as it takes about 3 to 6 months to market an object (i.e. to have it accepted by the auction house, to make photographs, to print and distribute the catalogues, to publish appropriate advertisements, etc.).

Moreover, asymmetric information is prevalent in many instances. Typically, sellers are better informed about the qualities of their art object (e.g., their provenance) than the buyers. In some cases, however, sellers know little about the art they own, largely because they did not purchase the objects personally in an organized art market; they may have inherited or received them as a gift. It has been claimed (e.g., Coffman 1991) that such sellers systematically undervalue their art, so that a professional buyer may attain very high returns by buying cheaply and selling on an organized market. In the age of well-publicized rocketing prices for art and antiques, the opposite may also be true: owners of art objects of little value expect much too high prices, so that no trade takes place and easy profits are excluded.

There is empirical evidence of striking anomalies in art markets. This, even in the market for prints which, due to multiplicity, is more liquid than that for other art objects (Pesando 1993). In general, however, especially top paintings of top artists are traded on a very thin market. Art speculators may correctly forecast rising demand for top paintings, but it is nearly impossible for them to foresee whether export, and other restrictions arbitrarily imposed by government in response to fickle public pressure, leads to a dramatic fall in price. The dependence of art prices on political and administrative interventions is a factor hindering successful arbitrage.

The incompleteness of art markets – which is partly institutionally induced – makes the study of average returns over, say, the market for paintings as a whole of limited interest. Important are the vast differences in the possibilities of exploiting market imbalances, which lead to some great gains, but also to some great losses. Further progress in the economics of the art market requires a thorough analysis of the actor's behavior, which depends crucially on institutional determinants, such as museum organization or government and public administration intervention.

4.   Art as an Investment or as a Consumption Good

The economic studies of the art market rightly distinguish two different sources of return or utility of holding art objects. The financial return is measured by the change in the monetary value; the psychic return or consumption benefit is indirectly measured by the difference between this financial return on the art object and the returns achievable by alternative investments, in particular in government securities and stocks. This residual approach presumes that the actors behave rationally, that all markets are in equilibrium and that the risk is comparable (i.e., the risk corrected returns in all forms of investment must be equal). It does not allow the testing of any theoretical proposition except one: provided the owners derive at least some consumption benefit, the financial rate of return on art objects should, in equilibrium, be *lower* than that in other markets with similar risk. This is indeed what most studies find (see e.g. Table 9-1). With few exceptions, the financial rates of return calculated are much lower than those for government bonds or stocks, even though the risk in terms of price variations (i.e. neglecting other forms of risk such as destruction) of art objects is larger than for financial investments. The psychic return, i.e. art is also a consumption good, has not been analyzed as such, though this aspect basically distinguishes the art market from pure financial markets. In the following, the determinants affecting the marginal choice between buying and holding art as an investment, or as a consumption good, are studied, taking into account the consequences for financial returns (see also Beltratti and Siniscalco 1991). The analysis also contributes to knowing what type of actors – in the extreme "pure collectors" and "pure speculators" – dominate the art market, and what short-run gains and losses occur due to adjustments during disequilibria.

4.1   Determinants of Investment or Consumption

1. *Change in risk.* "Pure speculators" cet. par. leave the market when unpredictable financial risk (price variations), as well as other risk factors (such as uncertain attribution), increase. "Pure collectors" are, at least in principle, insensitive to these risk factors; they buy and hold an art object because they like it and do not mind if its price variability increases or if its attribution becomes more uncertain. The more pure collectors dominate the market, the lower is the financial return in equilibrium; the major part of the return is made up of psychic benefits.

2. *Change in cost.* An increase in the cost of selling an art object, or a restriction in selling due to government intervention, tends to drive out pure speculators but should not affect pure collectors, because the latter do not intend to sell their holdings (though they sometimes actually do). A rise in the cost of storing and insurance may also systematically shift the balance between types of buyers and sellers, because they are likely to affect each differently.

3. *Unexpected change in taxes.* When transactions in art are taxed more heavily, speculators find it profitable to move to other markets. On the other hand, when the taxes are generally increased, people buying art only for financial reasons are attracted to the art market if it offers better chances of avoiding or cheating on taxes than investments in other assets. The art market is then increasingly dominated by pure speculators, and equilibrium financial net return equals that of any other market. A major consideration for collectors is whether an increase in the value of their holdings is taxed (in most countries, it should be, but taxation is often not carried out), or whether it is taxed only when sold. In the latter case, the market is made even thinner.

4. *Unexpected change in regulations.* Despite WTO liberalizations and large-scale integrations (the European Union), the restrictions on the trade in art are becoming more severe (Pommerehne and Frey 1993). This hampers international trade in art, leads to the establishment of local art markets and tends to favor pure collectors who do not intend to trade.

5. *Change in genres and tastes.* For some genres of paintings, demand follows a systematic time sequence. Portraits are at first of little interest, except for the person depicted and his or her family and company, and are therefore little traded. Provided the painter later turns out to be famous, the genre becomes unimportant and the picture is traded. An example would be portraits by Titian, where it matters little today who is portrayed. Social determinants affect the psychic benefits of owning particular genres of art objects. Today, for instance, religious pictures depicting the crucifixion or the torturing of saints, or which are offensive to other religions, paintings of bloody war scenes or of dead game, or which are for some other reason

"politically incorrect", are out of favor and therefore in lower demand by private collectors. The corresponding market, as far as it exists at all, is dominated by buyers who are little affected by such considerations, in particular by art museums, which can argue that they are only interested in the art historic aspects, or in their traditional area of collection. Thus, pure collectors tend to dominate the market, and in equilibrium psychic benefits are high and financial art market returns low in such paintings. Speculators will only be active in such art markets if they are able to foresee a change in taste – a rather unlikely event.

A related aspect is which kind of art is marketable at all. People interested in art solely as a financial asset shun away from art, which cannot be commercialized. However, there are art forms which only appear to remain outside the market, but which later turn out to be fully commercialized.

A pertinent example is Land Art which was termed to be "impossible" to market, essentially because it was thought to provide a pure public good. Beginning in the mid-sixties, mostly American and British artists started to work in so far "untouched" (at least by art) areas, such as deserts or industrial regions. Examples range from simple walks to gigantic constructions undertaken by bulldozers. The best known, and by now world famous, Land Artist is Javacheff Christo. Originally, the artists involved in Land Art revealed no interest in, and were occasionally hostile to, selling or even marketing their artistic products. More importantly, art experts considered it impossible to merchandise that kind of art. In some cases, the artists willingly destroyed their creations, or just left it up to nature to annihilate them.

Today, the view that Land Art cannot be commercialized looks rather naive. Christo, for example, is well-known for earning good money. Christo ranks ninth among the select groups of one hundred artists prominent in auctions (Frey and Pommerehne 1989a, Table 6.2). It is, indeed, surprising how well artists are able to market a creation which appears to be a public good par excellence. This shows that top artists are not only creative in their art, but also in merchandising it – though many of them would violently oppose this statement. The possibilities of making money involve selling sketches, or photographs, or using the often spectacular happenings going with Land Art to attract attention to directly saleable art. Land Art, and in particular Christo's self-financed wrappings, should perhaps be used by economists as an example of the innovative force of markets, even when the original (artistic) product has the nature of a public good. Ginsburgh and Penders (1997) document how this merchandising of Land Art has taken place. They are able to show that for the period 1972-1991, the annual nominal rates of return on Land Art of 20 percent are similar to those of Conceptual Art (18.9 percent) and Minimal Art (23.8 percent), and even higher than for European Great Masters (15.8 percent). The study thus reveals a really superb capability of marketing what was originally a public good.

4.2   Measuring the Psychic Benefits of Art

In the rate of return studies, the psychic benefits of art have so far been measured by comparing the differences between the financial returns of art investment with the respective returns on financial assets. This residual method is wrought with serious difficulties, for the reasons given above[4]. Three more direct approaches should therefore be considered:

1. *Rental fees for art objects.* The consumer then pays for enjoying art, while he or she is unaffected by changes in art prices. However, a market for renting art objects scarcely exists. This statement is based on our extensive survey of auction houses and major galleries. Of course, commercial art renting exists to a limited extent (examples are given by Stein 1977, p. 1029), but it is not of any great importance compared to say, car or house rentals; moreover, expensive works are explicitly excluded.

---

[4]   Similar conclusions have been drawn in growth theory, where it has turned out to be rather futile to analyze "technical progress" by looking at the difference between the output and input of labor and capital. The same holds for compensating differentials in labor theory.

Where commercial art renting exists, it is often connected with renting other objects, such as furnished houses, or museum rooms for special occasions. But even this is on a small scale only. However, in Europe, most art renting programs are heavily subsidized and concentrate on comparatively inexpensive contemporary art (examples are in the Netherlands and Denmark; for "artotheks" in general, see Dietze 1986). The prices asked have more the nature of a small fee than an (equilibrium) rental price corresponding to the exchange value of the art objects lent out. Some museums also lend out part of the stock not exhibited to private individuals, but only on a very small scale. The rentals charged are, also in this case, far from the market rate.

The question is why such a market, revealing "pure" psychic benefits from art, is absent. The arguments normally offered are not convincing: the risk of lending can be covered by appropriate insurance and by collateral; transaction costs are not higher than in other areas where a rental market exists.

We submit that the reason must be sought in the property rights and in a corresponding *ownership effect.* An art object yields *additional* benefits if it is owned (and not just rented) because the art object's "aura" (see Benjamin 1963) is therewith appropriated. Consequently, neither is a potential hirer willing to pay "market" rents (covering capital cost, insurance, etc.), nor could the present owners be sufficiently compensated by such rents for foregoing the art object when it is rented out. It may be argued that this holds for private collectors, but not for galleries and museums. However, most owners of private galleries are art lovers themselves, and often behave more like private collectors than like purely commercial enterprises. Indeed, many major gallery owners have a sizeable private collection of their own (Beyeler of Basle is a good example). Thus, museums and galleries, with very few exceptions, only *exchange* art objects among themselves, but do not unilaterally rent out (chapter 3 discusses further reasons). Finally, in purely commercial galleries – usually organized in chains – the managers are not subject to the ownership anomaly. We expect and predict that such firms will rent out paintings and other art objects in the future, but that this market will remain unimportant compared to the major galleries where important and expensive art is bought and sold. Thus, the art rental market is not likely to inform us about the *quantitative* aspect of the psychic benefits of art.

2. *Willingness to pay.* A more promising, yet largely untried, approach to measure the size of psychic benefits from art objects is to estimate the marginal willingness to pay for viewing art in museums, for which several approaches may be useful. One is to analyze the determinants of popular referenda on cultural budget expenditures or on buying specific works of art, such as the two Picasso paintings in Basle in 1967 (see chapter 7). A more indirect procedure is to infer the citizens' willingness to pay for museums from median voter models which, however, presuppose stringent conditions on the politico-economic process. For some museums located rather isolated in the countryside, the travel cost method may be appropriate. Hedonic property price and wage equations may be used when the respective markets are known to function well. In any case, such analyses require that unconnected aspects, such as the location and attractiveness of the museum building itself, be carefully separated from the benefits derived from the art objects. Finally, contingent valuation methods based on careful surveys may under some conditions be an appropriate procedure to elicit individuals' willingness to pay for viewing art. Most likely, a skilful combination of the estimates based on a variety of approaches will yield the most satisfactory and robust estimates of the psychic benefits from art.

3. *Prices for copies.* One may derive psychic benefit from consuming art by analyzing the prices paid for (near-perfect) copies of originals, assuming that such prices mainly or exclusively reflect user values (i.e. that such "industrially" manufactured copies are not themselves collectibles). In the case of corporate buyers, it may also be useful to look at the advertising effect to the firms, which can be captured by the cost of reaching the same effect by alternative means of publicity, e.g., newspaper or television advertisements.

5.   Concluding Remarks

The studies on the rate of return on investment in art yields interesting insights. There is now a better knowledge of the aggregate returns of various art objects. Economists can confidently respond to the claims made, and expectation held, in the media and in the public about the financial profitability of the art market.

At the same time, the existence of so many studies devoted to the subject has revealed strong existing limitations. What has become clear is the futility of treating the art market as any other, and to simply use it as another area to which analytical (technical) virtuosity can be applied.

It is crucial to take the intrinsic properties of the art market seriously, and to integrate the institutional and behavioral differences to other markets into the analysis. In particular, attention should be devoted to two aspects:

Firstly, transaction costs in the art market are so much larger than in other investment markets, especially in markets for financial assets. We have also pointed out the crucial importance of taxes for buying and selling decisions with respect to art. The size and nature of transaction costs and taxes depend on the particular institutions existing in a country and period, and may also differ widely between different types of art objects. The existence of these major cost and benefit factors intervening in trade prohibits the same kind of (generalized) efficiency obtained on financial markets from being obtained on most art markets.

Secondly, there are major behavioral differences between the various actors on art markets, which must be taken into account. We have argued that private collectors are more prone to falling prey to behavioral anomalies than speculators and professional dealers. What determines the size and development of the psychic benefits of owning art has received scant attention in the literature so far. Other actors subject to quite different preferences and constraints are the museum people and art dealers. Each of these groups earns quite different types of returns from acting on the art market, of which financial returns is only one, and perhaps not such a terribly important one.

The analyses of the art market so far bear little relationship to political development, which may have a major impact on its character, rate of returns and efficiency. The specter of arts trade restrictions hampering arbitrage looms large. Even the European Union, which otherwise champions free trade, has made no effort to keep the international trade in art open. The "unidroit convention", signed by many countries (but not by all), also serves to restrict the international trade in art by making it more risky.

Chapter 10 -
Evaluating Cultural Property*

1. Economics and Cultural Property

Decisions concerning cultural property are continually being taken by governments and public administrations. Preservation implies maintaining the stock and hindering its dilapidation and deterioration. The upkeep of the stock creates costs, as the resources involved (in the case of historic monuments, especially the sites) could potentially be used for alternative purposes. The costs involved consist of missed opportunities. They are real but not monetary, and they do not show up on any balance sheet. These opportunity costs, as economists call them, are often neglected in political and administrative decisions but should be taken into account in a socially-sound decision. In addition, the preservation of cultural property also requires current funds for repairing and safeguarding the objects. In order to be able to make reasonable decisions, an evaluation of the *value* of the cultural heritage (compared to relevant alternatives) is required.

Economics offers a wide range of approaches and techniques in helping with this decision. The goal is always to assess how much satisfaction *individuals* derive from cultural property. Section 2

---

*   This chapter is based on Bruno S. Frey (1997), "Evaluating Cultural Property", previously published in the *International Journal of Cultural Property*, pp. 231-246, used by permission of Oxford University Press.

critically analyses various procedures used in economics for evaluating cultural property. The following section 3 focuses on the specific problems when these procedures are applied to cultural issues. Section 4 presents a policy approach based on constitutional choice. It proposes an *integration of evaluation and decision* by using direct democratic institutions, i.e. popular initiatives and referenda. Section 5 offers conclusions.

2.   Evaluation Procedures

2.1   Impact Studies

The most popular way to measure the "value" of a piece of cultural property is to look at the *monetary revenue* created. Thus, for example, one looks at the expenditures incurred by the visitors to a theatre or opera house (entrance fee, meals in restaurants, transport, hairdresser's, formal dress etc.) and calculates the multiplier effect induced by these expenditures. A restaurant frequented by cultural visitors, for example, has to buy in such things as food and electricity, and has to pay various people, in particular the cook and kitchen staff, in order to be able to offer the meal. The recipients of these revenues in turn spend it on other goods and services, etc. Impact studies thus measure the monetary income which can be attributed to a particular cultural object.

Though such studies are largely in demand by the suppliers of cultural services (see e.g. Vaughan 1980 for the Edinburgh Festival or O'Hagan 1992 for the Wexford Opera Festival), they do not adequately capture the social value of a cultural object. It completely disregards those values *not reflected on the market*. As we have seen in chapter 6, they consist of option, existence, bequest, prestige and educational values, which are not revealed as market demands but are rather non-user values.

Empirical research has shown that, depending on the cultural sector considered, these non-market values are often of significant size. They need to be taken into account when undertaking the benefit-cost calculation of whether a cultural activity, or the price of cultural property, should be supported by the public. To use impact studies which disregard these values is very risky. It may well turn out that a non-artistic activity or object generates even higher revenues. If one relies on the logic of impact studies, one should then undertake these non-artistic activities, e.g. demolishing a historic building and substituting it with, say, a sports stadium or a shopping center. (Good) economists take great pains not to fall into this trap. But they are often offered substantial money to perform such studies because they may be in the interest of the institutions offering such activities.

2.2   Willingness-to-Pay

There is a well-established way to evaluate non-marketed goods: willingness-to-pay values measure the maximum price which would be paid by a person for the object or project in question. Several methods are available and have been empirically employed (Cropper and Oates 1992, see also Pommerehne 1987, Mitchell and Carson 1989). The two most widely used procedures are:

1. *The hedonic market approach.* The values attributed to a cultural object are measured by looking at private markets which indirectly reflect the utility persons enjoy. Consider a historic palace situated in a beautiful park located in the city center. All other things being equal, an individual attributing a value to the palace and park would be prepared to accept an equivalent job in such a palace at a *lower* wage than elsewhere. The difference between this lower wage and the wage elsewhere constitutes an indirect monetary measure of that particular individual's evaluation of the palace and park. The value attributed can also be derived from the *higher* rents, house and land prices which people are prepared to pay because they enjoy the palace and the park. Again, the price difference compared to an equivalent apartment, house or piece of land elsewhere constitutes a monetary evaluation of the palace and park.

   While such an indirect measure of the value of culture is intriguing, it is able to capture only part of the non-market values mentioned above. The option, existence, and prestige values tend to be integrated (and at least part of the bequest value in the case of house and land prices), but not the educational value.

The hedonic market procedure is quite intricate. Its reliability depends on two major conditions: the private markets for labor and housing or land must be in perfect equilibrium, and the "ceteris paribus" (all else being equal) assumption needed for the comparison must be fulfilled. These conditions are rarely completely met so that the corresponding monetary evaluation of the cultural object is biased, often to an unknown extent.

2. *Travel cost approach.* This method lends itself in particular to measuring the value of an object of the historic heritage, say a castle situated in the countryside. People spend money on the trip leading to the castle, as well as for the entrance ticket. This constitutes a lower bound for the utility they expect to derive from the visit.

The travel cost method relies on two major assumptions:

(a) The object in question must be the only purpose of the trip, and the trip itself does not yield any pleasure. In many cases, these assumptions do not hold true because people tend to combine various goals when making a trip. Moreover, the castle (in our example) may be located in an attractive landscape, or the trip is pleasurable because of one's company, so that the cost expended no longer reflects the utility attributed to the castle.

(b) Few of the non-market values listed above are taken into account; the method captures at best part of the prestige and educational value. Even under ideal conditions, the cost expended does not reveal the full value attributed to the cultural object, because it may well be that the people would have been willing to travel longer distances, and to pay a higher entrance price in order to enjoy the object.

As the essential assumptions required by the two approaches just discussed are in many cases not sufficiently met in practice to make the respective methods seriously applicable, most economists have turned to "Contingent Valuation" (CV). This uses *sample surveys* to elicit the willingness-to-pay for cultural objects. The questionnaire involves a hypothetical situation, the term "contingent" refers to the constructed or simulated market presented in the survey.

2.3   Contingent Valuation Surveys

Surveys have been widely used by economists to estimate people's willingness-to-pay. Over the years considerable experience has been gained. In their bibliography, Carson et al. (1994) list almost 1700 studies in over 40 countries. Early examples include evaluations of a reduction in household soiling and cleaning (Ridker 1967), the right to hunt waterfowl (Hammack and Brown 1974), reduced congestion in wilderness areas (Cicchetti and Smith 1973), improved air visibility (Randall, Ives and Eastman 1974), and the value of duck hunting permits (Bishop and Heberlein 1979). Most survey studies evaluate objects in their natural environment, but there are also other applications such as e.g. the reduced risk of dying from heart attack (Acton 1973), reduced risk of respiratory disease (Krupnick and Cropper 1992) and even improved information about grocery store prices (Devine and Marion 1979).

A politically important recent Contingent Valuation study (Carson et al. 1992) has been used to measure the environmental damage caused by the supertanker Exxon Valdez, which ran aground in March 1989 in Prince William Sund, Alaska, spilling 11 million gallons of crude oil into the sea. The enormous sums of money involved in the litigation connected with the Alaska oil spill has further drawn the attention of the economics community to this particular survey method. As a consequence, the Contingent Valuation method has come under careful scrutiny in the profession. The United States National Oceanic and Atmospheric Administration (NOAA) hired two Nobel prize winners (Kenneth Arrow and Robert Solow) to co-chair a panel with the task of assessing the Contingent Valuation method. The bottom line of the panel report (Arrow et al. 1993) concludes " . . . that CV studies can produce estimates reliable enough to be the starting point of a judicial process of damage assessment, including lost passive-use values". The term "passive-use values" refers to the non-use values of the environment composed of existence, option and bequest benefits. However, the report stated a large number of stringent requirements for that conclusion to hold. The most important are:

- personal interviews rather than telephone surveys, which in turn are preferable to mail surveys;

- the environment in which the object to be evaluated is situated must be described accurately and understandably;

- it must be made clear for what other purposes the money can be spent if the project or policy is not undertaken, i.e. the budget constraint must be well specified;

- the respondents must be reminded of the substitutes for the commodity in question. Thus, for example, it must be stated what other castles or palaces can be visited if the one in question were demolished;

- it must be ascertained that the respondents understand the question and the underlying choice.

These rather stringent conditions are rarely fully met in practice. It is therefore always necessary to evaluate whether the violations are so grave as to make the Contingent Valuation approach of little use.

3.   Applications of Contingent Valuation Surveys to the Arts

3.1   Existing Studies

So far, only a few studies use the Contingent Valuation procedure on cultural issues. There have been attempts to measure the broad support for the arts in terms of the desired government expenditures (e.g. Throsby and Withers 1983, Morrison and West 1986). Up till now, there seem to be only two serious studies where the procedure has been applied to measure the willingness-to-pay for specific cultural objects: Bille Hansen (1997) uses it for the Royal Danish Opera in Copenhagen, and Martin (1994) for the Musée de la civilisation in Quebec.

Yet, in cultural policy, decisions are continually taken whether to preserve an object of cultural heritage, to demolish it, or at least to let it deteriorate beyond repair. Relevant examples are the castles or palaces mentioned above. Others are villas in the "fin-de-siècle" style or "Jugendstil", which on the one hand are worth preserving and which, on the other hand, are situated in locations which can be most profitably used for other purposes (and which are often very expensive to repair and put to good use). Another example are the "galleries" (shopping malls of the late 19th and early 20th century) in Paris (and elsewhere) which are dilapidated, but which could still be restored.

In contrast, it makes little sense to evaluate the benefits and costs of preserving, say, the Colosseum or the Eiffel Tower, because it is beyond one's imagination that they will be torn down – if, for some reason, a demolition were planned, a Contingent Valuation survey would not change anything.

3.2   Problems of Survey Studies in the Arts

Where are the specific problems which arise when Contingent Valuation is applied to cultural heritage?

Four issues will be discussed.

1. *Marginal versus total.* Survey studies typically confront the respondents with an "all or nothing" choice, or with an indivisible good. Either the villa or the gallery is to be totally preserved, or not at all. Bille Hansen (1997) explicitly states, for example, that the Royal Danish Theatre is to be run at the *present* activity level. Clearly, it is always possible to vary the level – though that option is routinely and fervently rejected by the suppliers[1]. One possibility would be to give up the ballet section, or the opera

---

[1]   Such pronouncements are a reasonable strategy for the suppliers. They therefore induce the demanders to choose between having the cultural object and not having it at all. Provided the demanders choose the first option (which is very likely to be the case), suppliers can reap a rent. Such strategic action has been analyzed in the case of public bureaucracies' behavior vis-à-vis the parliament (see Niskanen 1971).

section, and the respondents could then be asked about their willingness-to-pay for these different activity levels. Even a villa or a gallery could be only partly preserved, without completely destroying the respective historical value. Constructing such a demand curve for various "sizes" or "qualities" of the cultural good is, in principle, possible but would involve much additional work because the survey must exactly specify the various levels, and do it in a way understandable to the persons asked.

2. *Non-optimizing.* This second issue is closely connected to the first, but is not identical. The survey approach does not include an optimizing algorithm, i.e. the historic object is presented to the respondents as it is. It is (implicitly) assumed that supply is already efficient in two respects:

   (a) The object's activities are so perfectly run that no improvement is possible without having to give up some other goal. This assumption is, to say the least, heroic; it is known from much research in the economics of art that large opportunities for improvements in technical efficiency exist.

   (b) Contingent Valuation studies also assume efficiency, in the sense that the consumers' preferences are met. Again, art economists provide strong evidence to the contrary. In particular, the directors of theatres, museums and also historic sites tend to follow their own preferences, which may systematically and significantly deviate from what the average citizens – who are relevant in willingness-to-pay studies – desire.

Survey studies thus do not take into account much of the insights and knowledge which have been accumulated in cultural economics. Excellent opportunities for improvements in the presentation and preservation of art are therefore overlooked. A most useful contribution by an economist to safeguard our cultural heritage is to suggest already known or innovative ways to put it to good use. Thus, for example, a Roman arena can be employed for all kinds of artistic, popular and sports performances and festivities, so that the respondents are likely to have a much greater willingness-to-pay because the arena has been put to good use and has been filled with life.

3. *What values?* It is not obvious what preferences should enter Contingent Valuation studies in the arts (and elsewhere). Two aspects are of particular importance:

(a) Psychological anomalies[2] play a major role. Most importantly, the disparity between gains and losses matters. This endowment effect leads to a major difference between willingness-to-pay and willingness-to-accept which, according to standard economic theory, should be equal. In a study of the valuation of the environment by duck hunters, for example, the willingness-to-pay to save a marsh area used by ducks was on average $ 47 per hunter, but they would on average demand $ 1044 – or 22 times as much – to accept the identical loss (Hammack and Brown 1974).

The endowment effect helps to explain the idea behind the "patrimoine nationale" of art. A loss is highly valued – imagine France losing the Mona Lisa, Rome the Colosseum, or the Uffici being destroyed. But imagine that none of these historic treasures was ever in the particular place it is now located: does the Louvre really need the Mona Lisa (it has hundreds of other masterpieces); does Rome really need the Colosseum (it has nearby the whole Roman Forum with the spectacular triumphal arches); and does Florence really need the Uffizi (it has other important museums as well as the Dome)? If this were true, the citizens would express a low willingness-to-pay to newly acquire these objects of culture. The question is what evaluation counts or, equivalently, what initial state is envisaged. Taking the status quo and inquiring how a loss would be evaluated leads to very high sums of money. But seen in the long run, the issue looks different. Once it is hypothesized that an art object never existed, or has been lost for a long time, the endowment effect vanishes and the evaluation of the respective art object is dramatically lower.

---

[2]   See e.g. Kahneman, Slovic and Tversky 1982, Arkes and Hammond 1986, Bell, Raiffa and Tversky 1988, Dawes 1988, Frey and Eichenberger 1989a,b, Thaler 1992.

(b) Art is international, and it isn't unusual for a country's culture to be more highly valued by foreigners than by the inhabitants of the country itself. Yet, Contingent Valuation studies normally only survey the inhabitants. Thus, Bille Hansen (1997) only surveyed residents of Denmark for her study of the Royal Theatre. While this may be admissible in this particular case, in other cases it would be seriously misleading. The Maya ruins in the jungles of Middle America, for example, are probably valued little by their inhabitants, but the North Americans and Europeans would certainly express considerable willingness-to-pay for their existence and preservation.

It might be argued that at least part of that willingness-to pay would be expressed by local respondents who include the prospects of attracting tourists in their evaluation. But option values are not taken into account, as they do not lead to actual visits. Under ideal conditions, only a minor part of the option value can be appropriated by the local residents in the form of royalties for the pictures taken and films made.

A similar problem arises with future generations who cannot be surveyed at all. Part of the value is taken into account by the bequest motive of the respondents, but again the questionnaire has to be very carefully designed. For objects belonging to the cultural heritage, the problem of capturing the willingness-to-pay of future generations is particularly intense because the issues involved are often extremely long term, and it is known that future preferences with respect to art systematically deviate from the values of the present generation. Older people tend to attach much less value to contemporary art than is attributed by the subsequent generations – at least from the vantage point of the latter[3].

4. *Specific versus statistical values.* Individuals evaluate specific objects – such as particular cultural monuments – quite

---

[3]   Today's younger generation values Jugendstil-monuments more highly than the past generation who produced it. But not all of what was called "art" in the past is considered such today.

differently from a non-specified, or statistical, object. This disparity was first found in the case of human lives (Schelling 1984). People are prepared to spend enormous sums of money on saving the life of an identified person, such as a child who has fallen into a well. They are prepared to spend much less on efforts to save yet unidentified lives, such as spending resources to reduce the number of fatal accidents on the road. This mirrors the two kinds of Contingent Valuation studies in art mentioned at the beginning. It follows that respondents would indicate a much higher willingness-to-pay for the Royal Danish Theatre and the Musée de la civilisation in Quebec than for public art expenditures in general.

3.3   Beneficial Aspects

As with any other evaluation method, Contingent Valuation surveys are confronted with problems and difficulties. Yet it is important to see that they also provide major insights.

1. *Serious research effort.* Contingent Valuation studies promise to yield worthwhile results because they force the researchers to undertake a determined, and extensive, analysis of the art object in question. The questionnaire has to meet stringent requirements to be usable at all. Even more importantly, the representative survey approach needs to address both visitors and non-visitors. The usefulness of a CV-study is further increased if the assumptions made in the course of the analysis are discussed and systematically varied so that the robustness of the results can be evaluated.

2. *Indirect benefits.* Contingent Valuation studies have the major advantage of being able to capture existence, option and bequest values: " . . . the contingent valuation method would appear to be the only method capable of shedding light on [such] potentially important values" (Portney 1994, p. 14). This is a decisive advantage over all those approaches – in particular the popular impact studies – which disregard non-user values. That such non-use values are of particularly great importance in the arts has already been pointed out.

3. *Quality, not just quantity.* A frequent accusation by "arts people" is that economic approaches can only measure the quantity of art but not the quality. Contingent Valuation proves such accusations to be wrong. The number of visits to a theatre, a museum or monument is only one part; it has to be weighted by how highly a visit is valued by the individuals concerned. Moreover, non-use values are also integrated. The respective evaluations are compared to alternatives, in particular to other uses of tax funds or to lower taxes and higher private consumption.

4. Combining Evaluation and Decision by Referenda

Public decisions on culture are taken in the politico-economic process in which politicians, public officials, interest groups and citizens/taxpayers interact within a given constitutional framework. Thus, some cultural decisions are to be taken at local, others at regional (cantonal, provincial) and still others at national level. These decisions are normally highly complex due to the many interactions. But the budgetary situation and the administrative constraints are always highly important and they determine to a large extent how much money is spent in various ways for the arts. In contrast, willingness-to-pay studies, which relate to social welfare and not to political exigencies, are of little importance. *Some* actors may under *some* circumstances use the result of such studies to bolster their arguments provided they suit their interests.

The major problem with the willingness-to-pay studies based on social welfare is that they are *divorced from political decisions*. It is therefore proposed here that the willingness-to-pay is revealed, and at the same time the decision made, by *popular referenda*. This proposal is theoretically cogent. Indeed, the panel mentioned above, headed by Arrow and Solow (Arrow et al. 1993), demand that "contingent valuation should use referendum format" (Portney 1994, p. 9). A well-designed Contingent Valuation study thus imitates a popular referendum – why then should it not be employed? As a decision mechanism, referenda have many advantages over democratic decisions via representation. In particular, it evades the principal-agent problem and constitutes an effective barrier against the "classe politique" (see e.g. Bohnet and Frey 1994). Both aspects are of particular importance with respect to cultural decisions, because the politicians and bureaucrats tend to have a larger discretionary room in this area than elsewhere. As has been empirically shown in chapter 7, individual citizens do not only evaluate the user-values but also existence, option and bequest values in their vote.

Five arguments are often raised against the use of popular referenda in cultural policy:

1. *Incapable citizens.* Voters are often claimed to be both uninformed and unintelligent with respect to cultural affairs. They therefore cannot be trusted to make "good" decisions. The criticism concerning the lack of information is doubtful because when citizens are given the power to decide, they will inform themselves. In contrast, as they cannot decide anything today, they do not acquire much information. The state of information is thus not given but determined by the participation possibilities. The discussion process *induced* by the referendum produces the necessary information to decide, a service which the researcher has to artificially perform when undertaking a survey. Concerning the claimed lack of intelligence with respect to art, referenda are, of course, in exactly the same position as the willingness-to-pay methods: in all cases individual preferences – and not the (supposedly) superior insights of a cultural or political elite – are important.

2. *Superficial citizens.* Voters are also claimed not to take referendum decisions seriously. Such decisions are indeed "low cost" (see Kliemt 1986, Kirchgässner and Pommerehne 1993), but this equally well applies to Contingent Valuation procedures (but not to the travel cost method which looks at revealed behavior). One may even argue that individuals take their response to a survey more lightly because the situation is purely hypothetical. Referendum voting is, moreover, connected with significant personal cost when the pre-referendum discussion is intensive. In that case, not having and not being able to defend a particular position (and voting decision) is negatively sanctioned by the citizen's social environment (for this argument, see Frey

1994). Intensive discussions are quite typical for referenda on culture because the citizens are often strongly involved emotionally. This was, for example, the case in the vote on the purchase of two Picasso paintings in the city of Basle discussed in chapter 7.

3. *Propaganda influence.* In referenda, interest groups and parties seek to affect the vote by newspaper, radio and television campaigns. But such efforts to influence the outcome are not in themselves bad, not least because they provide information and classify standpoints. What is essential is that an open society admits propaganda from *all* sides. Consequently, the outcome of propaganda is most uncertain. It should also be taken into account that propaganda from one side induces propaganda from the opposing side. Normally, the cultural interests are well organized and motivated. They emanate from the persons active in highly subsidized cultural institutions, such as museums, theatres, orchestras and other arts organizations, as well as from art lovers. Individuals uninterested or opposed to art are generally less educated and have low income and low political participation. They are rarely organized, so their propaganda influence is weak. Art lovers should therefore not be too concerned about the propaganda activity accompanying referenda.

4. *Restricted participation.* Referendum participation is constrained in two ways:

   (a) Some citizens decide not to vote. This is parallel to those individuals who refuse to answer the survey questions in a Contingent Valuation study. The motivation is not the same, but is likely to be similar. The major reason for non-participation is the lack of interest in cultural issues. It may well be argued that it is reasonable if such people do not vote or respond.

   (b) Some people, especially foreigners and future generations, are formally excluded from voting. As we have seen, this also applies to most surveys. Part of these interests are however taken into account by the voters themselves. As far as these interests are connected with business (tourism), propaganda is used to motivate voters to decide in their favor.

5. *Amount of knowledge gained.* In a popular referendum, voters may only decide between a "yes" and a "no" answer, while more information can be collected in surveys. This is a clear advantage of such studies. However, referenda outcomes can be analyzed by cross section (and sometimes time-series) methods which yield additional information. This has, for instance, allowed researchers to isolate various non-user benefits. Moreover, while the referendum decision itself is restricted to a simple yes or no, preference intensity is partly reflected in the decision to participate or not, and the fact that one's revelation of preference is connected with a binding democratic decision tends to raise the seriousness with which the decision is made.

The five arguments just discussed and often raised against the use of referenda in the arts are thus not compelling. Either they are unfounded as such – e.g. that citizens are incapable – or the shortcomings are shared by other methods of evaluating cultural property. No approach is ideal, but we should use those methods which best serve the purpose on hand. Popular referenda are certainly a good procedure in many cases, especially as they combine evaluation and decision. Once the voters have decided in a referendum, the constitution forces the government and its bureaucracy to undertake the corresponding measures. In contrast to all other approaches, evaluation and decision are integrated. This is the crucial advantage over all other methods, including Contingent Valuation surveys. These approaches only lay the ground for decisions. As is well known from everyday experience, as well as from Public Choice research (e. g. Mueller 1989, 1997), the political decision-makers in the public bureaucracy, government or parliament tend to disregard such "objective" information as the result of a Contingent Valuation survey. Rather, they decide on the basis of their (often short-term) interests. In that process, vested interests and interest groups play a large role – and not always to the benefit of the arts. For instance, the interests of the persons presently employed in the arts tend to have a determining weight. New projects and ideas in contrast are at a disadvantage.

5.   Conclusions

Willingness-to-pay procedures, and in particular Contingent Valuation, are useful but have a decisive disadvantage: they are not directly related to political decisions. Popular referenda combine the evaluation of competing alternatives with democratic decisions. This combination is particularly relevant and beneficial for cultural decisions. Academics who want to contribute to preserving the cultural heritage should not restrict themselves to undertaking willingness-to-pay studies, but should suggest constitutional changes, allowing and prescribing the use of popular referenda for cultural decisions.

Referenda on issues of culture, and cultural heritage in particular, are feasible. As was shown in chapter 7, in Switzerland such referenda are routinely undertaken at all governmental levels. At the national level, the propositions relate to general laws and constitutional provisions on the support of art. At the cantonal and, even more so, at the communal level, citizens decide directly on the amount of subsidies and other types of cultural support. Voters are prepared to support a substantial share of such cultural outlays. Indeed, they tend to be more favorably inclined to support culture than other types of expenditures. It can, of course, be argued that Switzerland is different from other countries. This is certainly true, but what the Swiss example does show is that referenda on issues of cultural heritage *can* be undertaken, and that one *can* put trust in the voters' judgement.

Chapter 11 -
Art Fakes – What Fakes?

1. A Widespread Activity

The discussion of art fakes is dominated by the legal and by the art historic points of view. Lawyers tend to look at fakes in terms of forgery and counterfeiting. Fraud should therefore be prohibited. Art historians emphasize the uniqueness or "aura" of the original work. Consequently, it has to be specially protected against imitation.

This chapter employs the economic point of view to consider fakes. Its analysis and conclusions differ substantially from the legal and art historic approaches, which both tend to have a negative attitude towards imitations, and often suggest a repressive policy. On purpose, no distinction is drawn between the various terms normally used in this context, such as copies, forgeries, fakes, imitations or counterfeits. They are often *not* relevant from the economic point of view. It is, however, not disputed that there are sometimes cases in which it makes economic sense to differentiate between e.g. legal and illegal copying[1].

A major conclusion drawn from the present analysis is that copies are not necessarily bad, but rather good: the fact that they are

---

[1] Useful classifications are provided, e.g. in Lazzaro, Moureau and Sagot-Duvauroux (1998), Benhamou and Ginsburgh (1998) or Benghozi and Santagata (1998).

undertaken on a grand scale indicates that such multiplication of the original creates utility for the persons demanding, and paying, for them.

Faking activities have always been widespread[2]. They range from the reproduction of art objects to written texts (such as the *Protocols of the Elders of Zion*), historical relics (such as most chastity belts or "Spanish Inquisition" torture chairs), musical works, forgeries undertaken for political purposes (such as the *Donation of Constantine*, which sought to establish the medieval Papacy's claim to temporal power), or for war propaganda or espionage, the counterfeiting of banknotes, and – very importantly – commercial copies of branded goods (such as perfumes by Chanel or Dior, watches by Rolex, Bulgari or Cartier, shirts by Versace, Lacoste or Giorgio Armani, or luggage by Gucci, Prada or Louis Vuitton[3]). This chapter focuses on fakes in the fine arts, especially in paintings (for an early bibliography of the extensive literature, see Reisner 1950).

As will be argued below, the economic view takes a rather positive attitude towards fakes (at least compared to the prevailing negative evaluation by law and art history), but this does not mean that forgeries do not create any problems. There are indeed significant costs created on both the demand and supply sides of the market. But many such problems can be mitigated or even overcome by appropriate legal constructs and institutional arrangements.

Section 2 of this chapter briefly discusses the dominant views held in law and in art history. The beneficial, and harmful, effects of fakes from an economic point of view are considered in sections 3 and 4, respectively[4]. The final section 5 discusses what possible

---

2   See the very useful book edited by Jones (1990), made for an exhibition on *Fake? "The Art of Deception"* in the British Museum. Other relevant works are e.g. Neuburger (1924), Kurz (1948), Isnard (1960), Savage (1963), Hamilton (1980), Waldron (1983) or Dutton (1983).

3   Estimates of the quantitative importance of commercial counterfeiting are given in Benghozi and Santagata (1998).

4   Most economic analyses have addressed the issue from a narrow property rights perspective, see e.g. Takeyama (1994), Deardorff (1995), Koboldt

consequences can be drawn. It rejects a repressive policy on copying and proposes a possible solution, namely, a general rule for "quotations in art".

2.   Dominant Views on Fakes

2.1   The Legal Position

Lawyers are concerned with fraud linked with copying activities, i.e. the production, sale, and purchase of reproductions. Two situations are prominent.

Firstly, a person *buys* a fake assuming it to be an original. He or she has acquired an art object and can have reasonable expectations that it meets the conditions under which it has been sold. Thus, a particular painting bought from a well-established art dealer, or at a serious auction, should indeed be an original. Most auction houses guarantee that if the painting does not turn out to be an original, as specified, it can be returned. However, in other cases where the seller deliberately cheats the buyer, the transaction constitutes an illegal act.

Secondly, an artist creates a tangible (a painting or sculpture) or intangible (a novel, play or piece of music) object, but steals the idea from another artist without the latter's consent, and without compensating him or her.

The two cases just discussed have been constructed to constitute a fraud, but a small variation makes it a legal transaction. If a buyer has unreasonable expectations (e.g. if he pays a low price for a "Rembrandt" at a country fair), the seller is not responsible because of the principle of "caveat emptor". In the second case, an artist may reproduce the style, or work closely within a movement (e.g. within Impressionism) without violating any rights, i.e. there are artistic ideas which cannot, and should not, be protected.

(1995), Hansman and Santilli (1997), and Burke (1998). Partial exceptions are Grossman and Shapiro (1988, 1989), and Mossetto (1993).

The legal norms in a particular country, and at a particular point in time, are not necessarily consonant with the *moral* views on faking generally held by art experts and artists. But the moral evaluation is, nevertheless, important because it affects behavior, at least to some extent. The sense of wrongdoing when copying art works has changed enormously over time. In former centuries in the West (and even more elsewhere), replicating the work of other artists was a perfectly acceptable activity. Michelangelo forged a work by his master Domenico Ghirlandaio in order to demonstrate his ability as an artist. (The forgery of *Cupid Asleep*, which was sold in 1496 as a classical sculpture, may not have been so innocent; see Wilson 1990.) There are even accounts of purchasers who welcomed a reproduction, even though they had bought it as an original. Thus, the buyers of the claimed Renaissance bust of Lucrezia Donati were pleased to discover that it was a fake; that an artist of such talent was still alive (Jones 1990, p. 15). As for religious relics, authenticity was not relevant, but their value depended on their ability to beget miracles. Sacred relics multiply without losing their value. Thus, five churches could lay claim to the original head of John the Baptist (Loewenthal 1990, p. 18).

In modern times, some artists, such as Salvador Dalí or Magritte, intentionally erased the difference between original and fake in order to revolt against the burden of the dead past. Obviously, if these artists and movements, such as performance art, auto-destructive art or earth art, refuse to make the distinction, there is neither a moral nor legal case against "fakes" – the term loses its meaning.

2.2   The Art Historic Position

The dominant position in art history is that the original has a special and unique quality which fakes lack. The original art work has an "aura" which, though invisible, is nevertheless real (Benjamin 1963). In many cases, it is no longer possible for a viewer to distinguish the original from a reproduction; not even sophisticated technical means are always able to differentiate them. It is therefore not the physical nor aesthetic aspect of the work of art, but rather the context and history of its creation, which marks the original.

This is somewhat difficult to follow for an economist, but even well-established art experts are at a loss to explain why a (perfect) copy is considered so much less valuable than the original. Thus the (former) director of the British Museum, Sir David Wilson, wonders: " . . . the final question is the one that appears unanswerable, although psychologists have tried to explain it: why does an object which is declared a fake lose virtue immediately?" (Wilson 1990, p. 9).

Yet the difference *is* real in the sense that most owners of art works are terribly disappointed when they detect that a presumably original piece is a copy – and that sentiment also applies to economists and other "rationalists". But it should nevertheless be noted that this "cult of the original" is not hard-wired for human beings but is historically dependent. As has already been pointed out, Michelangelo's copy of a statue by Ghirlandaio was neither a fraud nor of lower quality. Vasari actually considered it a triumph, establishing the young Michelangelo among the great sculptors of his time, and beyond.

In contrast, Van Meegeren's copies of Vermeer were considered much inferior once they were detected. David Wilson (1990, p. 9) calls them "ghastly" and Jones (1990, p. 15) speaks of "grotesquely ugly and unpleasant paintings, altogether dissimilar to Vermeer's". But, before the exposure, the great art historian Abraham Bredius wrote of Van Meegeren's "Vermeer" forgery *Christ at Emmaus*: "It is a wonderful moment in the life of a lover of art when he finds himself suddenly confronted with a hitherto unknown painting by a great master, untouched, on the original canvas, and without any restoration, just as it left the painter's studio! And what a picture! Neither the beautiful signature . . . nor the pointillé on the bread which Christ is blessing, is necessary to convince us that what we have here is – I am inclined to say – *the* masterpiece of Johannes Vermeer of Delft . . . " (*Burlington Magazine*, November 1937)[5].

---

[5]   An account of Van Meegeren's activities is given in Jones (1990, pp. 237-240).

More recently, some forgers such as Tom Keating (see Jones 1990, pp. 240-242) have become TV celebrities, i.e. their work is considered to be essentially worthless by art lovers, but they enjoy a certain measure of attention because they have been able to fool art experts. Partly as a result of these developments, many art historians now take a less sanguine view towards reproductions and fakes (Jones 1990), and no longer consider the "aura" to only be attached to the original. Rather, art works are taken to be part of history, which includes their modifications, renovations and copying. Indeed, in many cases, the distinctions are so blurred that they become meaningless. Leonardo da Vinci's often renovated and partly repainted *Last Supper* in Milan is a pertinent example.

But after all is said and done, the puzzle still is far from being solved: why are most owners totally disappointed when they detect that they have a copy instead of the original – even if these are virtually identical, and even if the resale value is of no importance, because one would never wish to sell it?

3.   Beneficial Aspects of Imitations

Three major benefits from copying can be identified from an economic point of view.

3.1   Revealed Demand

The fact that an original is imitated and reproduced indicates that the respective art work is in demand. This in turn shows that consumers experience a utility gain from viewing, reading or hearing the art object, which is reflected in a willingness-to-pay. Imitations serve to propagate the original to a wider audience, and therewith raise the total utility for prospective consumers. This "propagation effect" is produced irrespective of whether the copies are made legally or illegally. Recently, the owners of the original art work, among them most leading art museums, have been selling exact replicas of selected pieces of their collection in their museum shops. The propagation effect is also obtained when the copies are made illegally, such as the counterfeit of furniture, musical pieces, or art objects. Some museums even consciously mix copies with originals (Pommerehne and Granica 1995, p. 247). The former idea of museums composed solely of copies has recently been peddled again by Banfield (1984). It has been realized in many "museums" located in shopping malls and similar venues (Benhamou and Ginsburgh 1998).

The creator of the original work of art may benefit in two ways from such imitations:

1. He or she may receive royalties from legal copying. In the case of music, this is usually the artist's major source of income. It is of lesser importance for paintings, though in some cases the income therewith gained is substantial.

2. Even if copying is done without the consent of the creator of the original (i.e. illegally), he or she may nevertheless benefit *indirectly* from it. The creator's name is propagated, thus allowing him or her to sell future (original) works at higher prices. Interestingly enough, the more closely the work is imitated, the greater the beneficial effect for the creator. In particular, he or she reaps the highest benefits if the copy is formally attributed to his or her name. In contrast, if the original is modified without any attribution in order to escape royalty payments, the creator benefits the least.

The exact extent to which the "propagation effect" benefits the creator of the original depends on the specific conditions of the respective art market, as well as the extent to which the existence of copies provide an effective signal pointing to the original and its creator.

3.2   Raise in Artistic Capital

To produce faithful copies of great works has always been one of the major ways in which artists train themselves[6]. This applies not only

---

6   Two related functions of copying for education and preservation are no longer relevant today: transport costs have fallen so much that most artists and consumers may see the originals. Neither is it necessary to have painted

to lesser known artists, but also to painters who became great masters later in their lives. In addition, the existence of fakes presents a continuous challenge for art experts. It not only shows their fallibility (remember the evaluation of Van Meegeren's "Vermeers"), but also represents an important teaching device, which helps art experts to overcome their "tunnel vision" (for many examples, see Jones 1990).

3.3   Supporting Creativity

"Each society, each generation, fakes the thing it covets most" (Jones 1990, p. 13). The smaller the barriers against imitating, the greater is the scope for future artists to experiment. If the creator of the original can easily interfere by legal injunction, artistic creativity is hampered. There are few great artists who have not borrowed from earlier masters, and some of them have done so extensively (e.g. van Gogh or Dalí) – for the benefit of the arts.

Closely related is a view of the arts which welcomes blurring the distinction between originals and copies. Not only is the term "original" often poorly defined[7], but there is also a continuity of history in which copies, all sorts of reproductions and renovations also play a role; art does not end with the creation of the "original". A case in point may be Michelangelo's paintings in the Capella Sistina, where it is open to serious discussion what the original is, and where, in any case, the fundamental cleaning revealed a "new" art work to contemporary art lovers and art experts alike. The distinction between the original and copy has been further blurred in the digital age (Greffe 1998), which has made it possible to produce "identical" pieces of art at low cost.

---

copies to "secure" the original in case of loss or destruction, because this can be achieved by purely technical (photographic) means.

[7]   In some art forms such as music and prints (see Pesando 1993) the distinction is difficult to draw or is irrelevant.

4.   Harmful Aspects of Imitations

It is useful to distinguish between the demand and the supply side.

4.1   Demand

In the presence of fakes, buyers face a larger uncertainty about the art objects they intend to purchase. Hutter (1998b) even refers to it as "information destruction effect". There is a constant race between the forgers and the investigators, who both use increasingly sophisticated technical means. There are periods in which one side seems to prevail, but the incentives to forge originals, and to detect fakes, is so strong that it can safely be predicted that neither side will carry a final victory.

Such uncertainty induced by the existence of fakes, imposes costs on financial investors looking for a high monetary return from buying art. Provided that the indirect effect of propagation is small, they would suffer a loss from the manufacture of copies and, of course, from buying a piece of work, which is presumed to be original. However, such loss is smaller than it at first seems. Rational buyers are well aware of both problems, and are therefore prepared to pay a correspondingly lower price for the art work. In contrast, if the propagation effect is positive, they are even prepared to pay a higher price.

As has been discussed at the beginning of this chapter, it is a riddle why art lovers (without financial interests) should suffer a loss if they find out that what they presumed to be an original is indeed a copy. All the visible attributes are unchanged and should therefore not affect the aesthetic judgement. Nonetheless, it has been empirically shown (Pommerehne and Granica 1995) that the larger the number of reproductions, the more the aesthetic evaluation (measured by willingness to pay) falls.

Uncertainty due to fakes does create real resource costs in the form of outlays of time, effort and money for search and information activities. In an ideal world without forgeries, these costs would not arise – but such an ideal is unreachable, so that these resource costs have to be taken as a fact of life.

As can be predicted by economic theory, the existence of these costs has created incentives to mitigate them:

1. There are specialized suppliers who can be trusted, because they would otherwise lose their reputation, and therewith future business. Exactly because there is considerable uncertainty in art markets, there is a niche for serious art dealers and auction houses.

2. Legal rules exist which allow hedging against various degrees of uncertainty.

In both cases, higher certainty about the art work is reflected in higher purchase prices. There is thus a trade-off between risk and price, thus allowing prospective buyers to choose a particular degree of certainty. It is, therefore, wrong to think that buyers are solely the passive victims of forgers; rather they can react actively to the possibility of fakes.

4.2   Supply

Fakes affect the incentive to produce original art. This is the same problem as with innovation in general. There is a trade-off: free imitation of originals produces utility for consumers, but at the same time reduces the (direct) profitability of innovations to the producers. Most legal systems strike a balance by granting innovators a monopoly for a restricted period of time[8]. This also applies to some, but not all, artistic "innovations" in the form of originals.

In the case of art, two considerations must be taken into account:

1. In those cases in which the propagation of copies raises the willingness to pay for the original work of art, or for other art work produced by the artist, there is no case for a temporal

---

8   See the special issue of the *Journal of Cultural Economics* 19 (1995), on "The Economics of Intellectual Property Rights".

monopolistic protection[9]. On the contrary, the originator has an incentive to subsidize fakes.

2. A quite different, but essential, question is the extent to which artistic creativity depends on monetary incentives. Is it really the same as technical or scientific innovations, say, in devising a new motor for automobiles, or a new chemical drug?

Considerable empirical evidence points to *intrinsic* motivation as being crucial for artists' and other people's personal creativity[10]. Artists may be strongly interested in monetary income, but at least at the start of their careers – exactly in the period when they are generally most creative and innovative – they are primarily driven by inner motives (intrinsic motivation), perhaps even by a strong drive to embark on artistic endeavors. Only at a later stage in an artist's life does monetary income going beyond what is needed for subsistence seem to become more important, or even predominant. But then it is often doubtful whether the art produced is still really innovative.

It is thus rather unlikely that *personal* creativity can be simply and systematically raised by monetary incentives. It is, in particular, most doubtful whether a higher monetary income is really able to induce higher creativity in the later phase of an artist's life. The effect on an artist's creativity disappears, by definition, once he or she is dead. In that case, the monopoly granted to the heirs is a pure rent, and does not serve any socially beneficial allocative purpose.

---

[9]   There is an analogy to photocopying, see e.g. Liebowitz (1985).

[10] See, in particular, the social psychological experiments undertaken, and reported, by Amabile (1996; 1997; 1998), Loveland and Olley (1979), and Hennessey and Amabile (1988). A general discussion of how geniuses work and behave is given by Simonton (1984; 1988; 1994). Chapter 8 of this book differentiates between institutional and personal creativity in the arts, which is of considerable relevance for the issue discussed here.

5.   Quotations as Solution?

The discussion suggests that the beneficial aspects of fakes are rather strong and the harmful effects rather weak. Copying is a response to the demand by people, who are otherwise unable to enjoy the original work of art (which, *once produced*, should be offered at zero price to the public). The use (consumption) of a copy produces utility, and should therefore not be curtailed or prohibited. Moreover, faking benefits the originator when he or she thereby gains additional recognition and fame. The harmful effects of faking, by raising uncertainty with prospective buyers, are reduced or even eliminated by the development of legal guarantees. Uncertainty can also be reduced by buying from reputable art dealers and auctioneers. As monetary incentives are likely to have a minor impact on individual artistic creativity and innovation, granting a monopoly to the creator of the original piece of art, and therewith hindering its copying, has only weak, if any, beneficial allocative effects.

While faking does not have as harmful an effect as is often claimed, it nevertheless has cost implications. Some of these costs can be reduced without giving up the advantages of a liberal art market, i.e. the possibility of copying originals at low cost and therewith generating utility. As pointed out, one possibility is to exploit contract law (the provision of guarantees about the quality of a work of art) and to turn to reputable dealers and auctioneers. This raises transaction costs to some degree, but this cost increase is, under most circumstances, lower than granting exclusive property rights to the creators of the original work of art.

A repressive approach, tolerating copying only with the explicit consent of the creator, and where all other reproductions are automatically forgeries, imposes significant burdens on society. Two types of costs can be differentiated:

1. Considerable energy and material resources are wasted in fighting over which artist should get the property right for the original, and who "copied" from whom. Another issue to be settled is how

far the monopoly right should extend. As is well known, "quotations" have played a great role, not only in literature, but also in painting. If the monopoly right is extensively defined, artistic progress is hampered, because an artist must tediously seek the approval of the owner of the property right before he or she can make such a "quotation". This certainly interrupts the flow of artistic activity, and will therefore be avoided, at least by creative artists. A repressive approach to copying thus does not only waste material resources, but also biases artists' activities in an unproductive direction.

2. The repressive policy against copying produces its own costs. Resources have to be used for art lawyers and arts policemen and judiciary. But, more importantly, copying moves underground. This creates huge uncertainties for prospective buyers; guarantees, for instance, are of little value because they cannot be legally enforced. Organized crime is favored. The experience would not be unlike drug, prostitution and alcohol prohibition, all of which have been huge failures. As a consequence of both uncertainty and prohibition, prices rise, and a substantial part of the profits created by art are appropriated by persons outside of art.

For these reasons, a repressive policy against fakes makes little sense. On the other hand, the creator of an original piece of art should be given an incentive to pursue his or her activity – but this incentive need not be given by granting a monopoly right, and resulting in monetary returns. Rather, a different approach is needed, based on the fact that, in the world of art, *recognition* plays a central role. The prospect of getting famous is certainly a strong incentive to be creative. A good solution, to balance the benefit and cost aspects discussed, would be to force every copier to *acknowledge the creator of the original*. As no monetary costs are involved, the requirement to recognize the originator may be laid down in quite an extensive way. Each copier must acknowledge his or her sources of inspiration, even if the relationship is only rather weak. He or she may easily be induced to do so because no monetary compensation has to be paid. But once this acknowledgement has been made, the process of copying, imitating, faking or forging may run its course:

the distinction between these terms becomes immaterial. The suggestion of "art quotations" remains unaltered in the digital age. Indeed, it corresponds exactly to the need to compensate the creator of an original work of art at the very beginning, because imitations simply cannot be prevented[11].

This is, of course, the solution found in academic research. In all disciplines, elaborate systems of *quotations* have evolved. Plagiarism exists, but seems to be restricted to relatively few cases. The system of quotations provides recognition for the creators of an academic work, but no direct monetary payments are involved. The recognition received builds up reputation and fame, which can then be transformed into higher monetary income by better job offers, popular publications and well-paid talks.

The crucial question is whether this well-functioning and efficient system of quotations in academic research can be transferred to art. An important difference is that the former are normally paid by their institution for teaching, while the latter have to gain income by selling their products. Obviously, the form these quotations take must differ widely among the various art forms. In some areas of art, formal quotations already exist (e.g. in some parts of music). In others, the quotations are often implicit (e.g. in paintings or sculptures), or are otherwise non-existent. But it is highly possible that with the progress in electronics, quotations may be technically more feasible in many areas of art.

---

[11]   Greffe (1998) suggests a similar mechanism of front-end compensation, but refers to monetary payment.

References

ACA (American Council of the Arts) (1980). *Americans and the Arts. A Survey of Public Opinion*. New York: St. Martins Press.

Acton, Jan (1973). Evaluating Public Progress to Save Lives: The Case of Heart Attacks, RAND Research Report R-73-02. Santa Monica: RAND Corporation.

Adler, Moshe (1985). Stardom and Talent. *American Economic Review* 75: 208-12.

Albert, Steven (1998). Movie Stars and the Distributioon of Financially Successful Films in the Motion Picture Industry. *Journal of Cultural Economics* 22: 249-270.

Alpers, Svetlana (1988). *Rembrandt's enterprise*. Chicago: University of Chicago Press.

Amabile, Teresa M. (1979). Effects of External Evaluation on Artistic Creativity. Journal of Personality and Social Psychology 37: 221-233.

Amabile, Teresa M. (1983). *The Social Psychology of Creativity*. New York: Springer.

Amabile, Teresa M. (1985). Motivation and Creativity: Effects of Motivation Orientation on Creative Writers. *Journal of Personality and Social Psychology* 48: 393-399.

Amabile, Teresa M. (1988). From Individual to Organizational Innovation. In: Kjell Gronhang and Geir Kaufmann (eds.). *Innovation: A Cross-Disciplinary Perspective*. Oslo: Norwegian University Perss: 139-166.

Amabile, Teresa M. (1996). *Creativity in Context: Update to the Social Psychology of Creativity*. Boulder, CO.: Westview Press.

Amabile, Teresa M. (1997). Motivating Creativity in Organizations: On Doing What You Love and Loving What You Do. *California Management Review* 40: 39-58.

Amabile, Teresa M. (1998). How To Kill Creativity. *Harvard Business Review*: 77-87.

Anderson, Robert C. (1974). Paintings as an Investment. *Economic Inquiry* 12: 13-26.

Arkes, Hal R. and Kenneth R. Hammond (eds.) (1986). *Judgement and Decision Making: An Interdisciplinary Reader*. Cambridge: Cambridge University Press.

Arrow, Kenneth J., Robert S. Solow, Edward Leamer, Paul Portney, Ray Radner and Howard Schuman (1993). Report of the NOAA-Panel on Contingent Valuation. *Federal Register* 58 (10): 4601-4614.

Ashenfelter, Orley (1989). How Auctions Work for Wine and Art. *Journal of Economic Perspectives*: 23-37.

Austen-Smith, David (1980). On Justifying Subsidies to the Performing Arts. In: William S. Hendon, James L. Shanahan and Alice J. MacDonald (eds.). *Economic Policy for the Arts*. Cambridge, MA.: Abt: 24-32.

Austen-Smith, David and Stephen Jenkins (1985). A Multiperiod Model of Nonprofit Enterprises. *Scottish Journal of Political Economy* 32 (1): 119-134.

Avery, Albert A. and Carl M. Colonna (1987). The Market for Collectible Antique and Reproduction Firearms: An Economic and Financial Analysis. *Journal of Cultural Economics* 11 (2): 49-64.

Banfield, Edward C. (1984). *The Democratic Muse: Visual Arts and the Public Interest*. New York: Basic Books.

Barkema, Harry G. (1995). Do Job Executives Work Harder When they are Monitored? *Kyklos* 48: 19-42.

Baumol, Hilda and William J. Baumol (1984). The Mass Media and the Cost Disease. In: Hendon, William S., Nancy Grant and Douglas V. Shaw (eds.). *The Economics of Cultural Industries*. Akron: Association for Cultural Economics: 109-123.

Baumol, William J. (1979). On Two Experiments in the Pricing of Theatre Tickets. In: Michael J. Boskin (ed.). *Economics of Human Welfare*. New York: Academic Press: 41-58.

Baumol, William J. (1986). Unnatural Value: or Art Investment as Floating Crap Game. *American Economic Review* 76: 10-14.

Baumol, William J. (1993). Social Wants and the Dismal Science: The Curious Case of the Climbing Costs of Health and Teaching. Mimeo. C. V. Starr Center for Applied Economics, New York University.

Baumol, William J. and Hilda Baumol (1994). On the Economics of Musical Composition In Mozart's Vienna. *Journal of Cultural Economics* 18: 171-198.

Baumol, William J. and William G. Bowen (1966). *Performing Arts - The Economic Dilemma*. Cambridge, MA.: Twentieth Century Fund.

Baxandall, Michael (1972). *Painting and Experience in Fifteenth Century Italy. A Primer in Social History of Pictoral Style*. Oxford: Oxford University Press.

Bayart, Denis and Pierre-Jean Benghozi (1993). *Le Tournant Commercial des Musées en France et à l'étranger*. Ministère de la Culture et de la Communication. Direction de l'Administration Général. Paris: La Documentation Française.

Becker, Gary S. (1976). *The Economic Approach to Human Behavior*. Chicago: Chicago University Press.

Becker, Gary S. (1991). A Note on Restaurant Pricing and Other Examples of Social Influences on Price. *Journal of Political Economy* 99: 1109-1116.

Becker, Gary S. (1992). Habits, Addictions and Traditions. *Kyklos* 45: 327-346.

Becker, Gary S. (1996). *Accounting for Tastes*. Cambridge, MA. and London: Harvard University Press.

Becker, Gary S. and Kevin M. Murphy (1988). A Theory of Rational Addiction. *Journal of Political Economy* 96: 675-700.

Belcher, Michael (1991). *Exhibitions in Museums*. Leicester and Washington D.C.: Leicester University Press and Smithonian Institution Press.

Bell, David E., Howard Raiffa and Amos Tversky (eds.) (1988). *Decision Making. Descriptive, Normative and Prescriptive Interactions*. Cambridge: Cambridge University Press.

Beltratti, Andrea and Domenico Siniscalco (1991). Collezionisti, Investitori, Speculatori: La determinazione dei prezzi sul mercato dell' arte. *Giornale degli Economisti e Annali di Economia* 50 (1-2): 51-69.

Benghozi, Pierre-Jean and Walter Santagata (1998). Market Piracy in the Design-based Industry: Economics and Policy Regulation. Paper presented at the International Conference on "The Economics of Copying and Counterfeiting", Venice, 3-4 December 1998.

Benhamou, Françoise (1996). *L'économie de la culture*. Paris: Editions La Découverte.

Benhamou, Françoise and Victor Ginsburgh (1998). Copies and Markets. Paper presented at the International Conference on "The Economics of Copying and Counterfeiting", Venice, 3-4 December 1998.

Benjamin, Walter (1963). *Das Kunstwerk im Zeitalter seiner technischen Reproduzierbarkeit*. Frankfurt a.M.: Edition Surkamp (4. ed.).

Biermann, Franz W. and Ursula Krenker (1974). Publikumsuntersuchungen am Theaterwissenschaftlichen Institut der Universität München. *Bayrisches Schauspiel: Theaterzeitung* (January): 17-21.

Bille Hansen, Trine (1997). The Willingness-to-pay for the Royal Theatre in Copenhagen as a Public Good. *Journal of Cultural Economics* .21 (1): 1-28.

Bishop, Richard C. and Thomas A. Heberlein (1979). Measuring Values of Extramarket Goods: Are Indirect Measures Biased? *American Journal of Agricultural Economics* 61: 926-30.

Blattberg, Robert C. and Cynthia J. Broderick (1991). Marketing of Art Museums. In: Martin Feldstein (ed.), *The Economics of Art Museums*. Chicago and London: University of Chicago Press: 327-346.

Blau, Judith R. (1989). Culture as Mass Culture. In: Arnold W. Foster and Judith R. Blau (eds.), *Art and Society. Readings in the Sociology of the Arts*. Albany, N.Y.: State University of New York: 141-176.

Blaug, Mark (ed.) (1976). *The Economics of the Arts*. London: Martin Robertson.

Bohm, Peter (1979). Estimating Willingness to Pay: Why and How? *Scandinavian Journal of Economics* 81 (1): 142-153.

Bohm, Peter (1984). Revealing Demand for an Actual Public Good. *Journal of Public Economics* 24 (1): 135-151.

Bohnet, Iris and Bruno S. Frey (1994). Direct-Democratic Rules: The Role of Discussion. *Kyklos* 47 (3): 341-354.

B.O.R. (Bayrischer Oberster Rechunungshof) (1984). *Bericht des Bayrischen Obersten Rechunungshofes 1984*. Munich: B.O.R.

Börsch-Supan, Helmut (1993). *Kunstmuseen in der Krise. Chancen, Gefährdungen, Aufgaben in mageren Jahren*. Nördlingen: Deutscher Kunstverlag.

Boulding, Kenneth (1977). Toward the Development of a Cultural Economics. *Social Science Quarterly* 53: 267-284.

Bourdieu, Pièrre (1979). *La distinction: critique sociale du jugement*. Paris: Editions de minuit.

Bourdieu, Pièrre and Alain Dardel (1966). *L'amour de l'art: les musées et leur public*. Paris: Editions de minuit.

Brennan, Geoffrey and James M. Buchanan (1985). *The Reason of Rules. Constitutional Political Economy*. Cambridge: Cambridge University Press.

Brosio, Giorgio and Walter Santagata (1992). *Rapporto sull économia delle arti e dello spectacolo in Italia*. Torino: Fondazione Agnelli.

Bröker, Josef (1928). *Die Preisgestaltung auf dem modernen Kunstmarkt (mit besonderer Berücksichtigung des Bildes)*, Universität Münster.

Buchanan, James M. (1987). Constitutional Economics. In: John Eatwell, Murray Milligate and Peter Newman (eds.). *The New Palgrave: A Dictionary of Economics*. London: Macmillan: 585-588.

Buelens, Nathalie and Victor Ginsburgh (1993). Revisiting Baumol's 'Art as Floating Crap Game'. *European Economic Review* 37: 1351-1371.

Burke, Andrew (1998). Legal Structure, Strategic Regulation and Dividing the Spoils from R&D in Intellectual Property. Paper presented at the International Conference on "The Economics of Copying and Counterfeiting", Venice, 3-4 December 1998.

Butler, David J. and John D. Hey (1987). Experimental Economics: An Introduction. *Empirica* 14, 157-186.

Butler, David and Austin Ranney (eds.) (1994). *Referendums around the World. The Growing Use of Direct Democracy*. Washington, D.C.: AEI Press.

Cameron, Judy and W. David Pierce (1994). Reinforcement, Reward, and Intrinsic Motivation: A Meta-Analysis. *Review of Educational Research* 64: 363-423.

Canela, Guido and Antonella E. Scorcu (1997). A Price Index for Art Market Auctions. *Journal of Cultural Economics: Special Issue on the Art Market* 21 (3): 175-196.

Cantor, Jay E. (1991). The Museum's Collection. In: Martin Feldstein (ed.), *The Economics of Art Museums*. Chicago: University of Chicago Press: 17-23.

Carson, Richard, et al. (1992). *A Contingent Valuation Study of Lost Passive Use Values Resulting From the Exxon Valdez Oil Spill*, Report to the Attorney General of the State of Alaska, prepared by Natural Resource Damage Assessment, Inc., La Jolla, California.

Carson, Richard, et al. (1994). *A Bibliography of Contingent Valuation Studies and Papers*. La Jolla, California: Natural Resources Damage Assessment, Inc.

Cassady, Ralph, Jr. (1967). *Auctions and Auctioneering*. Berkeley and Los Angeles: University of California Press.

Chanel, Olivier (1995). Is Art Market Behaviour Predictable? *European Economic Review* 39 (3-4): 519-527.

Chanel, Olivier, Louis-André Gérard-Varet and Victor Ginsburgh (1994). Prices and Returns on Paintings: An Exercise on How to Price the Priceless. *The Geneva Papers on Risk and Insurance Theory* 19: 7-21.

Cicchetti, Charles J. and V. Kerry Smith (1973). Congestion, Quality Deterioration, and Optimal Use: Wilderness Recreation in the Spanish Peaks Primitive Area. *Social Science Research* 2: 15-30.

Clark, David E. and James R. Kahn (1988). The Social Benefits of Urban Cultural Amenities. *Journal of Regional Science* 28 (3): 363-377.

Coffman, Richard B. (1991). Art Investment and Asymmetrical Information. *Journal of Cultural Economics* 15 (2): 83-94.

Coleman, James S. (1990). *Foundations of Social Theory*. Cambridge, MA.: Harvard University Press.

Condry, J. (1977). Enemies of Exploration: Self-Imitated versus Other-Imitated Learning. *Journal of Personality and Social Psychology* 42: 789-797.

Conforti, Michael (1986). Hovings Legacy Reconsidered. (Special Section: Museum Blockbusters). *Art in America,* June 1986.

Coutts, Herbert (1986). Profile of a Blockbuster. *Museum Journal* 86 (1): 23-26.

Cowen, Tyler (1998). *In Praise of Commercial Culture*. Cambridge, MA.: Harvard University Press.

Cronin, Thomas E. (1989). *Direct Democracy. The Politics of Initiative, Referendum and Recall*. Cambridge, MA.: Harvard University Press

Cropper, Maureen L. and William E. Oates (1992). Environmental Economics: A Survey. *Journal of Economic Literature* 302: 675-740.

Curtis, Ruth (1990). Community and Small Scale Festivals. National Arts and Media Strategy Unit, Arts Council. London: 1-10.

Cwi, David (1979). Public Support of the Arts: Three Arguments Examined. *Journal of Behavioral Economics* 8: 39-68.

Dawes, Robyn M. (1988). *Rational Choice in an Uncertain World*. San Diego and New York: Harcourt, Brace, Yovanovich.

Deardorff, Alan V. (1995). The Appropriate Extent of Intellectual Property Rights in Art. *Journal of Cultural Economics* 19 (2): 119-130.

Deci, Edward L. and Richard Koestner and Richard M. Ryan (1999). A Meta-Analytic Review of Experiments Examining the Effects of Extrinsic Rewards on Intrinsic Motivation. *Psychological Bulletin* 125 (3): 627-668.

Devine, D. Grant, and Bruce Marion (1979). The Influence of Consumer Price Information on Retail Pricing and Consumer Behaviour. *American Journal of Agricultural Economics* 61: 228-37.

Dietze, Horst (ed.) (1986). Aspekte des Kunstverleihs. Berlin: Deutsches Bibliotheksinstitut.

DiMaggio, Paul (1985). When the Profit is Quality. Cultural Institutions in the Marketplace. *Museum News* 63 (5): 28-35.

DiMaggio, Paul (ed.) (1986). *Nonprofit Enterprise in the Arts*. New York and Oxford: Oxford University Press.

DiMaggio, Paul and Michael Useem (1978). *Studies of the Performing Arts and Museums: A Critical Review*. Washington D.C.: Research Division, National Endowment for the Arts.

DiMaggio, Paul and Michael Useem (1989). Cultural Democracy in a Period of Cultural Expansion: The Social Composition of Arts Audiences in the United States. In: Arnold W. Foster and Judith R. Blau (eds.), *Art and Society. Readings in the Sociology of the Arts*. Albany, N.Y.: State University of New York: 141-176.

DiMaggio, Paul, Michael Useem and Paula Brown (1978). *Audience Studies of Performing Arts and Museums*. Washington D.C.: National Endowments for the Arts.

Dolfsma, Wilfred (1997). A Status Quo in the Economics of Art and Culture. A View of Some Recent Developments. *De Economist* 145: 243-254.

Downs, Anthony (1957). *An Economic Theory of Democracy*. New York: Harper and Row.

Drey, Paul (1910). *Die wirtschaftlichen Grundlagen der Malkunst*. Stuttgart and Berlin: Cotta.

Dümling, Albrecht (1992). Vorsicht Kommerz! Musikfestivals am Scheideweg. *Neue Zeitschrift für Musikwissenschaft* 7/8: 8-12.

Duncombe, William D. and Jeffrey L. Brudney (1995). The Optimal Mix of Volunteer and Paid Staff in Local Governments: An Application to Municipal Fire Departments. *Public Finance Quarterly* 23: 356-384.

Dupuis, Xavier (1980). *Analyse économique de la production lyrique*. Dissertation, Universität Paris I - Panthéon - Sorbonne, Paris.

Dupuis, Xavier (1983). La surqualité: le spectacle subventionné malade de la bureaucratie? *Revue Economique* 34: 1089-1115.

Dupuis, Xavier (1985). La micro-économie du spectacle vivant. In: Augustin Girard (ed.). *L'économie du spectacle vivant et l'audiovisuel*. Paris: Ministre de la Culture et Association pour le developpement et la diffusion de l'économie de la culture: 71-97.

Dupuis, Xavier and Xavier Greffe (1985). Subsidies to Cultural Employment: The French Experiment. In: Waits et al. (ed.), *Governments and Culture*. Akron, OH.: Akron University Press: 164-173.

Dutton, Dennis (1983). *The Forger's Art: Forgery and the Philosophy of Art*. Berkeley: University of California Press.

Eichberger, Dagmar (1996). The Grand Louvre: A Change in Direction. *Bulletin of the Melbourne Fine Arts Society* 8: 3-5.

Eichenberger, Reiner (1992). Verhaltensanomalien und Wirtschaftswissenschaft: Herausforderung, Reaktionen, Perspektiven. Wiesbaden: Deutscher Universitätsverlag.

Eisenberger, Robert and Judy Cameron (1996). Detrimental Effects of Reward. Reality of Myth? *American Psychologist* 51: 1153-1166.

Eisenberger, Robert and Stephen Armeli (1997). Can Salient Reward Increase Creative Performance Without Reducing Intrinsic Creative Interest? *Journal of Personality and Social Psychology* 66: 652-663.

Eisenberger, Robert and Michael Selbst (1994). Does Reward Increase or Decrease Creativity? *Journal of Personality and Social Psychology* 66: 1116-1127.

Elsen, Albert (1986). Assessing the Pros and Cons. (Special Section: Museum Blockbusters). *Art in America,* June 1986.

Epstein, Max (1914). *Theater und Volkswirtschaft.* Berlin: Simion.

Farchy, Joelle and Dominique Sagot-Duvauroux (1994). *Economie des politiques culturelles.* Paris: Presses Universitaires de France.

Feld, Alan L., Michael O'Hare and J. Mark D. Schuster (1983). *Patrons Despite Themselves: Taxpayers and Arts Policy.* New York: New York University Press.

Feldstein, Martin (ed.) (1991). *The Economics of Art Museums.* Chicago: University of Chicago Press.

Filer, Randall K. (1986). The "Starving Artist" - Myth or Reality? Earnings of Artists in the United States. *Journal of Political Economy* 94: 56-75.

Foster, Arnold W. and Judith R. Blau (eds.) (1989). *Art and Society. Readings in the Sociology of the Arts.* Albany: State University of New York Press.

Frank, Robert H. and Philip J. Cook (1995). *The Winner-Take-All Society.* New York: Free Press.

Frey, Bruno S. (1983). *Democratic Economic Policy.* Oxford: Blackwell.

Frey, Bruno S. (1986). The Salzburg Festival – from the Economic Point of View. *Journal of Cultural Economics* 10: 27-44.

Frey, Bruno S. (1992). Tertium Datur: Pricing, Regulating and Intrinsic Motivation. *Kyklos* 45: 161-184.

Frey, Bruno S. (1992). *Economics as a Science of Human Behaviour: Towards a New Social Science Paradigm.* Dordrecht: Kluwer.

Frey, Bruno S. (1994). Cultural Economics and Museum Behaviour. *Scottish Journal of Political Economy* 41 (3): 325-335.

Frey, Bruno S. (1994). Direct Democracy: Politico-Economic Lessons from Swiss Experience. *American Economic Review* 84 (May): 338-348.

Frey, Bruno S. (1994). The Economics of Music Festivals. *Journal of Cultural Economics* 18: 29-39.

Frey, Bruno S. (1996). Has Baumol's Cost Disease disappeared in the perfoming arts? *Ricerche Economiche* 50: 173-182.

Frey, Bruno S. (1997). *Not Just for the Money. An Economic Theory of Personal Motivation.* Cheltenham, UK and Brookfield, USA: Edward Elgar.

Frey, Bruno S. (1999). *Economics as a Science of Human Behaviour.* 2nd revision and extended edition. Boston and Dordrecht: Kluwer.

Frey, Bruno S. (1999). State Support and Creativity in the Arts: Some New Considerations. *Journal of Cultural Economics* 23 (1-2): 71-85.

Frey, Bruno S. and Reiner Eichenberger (1989). Should Social Scientists Care About Choice Anomalies? *Rationality and Society* 1: 101-122.

Frey, Bruno S. and Reiner Eichenberger (1989b). Anomalies and Institutions. *Journal of Institutional and Theoretical Economics* 145 (September): 423-437.

Frey, Bruno S. and Reiner Eichenberger (1994). American and European Economics and Economists. *Journal of Economic Perspectives* 7 (4): 185-193

Frey, Bruno S. and Reiner Eichenberger (1995). Returns on Art. Critical Evaluation and Psychic Benefits. *European Economic Review* 39: 528-537.

Frey, Bruno S. and Reto Jegen (1999). Motivation Crowding Theory: A Survey of Empirical Evidence. Working Paper No. 26. Working Paper Series of the Institute for Empirical Research in Economics, University of Zurich.

Frey, Bruno S. and Felix Oberholzer-Gee (1997). The Cost of Price Incentives: An Empirical Analysis of Motivation Crowding-Out. *American Economic Review* 87 (4): 746-755.

Frey, Bruno S. and Felix Oberholzer-Gee and Reiner Eichenberger (1996). The Old Lady Visits Your Backyard: A Tale of Morals and Markets. *Journal of Political Economy* 104 (6): 1297-1313.

Frey, Bruno S. and Werner W. Pommerehne (1980). An Economic Analysis of the Museum. In: William S. Hendon, James L. Shanahan, and Alice J. MacDonald (eds.) *Economic Policy for the Arts.* Cambridge, MA.: 248-259.

Frey, Bruno S. and Werner W. Pommerehne (1987). International Trade in Art: Attitudes and Behaviour. *Rivista Internazionale di Scienze Economiche e Commerciali* 34 (6): 465-486.

Frey, Bruno S. and Werner W. Pommerehne (1987). L'art pour l'art. Behavioral Effects of Performing Arts Organizations. *Empirical Studies of the Arts* 5 (1): 59-78.

Frey, Bruno S. and Werner W. Pommerehne (1988). Is Art such a Good Investment? *Public Interest* 91: 79-86.

Frey, Bruno S. and Werner W. Pommerehne (1989a). *Muses and Markets: Explorations in the Economics of the Arts.* Oxford: Blackwell.

Frey, Bruno S. and Werner W. Pommerehne (1989b). Art: An Empirical Inquiry. *Southern Economic Journal* 56: 396-409.

Frey, Bruno S. and Werner W. Pommerehne (1995). Public Expenditure on the Arts and Direct Democracy: The Use of Referenda in Switzerland. *Cultural Policy* 2 (1): 55-65.

Frey, Bruno S. and Angel Serna (1990). Der Preis der Kunst. Kursbuch (booklet 99): 105-113.

Frey, René L. and Gregory Neugebauer (1976). *Theater und Oekonomie.* Basel: Universität Basel.

Fronville, Claire L. (1985). Marketing for Museums: For Profit Techniques in the Non-Profit-World. *Curator* 28 (3): 169-182.

Fullerton, Don (1991). Tax Policy Towards Art Museums. In: Martin Feldstein (ed.), *The Economics of Art Museums.* Chicago: University of Chicago Press: 195-236.

Galeotti, Gianluigi (1992). Riflettori sull'iposcenio: elementi per un'analisi economica del Festival di Spoleto. In: Giorgio Brosio and Walter Santagata (eds.). *Rapporto sull'economia delle arti e dello spettacolo in Italia.* Torino: Fondazione Agnelli: 125-147.

Gallais-Hamonno, Georges (1972). *Des loisirs: analyse économique de la demande de loisirs en France.* Paris: S.E.D.E.I.S. (Société d'Etudes et de Documentation Economiques, Industrielles et Sociales).

Ganzeboom, Harry B.G. (1987). Cultural Audience Formation in the Netherlands Between 1962 and 1983. In: Douglas W. Shaw, William S. Hendon, C. Richard Waits (eds.). *Artists and Cultural Consumers.* Association for Cultural Economics: 179-191.

Gapinski, James H. (1984). The Economics of Performing Shakespeare. *American Economic Review, Papers and Proceeedings* 74: 458-466.

Gapinski, James H. (1988a). Tourism's Contribution to the Demand for London's Lively Arts. *Applied Economics* 20: 957-968.

Gapinski, James H. (1988b). The Economic Right Triangle of Nonprofit Theatre. *Social Science Quarterly* 69: 756-763.

Gärtner, Manfred and Werner W. Pommerehne (1978). Der Fussballzuschauer - ein homo oeconomicus? In: *Jahrbuch für Sozialwissenschaft* 29: 88-107.

Gavin, David A. (1981). Blockbusters: The Economics of Mass Entertainment. *Journal of Cultural Economics* 5: 1-20.

Gerelli, Emilio (1974). *Economia e Tutela dell'Ambiente*. Bologna: Il Mulino.

Getz, Donald (1989). Special Events. Defining the Product. *Tourism Management*: 125-137.

Getz, Donald and Wendy Frisby (1988). Evaluating Management Effectiveness in Community-Run Festivals. *Journal of Travel Research* 27: 22-27.

Ginsburgh, Victor A. and Pierre-Michel Menger (eds.) (1996). *Economics of the Arts. Selected Essays*. Amsterdam: Elsevier/North Holland.

Ginsburgh, Victor and Philippe Jeanfils (1995). Long-term comovements in international markets for paintings. *European Economic Review* 41: 325-335.

Ginsburgh, Victor and Anne-Françoise Penders (1997). Land Artists and Art Markets. An Analysis of Works Sold at Auctions. *Journal of Cultural Economics: Special Issue on the Art Market* 21 (3): 219-228.

Goetzmann, William N. (1993). Accounting for Taste: Art and the Financial Markets over three Centuries. *American Economic Review* 83 (5): 1370-1376.

Goetzmann, William N. (1994). The Informational Efficiency of the Art Market. Mimeo. Columbia University, New York.

Graeser, Paul (1993). Rate of Return to Investment in American Antique Furniture. *Southern Economic Journal* 59 (4): 817-821.

Grampp, William D. (1983). On Subsidizing Art Museums. Mimeo. University of Illinois, Chicago.

Grampp, William D. (1986/7). Should the Arts Support Themselves? *Economic Affairs* 6: 41-43.

Grampp, William D. (1989). *Pricing the Priceless Art, Artists, and Economics*. New York: Basil Books.

Grampp, William D. (1989). Rent-Seeking in Arts Policy. *Public Choice* 60: 113-121.

Greffe, Xavier (1985). Le pot de terre et le pot de fer. In: Augustin Girard (ed.). *L'économie du spectacle vivant et l'audiovisuel*. Paris: Documentation Française: 18-33.

Greffe, Xavier (1990). *La valeur économique du patrimoine*. Paris: Economica.

Greffe, Xavier (1998). Intellectual Property Right in the Digital Age. Paper presented at the International Conference on "The Economics of Copying and Counterfeiting", Venice, 3-4 December 1998.

Greffe, Xavier (1999). *L'emploi culturel à l'âge du numérique*. Paris: Anthropos.

Greffe, Xavier, S. Pflieger and F. Rouget (1990). *Socio-économie de la culture. Livre, musique*. Paris: Anthropos.

Grossman, Gene M. and Carl Shapiro (1988). Counterfeit Product Trade. *American Economic Review* 78: 59-75.

Grossman, Gene M. and Carl Shapiro (1989). Foreign Counterfeit of Status Goods. *Quarterly Journal of Economics* 103: 79-100.

Grunfeld, Jean François (ed.) (1994). *International Exhibition Guide*. Paris: Editions Parama.

Guerzoni, Guido (1994). Testing Reitlinger's sample reliability. Paper presented at the 8th International Congress on Cultural Economics in Witten, Germany, August 24-27.

Haalck, Hans (1921). Die wirtschaftliche Struktur des deutschen Theaters, Universität Hamburg.

Hamilton, Charles (1980). *Great Forgers and Famous Fakes*. New York: Crown Publishers.

Hammack, J. and Gardner Brown (1974). *Waterfowl and Wetlands: Toward Bioeconomic Analysis*. Amsterdam: North Holland

Hansmann, Henry B. (1981). Nonprofit Enterprise in the Performing Arts. *Rand Journal of Economics* 12: 341-361.

Hansman, Henry B. and Marina Santilli (1997). Authors' and Artists' Moral Rights: A Comparative Legal and Economic Analysis. *Journal of Legal Studies* 26: 95-143.

Hauser, Arnold (1953). *Sozialgeschichte der Kunst und Literatur*. Munich: Beck.

Heilbrun, James (1991). Innovation in Art, Innovation in Technology, and the Future of the High Arts. *Journal of Cultural Economics* 17: 89-98.

Heilbrun, James and Charles M. Gray (1993). *The Economics of Art and Culture - An American Perspective*. Cambridge: Cambridge University Press.

Hendon, William S., Frank Costa and Robert A. Rosenberg (1989). The General Public and the Art Museum. *American Journal of Economics and Sociology* 48: 132-143.

Hendon, William S., Nancy Grant and Douglas V. Shaw (eds.) (1984). *The Economics of Cultural Industries*. Akron: Association for Cultural Economics.

Hennessey, B. A. and Teresa M. Amabile (1988). The conditions of creativity. In: R.J. Sternberg (ed.). *The Nature of Creativity*. Cambridge: Cambridge University Press: 11-38.

Herterich, Fritz (1937). *Theater und Volkswirtschaft*. München und Leipzig: Duncker und Humblot.

Hirschman, Albert O. (1970). *Exit, Voice and Loyalty*. Cambridge, MA.: Harvard University Press.

Hirschman, Albert O. (1989). Having Opinions – One of the Elements of Well-Being? *American Economic Review* 79: 75-79.

Hirshleifer, Jack (1985). The Expanding Domain of Economics. *American Economic Review* 75: 53-68.

Hogarth, Robin M. and Melvin W. Reder (eds.) (1987). *Rational Choice*. Chicago: University of Chicago Press.

Holub, Hans Werner, Michael Hutter and G. Tappeiner (1993). Light and Shadow in Art Price Competition. *Journal of Cultural Economics* 17 (June): 49-69.

Honolka, Kurt (1986). *Die Oper ist tot – die Oper lebt: Kritische Bilanz der deutschen Musiktheater*. Stuttgart: Deutsche Verlagsanstalt.

Horlacher, Felix (1984). *Kultursubventionen*. Berne, Francfort and New York: Lang.

Horowitz, Harold (1983). Work and Earnings of Artists in the Media Fields. *Journal of Cultural Economics* 7: 69-89.

Hughes, Gordon (1989). Measuring the Economic Value of the Arts. Policy Studies 9 (3): 33-45.

Hummel, Marlies (1992). *Neuere Entwicklungen bei der Finanzierung von Kunst und Kultur durch Unternehmen*. Ifo Studien zu Kultur und Wirtschaft. Munich: Ifo Institut für Wirtschaftsforschung.

Hummel, Marlies and Manfred Berger (1988). *Die volkswirtschaftliche Bedeutung von Kunst und Kultur*. Munich: Ifo-Institut für Wirtschaftsforschung.

Hutter, Michael (1986). Kunst als Quelle wirtschaftlichen Wachstums. *Zeitschrift für Aesthetik und Allgemeine Kunstwissenschaft* 31: 231-245.

Hutter, Michael (1987). Music as a Source of Economic Growth. In: Nancy K. Grant and et al. (eds.) *Economic Efficiency and the Performing Arts*. Akron, Ohio: Akron University Press: 100-117.

Hutter, Michael (1992). Kann der Staat Kunst fördern? Wirtschafts- und systemtheoretische Überlegungen zur Kulturpolitik. In: C.A. Andreae and Ch. Smekal (eds.). *Kulturförderung in den Alpenländern*. Innsbruck: Wagner: 45-59.

Hutter, Michael (1996a). The Impact of Cultural Economics on Economic Theory. *Journal of Cultural Economics* 20: 263-268.

Hutter, Michael (1996b). The Value of Play. In: Arjo Klamer (1996) *The Value of Culture. On the Relationship Between Economics and Arts*. Amsterdam: Amsterdam University Press: 122-137.

Hutter, Michael and Ilde Rizzo (eds.) (1997). *Economic Perspectives on Cultural Heritage*. Basingstoke, UK: MacMillan Press Ltd.

Hutter, Michael (1998a): Communication Productivity: A Major Cause for the Changing Output of Art Museums. *Journal of Cultural Economics* 22: 99-112.

Hutter, Michael (1998b). Again Fake? Three Frameworks for Models of Information Goods, and a Remark on Regulation. Paper presented at the International Conference on "The Economics of Copying and Counterfeiting", Venice, 3-4 December 1998.

ICARE- International Centre of Studies on the Economics of the Arts (1994). *I musei Veneziani. Indagine sulle strutture permanenti e temporanee*. Offerta culturale della città di Venezia, secondo rapporto. Venezia.

Institut für Museumskunde (ed.) (1992). *Erhebung der Besucherzahlen an den Museen der Bundesrepublik Deutschland für das Jahr 1991*, Heft 36, Berlin: Institut für Museumskunde, Staatliche Museen Preussischer Kulturbesitz.

Isnard, Guy (1960). *Faux et Imitations dans l'Art*. Paris: Fayard.

Johnson, Peter (1995). Cultural Economics and Museum Behaviour: A Comment. *Scottish Journal of Political Economy* 42 (Nov): 465-466.

Johnson, Peter and Barry Thomas (eds.) (1998). Special Issue on the Economics of Museums. *Journal of Cultural Economics* 22: 75-207.

Jones, Mark (ed.) (1990). *Fake? The Art of Deception*. London: British Museum Publ.

Kahneman, Daniel, Paul Slovic and Amos Tversky (eds.) (1982). *Judgement under Uncertainty: Heuristics and Biases*. Cambridge: Cambridge University Press.

Kavolis, Vyautas (1964). Economic Correlates of Artistic Creativity. *American Journal of Sociology* 70: 332-341. Reprinted in Foster and Blau (1989): 383-395.

Kelly, Frank S. (1994). A Rate of Return Analysis of Mettlach Beer Steins. Mimeo. Department of Economics, Ohio University.

Kindermann, Carl (1903). *Volkswirtschaft und Kunst*. Jena: Fischer.

Kirchgässner, Gebhard (1991). *Homo Oeconomicus. Das ökonomische Modell individuellen Verhaltens und seine Anwendung in den Wirtschafts- und Sozialwissenschaften*. Tübingen: Mohr (Siebeck).

Kirchgässner, Gebhard and Werner W. Pommerehne (1993). Low-cost Decisions as a Challenge to Public Choice. *Public Choice* 77: 107-115.

Klamer, Arjo (ed.) (1996). *The Value of Culture. On the Relationship Between Economics and Arts*. Amsterdam: Amsterdam University Press.

Klein, Hans Joachim (1990). *Der gläserne Besucher. Publikumsstrukturen einer Museumslandschaft.* Berliner Schriften der Museumskunde, Band 8. Berlin: Gebr. Mann Verlag.

Kliemt, Hartmut (1985). *Moralische Institutionen: Empirische Theorien ihrer Evolution.* Freiburg (Breisgau): Alber.

Kliemt, Hartmut (1986). The Veil of Insignificance. *European Journal of Political Economy* 2/3: 333-344.

Koboldt, Christian (1995). Intellectual Property and Optimal Copyright Protection. *Journal of Cultural Economics* 19 (2): 131-155.

Krupnick, Alan and Maureen L. Cropper (1992). The Effect of Information on Health Risk Valuation. *Journal of Risk and Uncertainty* 2: 29-48.

Kurz, Otto (1948). *Fakes. A Handbook for Collectors and Students.* London: Faber.

Landes, William M. (1999). Winning the Art Lottery: The Economic Returns to the Ganz Collection. John M. Olin Law & Economics Working Paper No. 76, University of Chicago.

Lazzaro, Elisabetta, Nathalie Moureau, and Dominique Sagot-Duvauroux (1998), From the Market of Copies to the Market of Fakes: Adverse Selection and Moral Hazard in the Market of Visual Arts. Paper presented at the International Conference on "The Economics of Copying and Counterfeiting", Venice, 3-4 December 1998.

Le Pen, Claude (1982). L'analyse microéconomique de la production dramatique et l'éffet des subventions publiques. *Revue Economique* 33 (July): 639-674.

Leroy, Dominique (1980). *Economie des arts du spectacle vivant: essai sur la relation entre l'économie et l'ésthétique.* Paris: Economica.

L'Expansion (1994). En avant la musique. Special été, No 481: 32-35.

Liebowitz, S. J. (1985). Copying and Indirect Appropriability. Photocopying of Journals. *Journal of Political Economy* 93 (5): 945-957.

Loewenthal, David (1990). Forging the Past. In: Mark Jones (ed.). *Fakes? The Art of Deception.* London: British Museum Publ.: 16-22.

Louargand M.A. and J.R. McDaniel (1991). Price Efficiency in the Art Auction Market. *Journal of Cultural Economics* 15 (2): 53-65.

Loveland, K.K. and Olley, J.G. (1979). The Effect of External Reward on Interest and Quality of Task Performance in Children of High and Low Intrinsic Motivation. *Children Development* 50: 127-1210.

Machina, Mark J. (1987). Choice Under Uncertainty: Problems Solved and Unsolved. *Journal of Economic Perspectives* 1: 121-154.

Mai, Ekkehard (1986). *Expositionen: Geschichte und Kritik des Ausstellungswesens.* München, Berlin: Deutscher Kunstverlag.

Maillard, Cécile (1994). A quoi servent les festivals? *Grandes Lignes TGV* 18: 65-66.

Malraux, André (1947). *Le Musé Imaginaire.* Paris: Gallimard.

Marggraff, Robert (1922). Organisation und Betrieb städtischer Theater unter besonderer Berücksichtigung ihrer finanziellen Verhältnisse, Universität zu Köln.

Marplan (1968). Marktforschung für das Theater: Motivforschung. In: Wilhelm Allgayer und Gustav Weidemann (eds.). *Handbuch der Theaterwerbung, Teil 3.* Cologne: Deutscher Bühnenverein.

Martin, Fernand (1994). Determining the Size of Museum Subsidies. *Journal of Cultural Economics* 18: 255-270.

Martorella, Rosanne (1977). The Relationship between Box Office and Repertoire: A Case Study of Opera. *Sociological Quarterly* 18 (2): 354-366.

Mazzocchi, Giancarlo (1971). *La crisi economico-finanziaria dell' attività teatrale: alcuni spunti interpretativi.* Mailand: Vita e Pensiero.

McKenzie, Richard B. and Gordon Tullock (1975). *The New World of Economics.* 2nd ed. Homewood, IL.: Irwin.

Menger, Pierre-Michel (1980). *The Serious Contemporary Music Market, the Conditions of the Composer and Aid for Composers in Europe.* Strassbourg: Council for Cultural Cooperation, Cultural Affairs.

Menger, Pierre-Michel (1983). *Le paradoxe du musicien; le compositeur, le mélomane et l'Etat dans la société contemporaine.* Paris: Flammarion.

Menger, Pierre-Michel (1991). Marché du travail artistique et socialisation du risque. Le cas des arts du spectacle. *Revue française de sociologie* XXXII: 61-74.

Merin, Jennifer and Elizabeth B. Burdick (1979). *International Directory of Theatre, Dance and Folklore Festivals.* Westport, CT.: Greenwood Press.

Milgrom, Paul and R.J. Weber (1982). A Theory of Auctions and Competitive Bidding. *Econometrica* 50: 1089-1122.

Ministère de la Culture de la Francophonie (ed.) (1994). *Festivals et Expositions. Le guide culturel de l'été.* Paris: Ministère de la Culture.

Mitchell, Claire J. A. and Geoffrey Wall (1989). The Arts and Employment: A Case Study of the Stratford Festival. *Growth and Change* 20 (4): 31-40.

Mitchell, Robert C. and Richard T. Carson (1989). *Using Surveys to Value Public Goods: The Contingent Valuation Method.* Washington, D.C.: Resources for the Future.

Mok, Henry M.K., Vivian W.K. Ko, Salina S.M. Woo, Katherina Y.S. Kwok (1993). Modern Chinese Paintings: An Investment Alternative? *Southern Economic Journal* 59 (4): 808-816.

Montebello, Philippe de (1981). Exhibitions and Permanent Museum Collections - Competition or Correspondence? In: Institut für Museumskunde (ed.), *Ausstellungen - Mittel der Politik?* Berlin: Gebr. Mann Verlag: 153-163.

Montias, J. Michael (1973). Are Museums Betraying the Public's Trust? *Museum News* (May): 25-31. Reprinted in the *Journal of Cultural Economics* 19 (1995): 71-80.

Montias, J. Michael (1982). *Artists and Artisans in Delft: A Socio-Economic Study of the Seventeenth Century.* Princeton: Princeton University Press.

Moore, Thomas G. (1968). *The Economics of American Theatre.* Durham, N.C.: Duke University Press.

Morrison, William G. and Edwin G. West (1986). Subsidies for the Performing Arts: Evidence on Voter Preferences. *Journal of Behavioral Economics* 15: 57-72.

Mossetto, Gianfranco (1992). A Cultural Good Called Venice. In: Ruth Towse and Abdul Khakee (eds.), *Cultural Economics.* Berlin, Heidelberg and New York: Springer: 247-256.

Mossetto, Gianfranco (1993). *Aesthetics and Economics.* Boston: Kluwer.

Moulin, Raymonde (1967). *Le marché de la peinture en France:* Paris. Editions du minuit.

Moulin, Raymonde (1986). Le marché et le musée: la constitution des valeurs artistiques contemporaines. *Revue Française de la Sociologie* 27: 369-395.

Mueller, Dennis C. (1989). *Public Choice II.* 2nd edition. Cambridge: Cambridge University Press.

Mueller, Dennis C. (1997). *Perspectives on Public Choice.* Cambridge: Cambridge University Press.

Myerscough, John (1988). *The Economic Importance of the Arts in Britain.* London: Policy Studies Institute.

National Audit Office (1993). *Department of National Heritage, National Museums and Galleries: Quality of Service to the Public.* London: HSMO.

National Audit Office (1993). Department of National Heritage. *National Museums and Galleries: Qualitiy of Service to the Public.* London: HMO.

Netzer, Dick (1978). *The Subsidized Muse: Public Support for the Arts in the United States.* Cambridge, London and Melbourne: Cambridge University Press.

Neuburger, Albert (1924). *Echt oder Fälschung*, Leipzig: Zentralantiquariat der DDR.

Niskanen, William A., Jr. (1971). *Bureaucracy and Representative Government*. Chicago: Aldine.

O'Hagan, John W. (1992). The Wexford Opera Festival: A Case for Public Funding? In: Ruth Towse and Abdul Khakee (eds.). *Cultural Economics*. Berlin: Springer: 61-66.

O'Hagan, John W. (1995). National Museums: To Charge or Not to Charge? *Journal of Cultural Economics* 19: 33-47.

O'Hagan, John W. (1998). *The State and the Arts: An Analysis of Key Economic Policy Issues in Europe and the United States*. Cheltenham: Edward Elgar.

O'Hagan, John W. and Christopher T. Duffy (1987). *The Performing Arts and the Public Purse: An Economic Analysis*. Dublin: Irish Arts Council.

O'Hagan, John W. and Christopher T. Duffy (1995). National Museums: Functions, Costs and Admission Charges. *European Journal of Cultural Policy* 1: 369-380.

O'Hagan, John and Mark Purdy (1993). The Theory of Non-Profit Organisations: An Application to a Performing Arts Enterprise. *Economic and Social Review* 24: 155-167.

Osterloh, Margit and Bruno S. Frey (1998). Managing Motivation and Knowledge in the Theory of the Firm. Mimeo, Institute for Research in Business Administration and Institute for Empirical Economic Research, University of Zurich.

Österreichischer Rechnungshof (1984). *Bericht über die Gebahrung des Bundes mit Mitteln der Kunst- und der Sportförderung*. Vienna: Österreichische Staatsdruckerei.

Österreichischer Rechnungshof (1988). *Nachtrag zum Tätigkeitsbereich des Rechunungshofes*. Vienna: Österreichische Staatsdruckerei.

Österreichischer Rechnungshof (1994). *Burgtheater*. Vienna.

Pahlen, Kurt (1978). *Erster Europäischer Festspielführer 1978*. München: Goldmann.

Parkhurst, C. (1975). Art Museums. In: S.E. Lee (ed.): *On Understanding Art Museums*. Englewood Cliffs, N.J.: Prentice-Hall: 68-97.

Peacock, Alan T. (1969). Welfare Economics and Public Subsidies to the Arts. *Manchester School of Economics and Social Studies* 37: 323-335. Reprinted in Blaug (1976): 70-86.

Peacock, Alan T. (1984). Economics, Inflation and the Performing Arts. In: Baumol and Baumol (eds.) *Inflation and the Performing Arts.* New York and London: New York University Press: 71-85.

Peacock, Alan T. (1988). Cultural Economics and the Finance of the Arts. Mimeo. Heirot-Watts University, Edinburgh.

Peacock, Alan T. (1993). *Paying the Piper. Culture, Music and Money.* Edinburgh: Edinburgh University Press.

Peacock, Alan T. (ed.) (1998). *Does the Past have a Future?: The Political Economy of Heritage.* London: Institute of Economic Affairs.

Peacock, Alan T. and Christine Godfrey (1974). The Economics of Museums and Galleries. *Lloyds Bank Review* 111: 17-28. Reprinted in Blaug (1976), *The Economics of the Arts.* London: Martin Robertson: 189-204.

Peacock, Alan T and Ilde Rizzo (eds.) (1994). *Cultural Economics and Cultural Policies.* Dordrecht: Kluwer.

Peacock, Alan T., Eddie Shoesmith and Geoffrey Millner (1983). *Inflation and the Performing Arts.* London: Arts Council of Great Britain.

Peacock, Alan T. and Ronald Weir (1975). *The Composer in the Market Place.* London: Faber Music.

Perrot, Paul (1992). Funding, Sponsorship and Corporate Support. In: Patrick Boylan (ed.). *Museums 2000. Politics, People, Professionals and Profit.* London: Routledge: 148-168.

Pesando, James E. (1993). Art as an Investment: The Market for Modern Prints. *American Economic Review* 83: 1075-1089.

Polanyi, Michael (1966). *The Tacit Dimension.* London: Routledge and Kegan Paul.

Pommerehne, Werner W. (1982). Steuern, Staatsausgaben und Stimmbürgerverhalten: Eine empirische Untersuchung am Beispiel der öffentlichen Subventionierung des Theaters. *Jahrbücher für Nationalökonomie und Statistik* 197 (5): 437-462.

Pommerehne, Werner W. (1983). Private verus öffentliche Müllabfuhr - nochmals betrachtet. *Finanzarchiv* 41: 466-475.

Pommerehne, Werner W. (1987). *Präferenzen für öffentliche Güter. Ansätze zu ihrer Erfassung.* Tübingen: Mohr (Siebeck).

Pommerehne, Werner W. (1992). Opernfestspiele – ein Fall für öffentliche Subventionen? *Homo Oeconomicus* 9: 229-262.

Pommerehne, Werner W. (1994). The Effect of Public Purchases of Paintings on Auction Prices. Paper presented at the 8th International Congress on Cultural Economics in Witten, Germany, August 24-27.

Pommerehne, Werner W. and Lars Feld (1997). The Impact of Museum Purchase on the Auction Prices of Paintings. *Journal of Cultural Economics: Special Issue on the Art Market* 21 (3): 249-271.

Pommerehne, Werner W. and Bruno S. Frey (1980a). Kunst zwischen Freiheit und Demokratie. *Wirtschaftspolitische Blätter* 27 (6): 27-37.

Pommerehne, Werner W. and Bruno S. Frey (1980b). The Museum from an Economist's Perspecitve. *International Social Science Journal* 32 (2): 323-329.

Pommerehne, Werner W. and Bruno S. Frey (1993). Justifications for Art Trade Restrictions: The Economic Perspective. *Etudes en Droit de l'Art* 3: 89-114.

Pommerehne, Werner W. and Martin J. Granica (1995). Perfect Reproduction of Works of Art: Substitutes or Heresy? *Journal of Cultural Economics* 19: 237-249.

Pommerehne, Werner W. and Friedrich Schneider (1983). Warum bloss ist ein Rauschenberg so teuer? In: Clemens-A. Andreae (ed.). *Kunst und Wirtschaft*. Cologne: Bachem: 50-81.

Portney, Paul R. (1994). The Contingent Valuation Debate: Why Economists should Care. *Journal of Economic Perspectives* 8 (4): 3-17.

Randall, Alan, Berry C. Ives, and Clyde Eastman (1974). Bidding Games for Valuation of Aesthetic Environmental Improvements. *Journal of Environmental Economics and Management* 1: 132-49

Reder, Christian (1988). *Wiener Museumsgespräche. Über den Umgang mit Kunst und Museen.* Wien: Falter.

Reisner, R. G. (1950). *Fakes and Forgeries in the Fine Arts: A Bibliography.* New York: Special Libraries Association.

Reitlinger, Gerald (1961). *The Economics of Taste, Vol. I. The Rise and Fall of Picture Prices 1760-1960.* London: Barrie and Rockliff.

Reusch, Hans (1922). Die deutschen Theater in volkswirtschaftlicher Beleuchtung, Universität zu Köln.

Ridker, Ronald (1967). *The Economic Cost of Air Pollution.* New York: Praeger.

Riley, J.G. and W.F. Samuelson (1981). Optimal Auctions. American Economic Review 71 (June): 381-392.

Robbins, Lionel C. (1963). Art and the State. In: Lionel C. Robbins (ed.): *Politics and Economics: Essays in Political Economy.* London: Macmillan, 53-72.

Robbins, Lionel C. (1971). Unsettled Questions in the Political Economy of the Arts. *Three Banks Review* 91: 3-19.

Rolfe, Heather (1992). *Arts Festivals in the U.K.* London: Policy Studies Institute.

Rosen, Sherwin (1981). The Economics of Superstars. *American Economic Review* 71: 845-858.

Rosenthal, Norman (1981). Loan Exhibitions at the Royal Academy of Art. In: Institut für Museumskunde (ed.), *Ausstellungen - Mittel der Politik?* Berlin: Gebr. Mann Verlag: 145-152.

Rosett, Richard N. (1991). Art Museums in the United States: A Financial Portrait. In: Martin Feldstein (ed.), *The Economics of Art Museums*. Chicago: University of Chicago Press: 129-177.

Ross, Myron H. and Scott Zondervan (1989). Capital Gains and the Rate of Return on a Stradivarius. Economic Inquiry 27: 529-540.

Roth, Alvin E. (1988). Laboratory Experimentation in Economics: A Methodological Overview. *Economic Journal* 98: 157-86.

Rouget, Bernard, Dominique Sagot-Duvauroux and Sylvie Pflieger (1991). *Le marché de l'art contemporain en France. Prix et stratégies*. Paris: La documentation française.

Sagot-Duvauroux, Dominique (1985). *Structure de financement et organisation d'un système: l'exemple du théatre*. PhD Dissertation, Université de Paris-I-Panthéon-Sorbonne.

Savage, George (1963). *Forgeries, Fakes and Reproductions*. London: Barrie and Rockliff.

Schelling, Thomas C. (1984). The Life You Save May Be Your Own. In: *Choice and Consequence. Perspectives of an Errant Economist*. Cambridge, MA and London, England: Harvard University Press: 113-146.

Schenker, Philipp (1988). Die Holbein-Sonderausstellung. Besucher und Meinungen zu ökonomischen Fragen. *WWZ-Studien* No. 5, University of Basle.

Schneider, Friedrich and Werner W. Pommerehne (1983). Macroeconomia della crescita in disequilibrio e settore pubblico in espansione: il peso delle differenze istituzionali. *Rivista Internazionale di Scienze Economiche e Commerciali* 33 (4-5): 306-320.

Schoemaker, Paul J. (1982). The Expected Utility Model: Its Variants, Purposes, Evidence and Limitations. *Journal of Economic Literature* 20: 529-563.

Schouten, Frans (1989). Trends and the Future. In: Van Mensch, Peter (ed.). *Professionalising the Muses*. Amsterdam: AHA Books: 107-116.

Schulze, Günther and Heinrich Ursprung (2000). La Donna e mobile – or is she? Voter Preferences and Public Support for the Arts. *Public Choice* 102: 131-149.

Schumpeter, Joseph A. (1942). *Capitalism, Socialism and Democracy*. 1st edition, New York: Harper.

Schuster, J. Mark (1998). Neither Public Nor Private: The Hybridization of Museums. *Journal of Cultural Economics* 22: 127-150.

Schuster, J. Mark (1999). The Other Side of the Subsidized Muse: Indirect Aid Revisted. *Journal of Cultural Economics* 23: 51-70.

Scitovsky, Tibor (1972). What's Wrong with the Arts is What's Wrong with Society. *American Economic Review* 62: 62-69.

Scully, Gerald W. (1992). *Constitutional Environments and Economic Growth.* Princeton, New Jersey: Princeton University Perss.

Seelig, Ludwig (1914). *Geschäftstheater oder Kulturtheater?* Berlin: Genossenschaft Deutscher Bühnen-Angehöriger.

Shanahan, James L. (1978). The Consumption of Music: Integrating Aesthetics and Economics. *Journal of Cultural Economics* 2: 13-26.

Shaw, George Bernard (1903). *Man and Superman.* New York: Bretano's.

Shiller, Rober J. (1989). *Market Volatility.* Cambridge: MIT Press.

Shiller, Robert J. (1990). Market Volatility and Investor Behaviour. American Economic Review, Papers and Proceedings 80 (2): 58-62.

Simon, Herbert A. (1978). Rationality as a Process and Product of Thought. *American Economic Review* 68: 1-16.

Simon, Herbert A. (1982). *Models of Bounded Rationality.* Cambridge, MA.: MIT Press.

Simonton, Dean Keith (1984). *Genius, Creativity, and Leadership: Historiometric Inquiries.* Cambridge, MA.: Harvard University Press.

Simonton, Dean Keith (1988). *Scientific Genius: A Psychology of Science.* Cambridge, MA.: Harvard University Press.

Simonton, Dean Keith (1994). *Greatness. Who Makes History and Why.* New York and London: Guilford Press.

Singer, Leslie and Gary Lynch (1994). Public Choice in the Tertiary Art Market. Mimeo. Indiana University Northwest.

Smith, Charles W. (1989). *Auctions. The Social Construction of Value.* Berkeley and Los Angeles: University of California Press.

Smith, Vernon L. (1989). Theory, Experiments and Economics. *Journal of Economic Perspectives* 3: 151-69.

Smolensky, Eugene (1986). Municipal Financing of the U.S. Fine Art Museum: A Historical Rationale. *Journal of Economic History* 46 (4): 757-768.

Stein, John P. (1977). The Monetary Appreciation of Paintings. *Journal of Political Economy* 85 (5): 1021-1035.

Stigler, George J. and Gary S. Becker (1977). De Gustibus Non Est Disputandum. *American Economic Review* 67: 76-90.

Takeyama, Lisa N. (1994). The Welfare Implications of Unauthorized Reproduction of Intellectual Property in the Presence of Demand Network Externalities. *Journal of Industrial Economics* 42 (2): 155-166.

Thaler, Richard H. (1980). Toward a Positive Theory of Consumer Choice. *Journal of Economic Behaviour and Organization* 1: 39-60.

Thaler, Richard H. (1992). *The Winner's Curse. Paradoxes and Anomalies of Economic Life.* New York: Free Press.

Thaler, Richard H. (1993). *Advances in Behavioural Finance.* New York: Russel Sage.

Throsby, David C. (1994). The Production and Consumption of the Arts: A View of Cultural Economics. *Journal of Economic Literature* 33: 1-29.

Throsby, David C. (2000). *Economics and Culture.* Cambridge: Cambridge University Press.

Throsby, David C. and Glenn A. Withers (1979). *The Economics of the Performing Arts.* London and Melbourne: Arnold.

Throsby, David C. and Glenn A. Withers (1983). Measuring the Demand for the Arts as a Public Good: Theory and Empirical Results. In: William S. Hendon and James L. Shanahan (eds), *Economics of Cultural Decisions.* Cambridge, MA.: Abt: 177-91.

Throsby, David C. and Glenn A. Withers (1986). Strategic Bias and Demand for Public Goods: Theory and an Application to the Arts. *Journal of Public Economics* 31: 307-327.

Tietzel, Manfred (1995). *Literaturökonomik.* Tübingen: Mohr (Siebeck).

Torrence, E. P. (1970). *Encouraging Creativity in the Classroom.* Dubuque, IA: Brown.

Touchstone, Susan K. (1980). The Effects of Contributions on Price and Attendance in the Lively Arts. *Journal of Cultural Economics* 4: 33-46.

Towse, Ruth (1991). Venice as a Superstar. Mimeo, Department of Economics, University of Exeter.

Towse, Ruth (1993). *Singers in the Marketplace: The Economics of the Singing Profession.* Oxford: Clarendon Press.

Towse, Ruth (ed.) (1997a). *Cultural Economics: The Arts, the Heritage and the Media Industries.* Two Volumes. Cheltenham, U.K. and Lyme, U.S.: Edward Elgar.

Towse, Ruth (ed.) (1997b). *Baumol's Cost Disease. The Arts and other Victims.* Edward Elgar: Cheltenham U.K. and Northampton, USA

Towse, Ruth and Abdul Khakee (eds.) (1992). *Cultural Economics*. Berlin: Springer.

Trimarchi, Michele (1985a). Il Finanziamento pubblico degli Spettacoli. *Economia delle Scelte Pubbliche* 1: 37-54.

Trimarchi, Michele (1985b). La Domanda di Performing Arts: Una Analisi Preliminare. *Atti Accademia Peloritane dei Pericolanti* 54 (54): 3-26.

Trimarchi, Michele (1994). The Funding Process in a Comparative Perspective: Some Methodological Issues. In: Alan Peacock and Ilde Rizzo (eds.), *Cultural Economics and Cultural Policies*. Dordrecht: Kluwer: 23-31.

Tweedy, Collin (1991). Sponsorship of the Arts - An outdated Fashion or the Model of the Future? *Museum Management and Curatorship* 10: 161-166.

Vaughan, David Roger (1980). Does a Festival Pay? In: James L. Shanahan, William S. Hendon and Alice J. MacDonald (eds.), *Economic Policy for the Arts*. Cambridge, MA.: Abt: 319-331.

Vautravers-Busenhart, Isabelle (1998). *Kultur- oder Sparpolitik. Eine ökonomische und institutionelle Analyse für die Schweiz*. PhD Dissertation, Faculty of Economics, University of Zurich.

Velardo, G. (1988). *Designing Exhibitions*. London: Design Council.

Vesselier, Michèle (1973). *La crise du Théâtre privé*. Paris: Presses Universitaires de France.

Vickrey, William (1961). Counterspeculation, Auctions and Competitive Sealed Tenders. *Journal of Finance* 16: 8-37.

Villani, Andrea (1978). *L'economia dell' arte*. Mailand: Vita e Pensiero.

Volckart, Oliver (1997). Politische Zersplitterung und Wirtschaftswachstum im Alten Reich, ca. 1650-1800. Diskussionsbeitrag 04-97, Max-Planck-Institute for Research into Economic Systems, Jena.

Wagenführ, Horst (1965). *Kunst als Kapitalanlage*. Stuttgart: Forkel.

Wahl-Zieger, Erika (1978). *Theater und Orchester zwischen Marktkräften und Marktkorrektur*. Göttingen: Vandenhoeck and Ruprecht.

Waldron, A. (1983). *True or False? Amazing Art Forgeries*. New York: Hastings House.

Walsh, Richard N. (1991). Art Museums in the United States: A Financial Portrait. In: Martin Feldstein (ed.), *The Economics of Art Museums*. Chicago: University of Chicago Press: 129-177.

Warnke, Martin (1985). *Hofkünstler. Zur Vorgeschichte des modernen Künstlers*. Cologne: DuMont.

Weisbrod, Burt A. (1988). *The Nonprofit Economy*. Cambridge, MA.: Harvard University Press.

Wellington, Donald C. and Joseph C. Gallo (1984). Investment in a Small Antique. *Journal of Cultural Economics* 8 (2): 93-98.

West, Edwin G. (1985). *Subsidizing the Performing Arts*. Toronto: Ontario Economic Council.

Wiersma, Uco J. (1992). The Effects of Extrinsic Rewards on Intrinsic Motivation: A Meta-Analysis. *Journal of Occupational and Organizational Psychology* 65: 101-14.

Wilson, David M. (1990). Preface. In: Mark Jones (ed.). *Fakes? The Art of Deception*. London: British Museum Publ.: 9.

Winston, A. S. and J. E. Baker (1985). Behavior Analytic Studies of Creativity: A Critical Review. *Behavior Analyst* 8: 191-205.

Withers, Glenn A. (1981). Principles of Government Support to the Arts. *Meanjin* 40: 442-460.

Index of Names & Authors

Subject Index